(o'briens
fine wines

Two years ago, after 35 years on the wine circuit, I decided to hang up my boots. When Brendan O'Brien approached me with this plan to upgrade and expand his long established family company. I was excited enough to put on the proverbial old boots again and to take the position of Director of wine.

Already, in my short review of their portfolio of wines, it is apparent that O'Briens have some outstanding suppliers both from the New World and Europe. Their range of Fine Bordeaux and Vintage Ports is sensational!

O'Briens ship a large per
the producers and I w
dedication to finding wi
you the best quality and

I hope you enjoy the v
exclusive range of wines

GW00705999

T. P. Whelan

TP Whelehan
Director of Wine.

Exclusive Stockists of these highly recommended award winning wines:

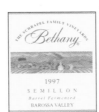

• blackrock • bray • dalkey • donnybrook • dun laoghaire •
greystones • glasnevin • malahide • navan rd • rathgar • rathmines
• sandymount stillorgan • templeogue • vevay

The Best of Wine in Ireland 2000

Editorial Director: Anna Farmar
Production and Design Director: Tony Farmar

Wine and Food Editor: Sandy O'Byrne

Cover design: Space
Text design: A. & A. Farmar
Typesetting: K. R. Farmar
Sales and Promotion: Siobhán Mullet
Distribution: Columba Mercier Distribution

Printed by Betaprint

Members of the Tasting Panel

Liam Campbell, Tony Cleary, Catherine Griffith
David Lonergan, Canice McCarthy, Julie Martir
Anne Mullin, Monica Murphy, Mary O'Callagha
Gerry Fitzsimons, Evelyn Jones, Andrew Tidey, A
O'Toole, Patricia Carroll, Jacinta Kennedy, Pete
Roycroft, Niamh Boylan, Gerry Gunnigan, Dait
Kelleher, Michael Anderson, Martina Delaney, Br
Brady, Fergal Tynan, Ciarán Newman, Peter Dun
Martin Moran, Fiona Conway, Maureen O'Har
Sinead O'Sullivan, Matt Quigley, Jean Smullen
Nigel Donnan and Terry Greene

A. & A. Farmar's
Best of Wine in Ireland 2000

Wine and Food Editor
Sandy O'Byrne

A & A
Farmar

British Library Cataloguing in Publication data
A CIP catalogue record for this book is available from
the British Library.

ISBN 1-899047-62-X

Published by
A. & A. Farmar
Beech House
78 Ranelagh Village
Dublin 6
Ireland

Tel: (01) 496 3625 Fax: (01) 497 0107
email: afarmar@iol.ie

Contents

The Wines

Publishers' preface

The title of this guide—*The Best of Wine in Ireland*—becomes more challenging with each edition. There are now more than 5,000 individual labels on the Irish market, in different styles and from all over the globe. Our aim is to provide a map through this maze for enthusiastic consumers.

There are more wines than ever in this year's edition, from more importers, reflecting among other things a general improvement in the quality of wines on the market. However, it has never been the policy of *The Best of Wine in Ireland* simply to reflect the market. Since perhaps two-thirds of the wine sold in Ireland costs less than £6 a bottle, and twenty brands make up a large proportion of the total, such a book would be both short and dull. (As it happens, over half of the wines submitted to us costing less than £6 failed to demonstrate sufficiently distinctive character or quality to get into the book.) Eighty-five per cent of the wines tasted are priced at over £6, with 60 per cent being between £6 and £12.

The guide's judgements are based on the recommendations of a panel of tasters who bring training, expertise and experience to the task in hand. As before, the panel was drawn from the wine trade, the catering industry and knowledgeable amateurs, all of whom hold the Wine and Spirit Education Trust Diploma. We as publishers have been particularly impressed by the degree of consensus arrived at by the tasters in assessing the wines for quality, value for money, typicité etc.

This edition includes an index of the suggestions for food to accompany the recommended wines, cross-referenced to the individual wines. So whether you are looking for a dish to match a particular wine, or for a wine to complement a favourite dish, you can now easily find

Wine and Food Editor Sandy O'Byrne's suggested matches.

We are extremely grateful to the tasters for giving so freely of their time and experience to evaluate the wines. The book would not be possible without the generous contribution of the wine importers who submitted wines for tasting, and patiently answered our requests for further information about their wines.

Anna and Tony Farmar
November 1999

Editor's introduction

The closing decades of the twentieth century have been a time of dramatic change for wine in the vineyard, cellar, bottle and on the table. My grandparents would not have drunk wine from the Midi; my parents would have questioned the idea of Californian wine; I can remember the first Australian wine to appear in Ireland and its rather cautious reception. A description of the creation of this revolution in the wine world would require a book of its own. However, a few key facts are worth mentioning before we all face, glass in hand, into the third millennium.

The impact of New World and latterly southern hemisphere winemaking cannot be over-emphasised. Winemaking used to be a natural, partially understood process; the winemaker stood back, often helplessly, and hoped for good wine. But with the new age of winemaking technology pioneered by California and Australia the winemaker took centre stage monitoring, controlling and adjusting every step of the vinification. These countries proved that good, even fine wine could be made in hot countries and provided the expertise and knowledge necessary to extend the whole geography of viticulture. For the consumer, technological advance set new standards of consistency and quality. Above all, New World winemakers showed that good wine could be made to appeal to more people and at a price more could afford.

As the research students at Davis and Roseworthy Universities were beavering away at understanding wine from the rootstock to the redox potential, the market for wine was changing too. A number of factors had led to the decline in sales of vin de table or basic table wine in producing countries. Overall, people were drinking less due to urban lifestyles, more sedentary occupations, health concerns, more choice and variety in beverages and less formal meals and mealtimes. The one or two litre a day consumption common in wine-producing areas in the middle of the century swiftly declined and with it the market for much of Southern Europe's wine. Wine had become one choice among many and the demand was for better quality.

The establishment of the middle ground between quaffing and connoisseurship helped to debunk the mystifying subject of wine for the majority of consumers. The image of wine as an élitist drink surrounded by all kinds of meaningless snobbery and affectation, began to disappear as more and more people outside producing countries began to enjoy wine as a drink with or without food. Again, the New World producers with simple labels, varietal wines and easy approachable styles, reinforced the modern image of wine. The market had changed. Wine was now a young drink in restaurants and wine bars and at barbecues and parties at home. It was to drink and enjoy, not to cellar and savour.

The combination of the New World challenge and the dynamics within the home and export markets forced a new attitude among winemakers in traditional areas. For the first time in history, winemaking was driven by its market.

Yet not all of the market influences have been for good. The first-growth wines of Bordeaux and their equivalents in other classic regions along with a handful of New World superstars, have become commodities rather than wines. Before they leave their original cellar they are bought and sold, traded as futures and eventually sold to the highest bidder in maturity. Many enthusiasts will never taste the best and much of the best will be drunk by those more interested in the outside than the inside of the bottle. Most such wine will be drunk long before it has reached its best or, even worse, will never be drunk at all.

At the other end of the spectrum, pressure on price points and the volume demands of large-scale retailers are beginning to show in some pretty poor wines. Over half the wines tasted this year in the under £6 category were rejected as unbalanced, badly made, or just plain dull.

The pressure on newly popular regions, often trendy too soon through media hype, has caused price rises, higher than desirable yields and, eventually, lower quality.

In this year's tastings new directions were apparent on a number of fronts. California and Australia are both playing it cool with a marked shifted towards cooler regions for their better wines. Oak is much more subtle and fruit more restrained, at least by Australian standards. Complexity and elegance drive these wines rather than the power and punch of some years ago.

Argentina and South Africa have each shown an impressive ability to break into the market and offer something different within a definite southern hemisphere style. Argentina is developing a portfolio of grapes and blends with individual style and character. South Africa has really taken a quality leap, especially in red wines and is producing wines of extraordinary sophistication even from the notorious *enfant terrible*, the Pinot Noir.

In Europe, Italy continues to impress with its quality and the range of new regions producing great, very different wines. Portugal, too, has come into its own with its enviable range of grape varieties displaying their full potential.

The South of France still remains exciting. Now the South West is beginning to emerge with more traditional regional wines, given a light polish by modern hands. In these areas, and throughout the regions, France has really met the challenge of the New World. Its winemakers—or at least a majority of them—have succeeded in retaining the character, the terroir of their regions while absorbing the consumer-friendly lessons of newer areas.

Much of the monumental change in wine in the last decades came, directly and indirectly, from you, the consumer. Thankfully, there were enough creative and open-minded producers to respond so successfully. But now and forever, wine and winemaking are driven by the market. So whatever glass you raise on New Year's Eve, remember that the future of that wonderful drink is in your hands!

Sandy O'Byrne
November 1999

Editor's Choices

The tastings and awards

For this year's *Best of Wine in Ireland* we conducted numerous tasting sessions between July and November 1999, handling nearly 1,600 wines submitted by 39 importers, of which some 1,250 were regarded by the panel as worth recommending as good buys. Some of the wines included this year were also in previous editions, with the same or different vintages. However, every single wine included in the book is *re-tasted* each year. Occasionally this has allowed the editor to comment that such and such a wine is 'ageing well', or is perhaps 'still too young' for optimum value.

Although many of the wines included will continue to improve for some years, the tasters judged the wines as if they are to be drunk during the next twelve months. Wines submitted that were judged likely to be past their best during the lifetime of this edition (even if still acceptable at the time of tasting) were excluded.

Assessing the wines

Each wine was tasted 'blind', that is, with the label concealed, and was assessed for:

■ nose—aroma, intensity, complexity
■ taste—balance, structure, extract, complexity, length
■ value—price/quality ratio.

Only those wines gaining at least 60 per cent of the available marks qualified for inclusion. As a result, *every wine listed is recommended as well-made and of reasonable value for money.* A number have been singled out for commendation, 'star' status, or as presenting particular value for money. The published tasting notes are a distilled version of those written by the members of the panel, edited by Sandy O'Byrne.

What the awards mean

☆☆☆ — exceptional wines of considerable complexity and classic balance from a very good vintage which reward serious tasting. Such wines show a classic balance and are some of the best examples of their type and origin. They are wines to drink, taste and enjoy for themselves.

☆☆—elegant wines which show character and complexity above expectations, with balance, subtlety and 'typicité'; ideal to accompany carefully prepared food at a special dinner party.

☆—wines which show character and style and are particularly good examples of their region and winemaking. The quality of these wines generally exceeds the expectations of the label and the price

C—commendation: wines that are good, interesting and merit attention but not quite a star. The category includes wines which are good examples of particular regional styles or which are a little young but show good potential.

££—value award: wines that offer exceptional value for money in comparison with others within its type/ region; these are mainly lower-priced wines but include those from classic areas which are attractively priced.

How the wines are listed

Apart from sparkling and sweet wines, which appear in separate chapters, the wines are listed by country of origin (and region in the case of France and USA); then by colour (white, red and rosé); then by price band; then by name, with the award winners coming first. In interpreting the often confusing layout of labels, we have tried to present the essential information that will enable the consumer to identify particular wines on the retailer's shelves.

An important part of any wine-purchasing decision is value for money, and we have indicated where particular value may be found. However, wine prices are not fixed. Different retailers may raise or lower the price of individual wines as they choose. On the other hand, we felt it desirable to indicate the approximate price. All the wines are therefore listed in order of price band.

We have made every effort to assign wines to their appropriate price bands, but please remember that these are guide prices only: prices may vary from one outlet to another, because of promotions, for example, or bulk buying; they may change because of fluctuations in exchange rates, changes in taxes and excise, and so on.

Editor's choice: personal favourites

Personal favourites from this year's Best of Wine

Rocca delle Macìe Ser Gioveto 1995

Antinori Tignanello

Luis Pato Vinha Pan DO Bairrada 1995

Quinta dos Rogues Touriga Nacional 1996

Guelbenzu Evo DO Navarra 1994

Ch. Ste Michelle Cold Creek Cabernet Sauvignon 1995

Clos du Bois Sonoma County Chardonnay 1997

Clos du Chapitre AC Fixin 1ère Cru 1996

Pascal Jolivet AC Sancerre 1998

Ch. Tertre Rôteboeuf AC St Emilion Grand Cru Classè 1996

The tasting panel

Liam Campbell lectures extensively on wine for the Wine Development Board and for off-licences and wine clubs.

Tony Cleary, who has worked for over twenty years in the wine trade, is now with Barry & Fitzwilliam, specialising in Central and South Eastern Europe

Catherine Griffith is wine consultant to Molloy's Liquor Stores and lecturer for the Wine Development Board.

David Lonergan is the manager of The Vintry Wine shop in Rathgar, Dublin 6. He lectures for The Vintry Wine Club where his particular forte is the Rhône valley.

Canice McCarthy is an off-licence manager for O'Brien's Fine Wines in their Malahide branch. He is a member of the Guild of Sommeliers, teaches a wine appreciation course at Malahide Community School and is a wine columnist for the People Group of newspapers.

Julie Martin is the first Irish woman sommelier; she has worked at Ashford Castle and Restaurant Patrick Guilbaud, is Secretary of the Irish branch of the Champagne Academy and Commandeur in the Association Internationale des Maîtres Conseils en Gastronomie Française.

Anne Mullin is a director of an international freight forwarding company specialising in the importation of wines and spirits, council member of the Irish Guild of Sommeliers and founder member of the Premier Cru Wine Club.

Monica Murphy of Febvre is a professional wine and cheese consultant, lecturer and writer.

Mary O'Callaghan holds the Advanced Diploma from the Court of Master Sommeliers; she is Wine Consultant to the Cheers! Take Home Group and lectures on wine for the Dublin Institute of Technology and the Wine Development Board.

Gerry Fitzsimons is a member of the Irish Guild of Sommeliers and a winner of the George O'Malley tasting trophy.

Evelyn Jones is the proprietor of The Vintry Wine Shop, Rathgar, Dublin 6 and winner of the Gilbey/NOFFLA Dublin Off-licence of the Year Award, 1996. She is a member of the Champagne Academy and runs wine appreciation courses as well as a wine club.

Andrew Tidey is the beers, wine and spirits marketing and development manager for Tesco Ireland.

Alan O'Toole is the sales manager of Fields Wine Merchants. He lectures for the Wine Development Board

Patricia Carroll is a food and wine editor and member of the Premier Cru Wine Club.

Jacinta Kennedy, formerly of the Mill Wine Cellar, Maynooth, is now sales representative with Taserra Wine Merchants.

Peter Roycroft is Manager of Mitchell & Son Wine Merchants, Glasthule, Co. Dublin.

Niamh Boylan is a longtime foodie and ex restaurateur; she is currently a food and wine lecturer/consultant

Gerry Gunnigan now works for Wines Direct, having worked in the UK wine trade and in vineyards in Alsace.

Daithi Kelleher is marketing manager of the Molloys Group and a winner of the George O'Malley tasting trophy.

Michael Anderson has been with Searsons since 1996, having previously lived in France for nine years.

Martina Delaney is sommelier at L'Ecrivain Restaurant since 1993.

Brian Brady is catering manager at a leading private club in Dublin.

Fergal Tynan is the manager of Raheny Wine Cellar, Dublin. He obtained a distinction in the WSET Diploma, 1998.

Ciarán Newman, is a director of Cheers! Take-home.

Peter Dunne is a director of Mitchell & Son Wine Merchants.

Martin Moran MW is Wine Development Manager for Gilbeys of Ireland.

Fiona Conway works with Findlaters Wine Merchants, Dublin.

Maureen O'Hara is a manager with Findlater Wine Merchants, Dublin.

Sinéad O'Sullivan works with Mitchell & Son Wine Merchants, Dawson St, Dublin 2.

Matt Quigley works with Dun Laoghaire Rathdown County Coumcil.

Jean Smullen was the Administrator of the Wine Development Board for the past eight years. She is now working on a consultancy basis, specialising in wine education and wine promotion.

Nigel Donnan has worked for winemakers in both Provence and Burgundy during harvest time.

Terry Greene owns and runs Vinovate and Winebrief, two independent consultancy services for the trade and public; he lectures for the Wine Development Board and has judged at the International Wine and Spirit Competition, London in 1998 and 1999.

Wine styles and typical examples

Although every wine is more or less different from every other, it is possible to classify them into 'styles'. Such classifications help wine drinkers in a wider exploration of the pleasures of wine-drinking by making it easier to choose a wine appropriate to the occasion. Each wine included in *The Best of Wine in Ireland* (apart from sweet and sparkling) has been broadly categorised by style according to 'weight' in the mouth. Below is a list of the style classifications used in this guide with a typical example given for each style.

Using the weight of wine as a system of classification means classifying primarily by what winemakers call 'structure', rather than taste, although both taste and aroma also enter into some of the classifications. The structure of the wine is the frame which carries the taste. The wine notes describe the aromas, tastes and length of the wines.

Some of the red wines are described in the tasting notes as tannic. This does not mean that they are in any way imbalanced. It is simply drawing attention to another characteristic aspect of a particular style, that the tannins are noticeable unlike many of today's wines which have very soft tannins indeed. The wines described as tannic have firm structures.

Light dry white
Light and crisp, with neutral or delicate fruit character, no oak influence, to be drunk young
Muscadet de Sèvre et Maine sur lie
Light fruity white
Ripe fruit flavours and balanced acidity, no oak influence, to be drunk young
Unoaked Chilean Chardonnay

Light fruity white, off-dry
Light, ripe fruit flavours with obvious residual sugar
German Riesling
Aromatic white
Made from a particularly aromatic grape variety, from a cool or relatively cool climate, with no apparent oak influence, usually best drunk young
Rueda
Aromatic white, classic
Highly aromatic but with restrained fruit and typical regional character, usually of a northern region
Sancerre; Mosel Riesling Kabinett
Aromatic white, fruit-driven
Fruit-driven from an aromatic grape variety to express the exuberant qualities of the fruit in an exotic and ripe style
New Zealand Sauvignon Blanc

Medium-bodied white
Rounded white wine with moderate weight of fruit and a small amount of oak ageing
Mâcon-Lugny
Full-bodied white
Full, rounded fruit and moderate to high supporting alcohol to give a rich wine
Châteauneuf-du-Pape blanc
Full-bodied white, classic
Full and rounded white wine with relative complexity of flavour and definite structure
Puligny-Montrachet
Full-bodied white, oak
Obvious oak influence from fermentation and/or ageing in barrel, usually strongest in young barrique-aged wines
Californian barrel-fermented Chardonnay
Light fruity red
Light, with lots of typical berry fruit flavours, lively acidity and minimal, soft tannin, to be drunk young and possibly cool
Beaujolais
Medium-bodied red
Moderate weight and rich, rather than simple, fruit character with balanced acidity and some tannin to give structure and dryness, usually with oak-ageing, which may be obvious in the taste
Montepulciano d'Abruzzo
Medium-bodied red, classic
Medium weight with the complexity and typical character of its origin, moderate tannin and generally well-balanced, usually with the ability to age
Volnay
Medium to full-bodied red
Weight of fruit and supporting alcohol with some intensity and a balanced structure, often a medium-bodied wine in a warm vintage.
Côtes du Rhône-Villages

Medium bodied red, fruit-driven
Moderate weight and alcohol with rich and expressive fruit character and usually oak ageing
Chilean Cabernet/Merlot
Full-bodied red
Full-bodied with ripe fruit, plenty of extract, balanced tannin and acidity, aged in oak and usually capable of further development in bottle
Rioja Gran Reserva
Full-bodied red, classic
Full and structured with firm, tightly-knit palate of well extracted but restrained fruit and oak, obvious tannin and usually considerable length in the aftertaste; will age in bottle and develop complexity of flavour
Pauillac
Full-bodied red, fruit-driven
Full and rich with extract, fruit, usually high alcohol and a weight of very ripe, warm fruit, very well-flavoured and big in taste with a long finish and varying ability to age in bottle
Australian Shiraz
Rosé
Light, fruity, made by short maceration, either very dry or relatively fruity
Rosé de Provence
Rosé, off-dry
Light, fruity with obvious residual sugar
Rosé d'Anjou

Matching wine and food

Sandy O'Byrne

Attitudes to matching wine and food depend on nationality. In France wine is as much a part of a meal as the sauce, in fact it is often called the 'second sauce', and appropriate combinations are taken for granted within the cuisine of the country. Drinking the 'wrong' wine would seem as extraordinary as pouring ketchup over oysters.

The didactic, traditional and highly successful French attitude to food and wine works within their own gastronomy. However, non-producing countries, where food traditions may be less defined than those of France, are really spoiled for choice.

It is quite true that the combination makes all the difference, and while nobody would wish to lay down rules, logical guidelines are needed for the great variety of food and wine available today.

The old rules of 'red wine for red meat and game; white wine for white meat and fish' are generally accurate though very limited advice. It is more a question of the weight or balance of a wine than its colour. Many red wines are more robust, full-bodied and structured than many whites and therefore suit more textured, substantial foods which meat and game usually are. White wines are usually lighter and better with fish and delicate meats such as chicken or veal. The theory falls down however, with textured fish like tuna or with a very light red wine. A less traditional method of cooking, such as a stir-fry of beef, changes the texture and introduces spices which are less happy with full-bodied red, while roasting cod can make it meaty and substantial enough for a middle-weight red like Pinot Noir or Chinon.

It is therefore the balance of weights between wine and food that is most important. To enjoy both, one must be able to taste both, and neither should overpower the other in weight (body) or intensity of flavour.

Apart from weight and body, other aspects of wine affect food in particular ways. Acidity is essential to all wine, it keeps it fresh, makes it appetising and produces the bouquet. Acid stimulates the palate and so cuts through fat and richness in food. A crisp fresh white wine acts like a squeeze of lemon on a buttery fish. Tannin which comes from the skins and stalks of grapes in red wine making, helps the wine to age and gives it bite. High tannin has a drying effect on the palate like cold, strong tea; in very young wines it can be quite astringent. Tannin interacts with protein and tough young reds are softened by rare lean meat which protects the palate. More moderate tannin is dry and appetising and an excellent foil to rich foods like game, casseroles and many classically cooked dishes.

Certain combinations of wine and food clash either because of something in the food, which reacts with wine, or something which affects the ability to taste.

Hot spices burn so that tasting anything is impossible. Mild spices can work with light fruity wines, but hot chilli, lots of ginger or crushed pepper are better with beer or water. Beware of horseradish and mustard which can be very hot and really spoil a fine red wine intended for the beef.

Some foods are difficult because of texture. Chocolate is notorious for coating the palate with a layer of fat which dulls all other flavours. High alcohol and sweetness in a fortified dessert wine such as Port, Banyuls, or Liqueur Muscat usually do the trick. Egg yolks in sauces like mayonnaise, have a similar effect, so can a lot of oil. For these, oak and high acidity work.

Acids are less a problem than might be thought. While I cannot think of any wine which would benefit from being drunk with grapefruit, it is principally fine and mature wines which suffer from vinaigrette sauce or the sweet sour effect of tomatoes. Such foods are best with wines which have lots of lively fruit.

Artichokes and, to a lesser extent asparagus can make wine taste metallic, while vegetable-based dishes in general need rather fresh, lively whites or soft, rich, red wines with little oak.

Sweet food is often just too sweet for even the most luscious wine. Natural fruit ripeness together with the acidity of a dessert wine are no match for a pudding based on refined sugar. The wine must be as sweet or preferably sweeter than the food it accompanies which means serving simple, fruit or nut-based puddings with the best dessert wines.

The taste of wine comes from the grape, soil, climate, winemaking, vintage and age. When considering wine and food combinations it often helps to start with the grape variety, then to decide which style of that grape might suit a particular dish or vice versa. (See the chart of major grape varieties on pages 14–15 below).

Varietals tend to have fairly direct fruit flavours, which are good with strongly flavoured dishes and relatively complex foods. Where soil and terroir dominate the grape variety, the wine is often drier and more austere and will suit more integrated flavours and richer foods and cooking methods. Hot climates give very ripe, rich flavours and plenty of alcohol as well as less obvious acidity. Such wines will go with strong flavours but with food that is less rich, less protein and dairy-based, and it can tolerate spices. Oak-ageing adds to the structure of the wine therefore needs more substantial food. Its drying effect is also good with rich and creamy sauces. Strong oak flavours respond best to char-gilled or barbecued foods. Maturity makes a wine more complex in flavour, but more fragile. An old Bordeaux will need quite simple meat with a carefully made sauce and subtle flavours. Old Burgundy is rather more robust but will still benefit from classically cooked food.

This year for the first time in the guide we have included individual food notes for most of the wines. These

Classic Varietals and Food

Whites	Characteristics	Food Matches
Riesling	Dry to sweet, high acidity, light to medium body, fine and aromatic, ages well	Delicate foods like fish, richness in sauces, cooking methods and ingredients. Off-dry versions with spices, light aromatic fruit with rich sauces
Chardonnay	Balanced acidity, medium to full body, usually oaked though amount of oak varies, apple to peach or melon-type fruit, creamy and buttery flavours with toasted influence ripeness, medium to high alcohol level	Depends on style and amount of oak influence. Main course foods, fish with sauces, chicken and light meats, smoked foods, fruit-influenced savoury dishes, pasta with cream sauces, creamy cheeses
Sémillon	Dry or sweet and botrytized full-bodied, waxy, honeyed character with citrus-type fruit acidity when young	Dry—with textured fish, chicken andlight meats, spices and many Chinese dishes Sweet—nutty puddings, light cakes and pastries, blue cheese, foie gras and similar rich pâtés
Sauvignon Blanc	Dry, crisp acidity, medium body, very aromatic and intense, from gooseberry to green apple, citrus type fruit to limes, green peppers and grassy influences. Classically minerally, flinty overtones	Well-flavoured fish, some chicken and light meats, vegetable and tomato based pasta, smoked salmon, spicy and herb flavoured food, goats' cheese, some blue cheese and strong cheeses in general
Chenin Blanc	Dry to sweet, high acidity, medium to full-bodied, aromatic citrus, apple, floral and honeyed fruit, ages well	Dry—rich food especially fish with sauces, pâté and charcuterie, salads and some spices Sweet—depending on sweetness, some spicy savoury food, goats' cheese and strong cheeses; also fruit-based puddings

Reds	Characteristics	Food Matches
Cabernet Sauvignon	Tannin, medium acidity, full body, typically blackcurrant-type fruit with mint, cedar and cigar-like aromas, ages well	Protein, especially red meat, matches rich meats like lamb and duck, rich meat sauces and game like widgeon
Pinot Noir	Medium tannin, medium to upper acidity, elegant body, rich fruit, typically strawberry type with spicy overtones, develops gamey vegetal character, moderate to long ageing	Red meat and some cheeses, typically game or beef, also casseroles and wine-based sauces. Lighter, fruity styles with textured fish, some spices and mushroom pasta or risotto
Syrah	Tannin, acidity, high alcohol, full body, can be firm and dense in structure or rich and fruit driven, dark fruit character of brambles, dark plums, violets with very spicy peppery overtones, ages well	Depends on structure and tannin, red meat, grilled and barbecued meats, game, casseroles, substantial pasta and grain-based dishes which include meat; richer styles can match spicy food
Merlot	Low to moderate tannin, higher alcohol, medium to full body, ripe, rich fruit character typically raspberries, plums and chocolate, can be fruity and simple or layered, rich and complex, ageing depends on style, generally moderate	Depends on tannin and oak influence, meats like beef, game like quail, pasta dishes and vegetarian food if not too oaky. Sausages, salamis and pâtés with fruity versions, some cheeses

are intended to indicate the sort of food the wine suits through examples of successful combinations. If a wine goes well with lamb steaks it is likely also to suit beef steaks; if it works with garlic flavours, it is probably also successful with herbs; a wine which suits a tomato and pasta dish may also work with pizza. There is always more than one wine for a particular dish, and each wine suits many different foods.

Further reading: Sandy O'Byrne goes into more detail on the principles and practice of *Matching Food and Wine* in her book of that name.

The mystery of vintages

Alan Crowley, Master of Wine

A great part of the mystique of wine is the importance of the 'vintage', and which are the better or lesser years. Unfortunately, to many consumers the concept of a vintage represents yet another unknown in the wine maze.

Put simply, a vintage is the year in which the grapes were picked and the wine was made. It is therefore an indication of how old the wine is. However, as with other agricultural products, the critical importance of the vintage lies in the variability from year to year of weather conditions during the growing season. In some regions, notably in Europe, the effect is of a particular importance on the potential quality of the final wine. Thus, in good vintage years, when there have been sufficient rainy and dry periods, with sufficient sunshine and warm temperatures at the right time, grapes can be produced of a better quality to make a superior wine, as opposed to those in lesser years when the weather is not so right for quality grape production.

The effect of the weather, and hence the reputation of the vintage, is usually more important in wine regions whose climate is more marginal for the growing of grapes. Generally such regions are in Europe—in Germany, in Burgundy and Bordeaux in France, in Spain and Italy. Wine regions with more or less regular weather conditions produce wines where vintages year to year assume less importance. Such wine regions include the New World vineyards of South Africa, California, Australia and Chile. In these cases the vintage serves the consumer simply as a reminder of how old the wine is, and hence when it should be drunk. Of course, even in these regions knowledge of the vintage and wine style is important to ensure the optimum time for drinking the wine.

Because European wines in particular are so dependent for their quality on the weather conditions of any one year, for many wine lovers the vintage is one of the keys to the quality of any particular wine. As such there is a benefit in having vintage knowledge, as it will assist in:

- Selecting wines from better years rather than lesser years.
- Ensuring a wine which is meant to be drunk young, or is better after a few years ageing, is at the correct age at the time of drinking.

Some wines are best consumed while still young. For example, Muscadet and Valpolicella are best consumed up to three years after their production or vintage as their charm lies in their fresh, youthful character.

On the other hand some wines, while generally not changing much in quality from vintage to vintage, benefit from two to three years' bottle maturation before consumption, for example, Australian Shiraz or Californian Cabernet Sauvignon.

As a very general guide, it can be said that most New World quality red wines benefit from having two to three years' maturation from the date of vintage before consumption, while most New World whites do not benefit from long maturation and are best consumed within three to four years after their vintage.

Identifying which European wines and which vintages have produced wine of superior quality depends more on detailed knowledge of the wine region than on general country classification. This can only be gained by wine education and experience. However, many regions are historically famous for producing fine 'vintage' wines such as Bordeaux, Burgundy, Barolo and Rioja, to name a few.

As a guide to the reputation of each year's vintage since 1985, a quick reference vintage chart is attached.

Vintage chart compiled by Alan Crowley, Master of Wine (revised November 1999)

Region	97	96	95	94	93	92	91	90	89	88	87	86	85	Classic vintages
Bordeaux red	7	8	8	7	6	4	4	10	10	9	5	8	9	82, 78, 70, 61
Sauternes	8	8	8	5	5	4	3	10	10	8	5	9	7	80
Burgundy red	7	8	8	6	8	6	7	10	9	9	7	7	9	83, 78
Burgundy white	8	9	8	6	7	7	5	9	9	8	5	8	9	83, 78
Rhône	8	7	8	7	5	5	7	10	9	8	7	8	8	78, 67, 61
Champagne	8	-	8	-	7	7	6	8	8	-	-	8	9	79
Germany	8	7	8	8	8	7	6	10	8	7	6	6	8	76, 75
Spain	8	7	9	10	4	6	8	6	6	5	7	6	6	82, 64
Italy	8	8	7	8	8	4	5	9	7	8	6	7	9	78, 71
Port	8	-	7	10	-	8	8	-	-	-	-	-	9	77, 70, 66, 63
Australia	7	8	7	8	7	7	8	7	6	7	7	8	8	82, 79
California	6	6	7	8	7	8	9	8	7	7	8	7	8	74

Each region for each year is given a mark out of ten for its vintage.

Of course, any vintage chart is only a general guide—the best producers can make a good wine in 'off' years, and in some years a winemaker, or part of a wine region, can experience local problems resulting in quite ordinary or inferior wines in an otherwise good year.

Editor's choice: wines for spicy food

Although really spicy foods do not come from wine-drinking areas, there are some very good combinations and a number of wines can withstand all but the hottest chillis. In general, wines with lots of lively, direct fruit or maybe a touch of sweetness work best, while excess oak or tannin are best avoided. This selection concentrates on wines that have plenty of fruit and direct flavour. Some, such as the Gewürztraminer and Shiraz, have a touch of spice themselves which forms a special bond. Others, the Marsanne and Tokay Pinot Gris, are rich and full and envelop the hot food beautifully while maintaining their own character. Others simply provide a refreshing contrast of lively fruit. Perhaps best of all is Champagne which refreshes and cleanses the palate and provides a long lingering flavour of its own.

Sipp Mack Gewürztraminer Réserve AC Alsace 1997

Billecart-Salmon Rosé nv Champagne

Turckheim Tokay Pinot Gris Cuvée Réserve AC Alsace 1997

Ch. de Sours Rosé AC Bordeaux 1998

Ch. Tahbilk Marsanne (Unwooded) 1996

Hardys Nottage Hill Sparkling Chardonnay 1997

Chatsfield Mount Barker Cabernet Franc 1997

Wolf Blass Shiraz 1997

Kendall-Jackson Vintners' Reserve Pinot Noir 1997

Shingle Peak Marlborough Riesling 1997

From cellar to glass

Liam Campbell

How to taste wine

The difference between drinking a wine and tasting a wine is reflection. The ordinary casual drinker might enjoy a particular bouquet, a more or less pleasant taste, a tingle of alcohol at the back of the throat, and so on, but hardly allows the wine to reveal all its character. The taster, on the other hand, looks closely at a wine to examine it, sniffs in the wine's aroma and then tastes the wine, letting it coat the palate in its entirety. At each stage the taster reflects and considers many things, looking for clues to help understand what messages the wine is giving about itself.

The three stages in tasting a wine follow a very logical sequence—look, sniff and sip.

A wine can tell you so much by its appearance and scent alone. The taste sensations (flavours) of a wine confirm the signals given by the former two. The secret of wine tasting is to sensitise all of these three senses and to train them to work together better to translate your own thoughts and impressions of a wine.

To begin, pour a relatively small amount of wine into your glass. (Incidentally, leave the cut crystal in the cabinet, and invest in ISO tasting glasses available from some specialist wine shops. These glasses are the ones professional wine tasters use, and they do make a difference by emphasising aromas and flavours.)

Swirl the wine gently in the glass. By filling your glass to no more than a quarter, you can swirl sufficiently without adding to your laundry bill. The swirling action does a number of things. Primarily, however, it increases the wine's surface area and the energy imparted by the swirling helps aerate the wine and release more rapidly its aromas. The swirling should coat the inside of the glass which slowly or rapidly forms little rivulets which run down the inside of the glass. These little streams are called 'tears' or 'legs'. As a general rule of thumb, the more pronounced the tears and the closer they run together down the glass, the more viscous the wine. This may indicate a wine made in a hot climate, a wine high in alcohol or long ageing in bottle.

The colour of the wine is brimful of clues about itself—its likely origins, possible grape varieties, alcohol content, age, even details of the way the wine was made, for instance, what maturing vessels were used, whether new oak or some inert container such as steel or concrete. To read the signals, consider the following generalisations. White wines begin life pale and (un)interesting. With age they develop and evolve a deeper colour. Typically, a wine when bottled begins with a pale lemon or lime colour which deepens with time into straw and gold. (As so often in wine, the rule cannot totally be relied on. Exceptions occur if a wine has been aged in new oak or if the wine is a sweet dessert wine. However, a quick sniff will quickly tell you whether your glass of rich golden wine is a young oak-aged wine, a sweet wine or a very old mature wine.) Swirl the wine again to release more vapours and aromas. If a wine smells of a mature non-fruity bouquet or of oaky vanilla or of waxy honey you can begin to guess what the wine is.

Conversely, red wines grow paler with age. Because the wine's colour is derived from the grape skins, the warmer the climate, the riper the grapes and the richer and probably deeper the colour the wine. As the wine matures, the colouring matter in the skins, the *anthocyanins,* connect with the tannin in the wine like two pieces in a jigsaw, become solid matter and fall as a harmless, if astringent and bitter, sediment in the wine.

This reaction explains how some quite tannic wines soften and improve by becoming smoother with age because the mouth-puckering, gum-tingling tannins literally fall from the wine.

Also in youth the colour forms right up to the edge. By tilting the glass away from you at a 45° angle and looking at the border of the wine furthest from you, a clearer impression is given. The more the colour fades from the edge of the wine the greater the age. The colour itself speaks volumes. Wine within its first year of bottling will appear a purple colour. Shortly afterwards the blue hue disappears to reveal a ruby colour. With time the ruby is transformed into mahogany and eventually a tawny orangey tinted colour with very noticeable fading from the rim to the deeper coloured core of the wine. As a red wine matured in new oak matures further in bottle, when poured a faint brick orange or yellow halo appears around the rim of the wine according to age.

Again, the bouquet will confirm much about the wine. Youthful berry fruit aromas suggest a young wine. Spice, cinnamon, clove, oak and vanilla suggest a wine matured in new oak. As the wine matures, it loses its exuberant, youthful fruitiness; it may even close up temporarily into sulky adolescence to emerge later as a mature, more complex and 'winey' bouquet.

Now start actually tasting the wine. Do not be intimidated by a fancy label or a grand image. First sip a little wine and swallow, just to let the brain register that it is dealing with alcohol. Next sip again, (enough this time to cover the whole tongue) purse the lips and suck in a little air. This aeration has a similar effect as swirling the wine in the glass to open up the bouquet. Then, with lips closed, roll the wine all over and around your tongue. Think of your tongue as an antenna picking up signals. Finally, either spit into a spittoon or swallow depending on the occasion. Wait a few seconds to let the signals register on your palate. The length of time the memory of the flavours on the centre of the palate remain, the better the quality of the wine. To quantify the length count from 1001, 1002, 1003 etc. Up to 1010 is a fair to good length. 1015 is even better and over 1020 is worth stocking up on providing you actually like the wine.

Your tongue has several hundred tastebuds, so do not deprive any of them when tasting wine. Different parts of the tongue and palate are affected by different substances in a wine. For instance, the tip of the tongue senses any sweetness, while the sides of the tongue detect the acidity and make you salivate. Ripe fruits, oak, spice etc. and the character of a wine are sensed in the middle of the tongue. However, tannins in red wine are sensed on the teeth and gums and have a drying effect on the saliva ducts. Alcohol is felt at the back of the throat and gives a very warming sensation if alcohol content is high. If very high in alcohol the sensation is more burning.

How do you tell if a wine is immature, ready to drink or past its best? If the wine in the glass continues to improve in aroma and/or flavour over some hours it is possibly still immature. If the wine changes little it is most likely on its plateau of perfection. However, if the wine's taste disimproves over a few hours in the glass, then it is most likely past its peak and its companion bottles should be drunk soon.

It is easy to confuse some of the characteristics of a wine as the senses are assaulted by often contradictory flavours. For instance a bone-dry wine from a warm sun-ripening climate can give a misleading impression initially of being off-dry or medium sweet because of the super-ripe fruit sensed in the middle palate. However, if no sweetness is detected on the tip of the tongue, then the wine is in fact dry.

Another area of easy confusion lies in a tart wine with high acidity but little other flavour. When counting the length of the wine after spitting/swallowing concentrate on your middle palate and do not be tempted to let the shrieking acidity alone on the sides of the tongue grab all your attention. A persistent acidic finish on a wine alone is not a sign of quality if unpartnered by flavours on the centre of the tongue.

My parting advice is:

1. Remember you are the master of your own palate. But like any craft, tasting improves with practice.

2. Your opinion of a wine is perfectly valid for you. Have faith in your first impression rather than let others influence you if you disagree.

3. Keep an open mind about all wines. Your tastes, like fashion are forever changing. Remember flares? Do not deprive yourself today of a wine that may become your favourite tomorrow.

Buying wine

When buying wines for different reasons and for different occasions, one supplier usually suits better than another for that particular reason and occasion. The basic choices are: from the winemaker directly, the wholesaler/importer, the supermarket, by mail order, from a specialist wine shop, an off-licence or a grocery store.

Because of the vulnerability of wine to its conditions of storage, the same bottle of wine, handled by different suppliers could taste notably different depending on how conscientiously the bottle was handled and cared for or not. A reliably tried and tested *winemaker* will have a pride in his or her wine and an understanding for taking care of the wine when bottled. *Wholesalers* also understand about correct storage but may not have a licence to sell direct to the consumer.

Supermarkets offer a wide range of wines but untutored staff may not always appreciate that wine is a living organism that can deteriorate if exposed for prolonged periods to heat and light. White wine in clear glass is particularly vulnerable. A fast turnover of sales and a regular rotation of stock on the shelves will help prevent a wine being damaged. All too seldom does one find staff dedicated to the off-licence section with wine knowledge.

Mail order can offer good value because there is no high street rent to pay and it is very convenient for customers whose access to wine outlets is restricted. Wines offered are usually for early consumption and are usually sold by the case. Recent innovations include gift presentations for special occasions. Often wines offered are from winemakers of unknown reputation thereby placing all one's trust in the reputation of the mail order company.

Specialist wine merchants offer a more limited range than a supermarket but compensate with expert advice and a knowledge of their wines. In the absence of the same economies of scale, the wines may cost a little more but reliable producers and vintages should dominate the shelves.

Off-licences vary greatly, from those who stock a range of wines rivalling a supermarket to ones whose main speciality is cans of beer. The former can offer a surprisingly good range of wines at keen prices with an occasional 'find' if you rummage around the back of the shelves.

The *grocery shop* offers convenience at a price, but is usually limited in range and wine expertise.

Taking wine home

Like all living things, wine benefits from a little love and kindness. It does not react well to noise, vibrations, strong odours and direct light. It detests sudden erratic changes in temperature. While it is more forgiving of the cold, it can be damaged and taste 'soupy' if exposed to prolonged heat above 25°C.

It is best to transport the wine bottles upright to minimise the 'slosh-about' factor, especially if the wine has not been heavily filtered and has thrown a deposit, or is maturing and healthy but harmless sediment is present and clouds the agitated wine.

When safely home, before you are tempted to reminisce and open a bottle, allow the wine a few days' rest to recover from the journey.

Storing wine

Much is made of the correct storing and cellaring of wine. If circumstances and space dictate that you buy wine only to consume it immediately or within a few weeks or so, then wine is quite tolerant of uncomfortable surroundings, providing it is not stored near immediate heat. So do not set up your wine rack near a hot radiator, water pipes or in the airing cupboard beside the immersion heater.

Sooner or later you will be tempted to lay down some wine for rather longer, perhaps as a result of discovering some irresistible bargains or rarities never to be seen in our time again. Since monitoring the evolving quality of the wine as it ages is part of the fun, there is hardly any point in buying less than, say, a case of any one vintage. Then attention to preparing a storage area or wine cellar is vital to the health and longevity of your wine.

Golden rules for wine storage

Store the bottles horizontally on their side with the label facing upwards, for easy identification. Maintain a regular temperature hovering between 10°C and 15°C. Avoid light, noise, vibrations and strong odours.

If your house does not run to a cellar, improvise with a wardrobe or sturdy chest of drawers, ideally in a cool north-facing room. Special wine racks are widely available. Avoid hot spots such as radiators and water pipes. If an offspring or a sibling's bedroom is adjacent, with a state-of-the-art music centre with giant speakers consider a different location for the wine—or for your offspring/

sibling. To keep the wine as cool as possible, store it against an outside wall in the room. Exclude sunlight by closing the curtains or by covering the wine with a blanket.

The finer wines, requiring long ageing, should be stored at the lowest level, and this is also the coolest part of a room. Do not be tempted to use the top of the wardrobe as the fine wine will mature less effectively at the warmer temperatures over time. Store wines intended for earliest consumption within easy reach, e.g. the top drawer or top row of a wine rack. Finally, a cautionary tale about the effects of poor wine storage. In 1994 a New York investor purchased a 1787 Chateau Margaux for £287,000 from Thomas Jefferson's cellar. The bottle was proudly displayed, upright, in a glass case under hot lights. Inevitably, the antique cork slowly shrivelled and silently sunk into the wine, thus creating the world's most expensive bottle of vinegar.

Professional wine storage

If it is not possible to store your wines at home, look into trusting your finest wines to professional storage by a specialist in wine storage who understands and appreciates a wine's preferred habitat. To protect the legal health of your wine, ensure the specialist is financially secure and that each case of wine is clearly and unambiguously marked identifying you as the owner.

Cellar records

A written record of your cellar's consumptions and replenishments greatly adds to the enjoyment of the cellar. Allow a large page per case of wine. The heading should give price, supplier, quantity bought and purchase date. As the wine gently ages, you should sample a bottle from time to time. List a tasting note for each bottle sampled with date and details of the occasion. This monitoring of a wine's progress towards maturity will indicate to you when is the optimum time to drink up according to your personal preference. Records will also help you to keep track of which wines are stored where, helping you avoid disturbing the sleeping beauties.

If professional wine storage is used then cellar records should account for where, when, which and how much wine has been stored.

Serving wine

First remove the foil using a knife or a foil cutter just below the lip of the bottle. Old bottles that have been stored in damp cellars may have a slight mould round the lip which should be wiped. (The damp helps to preserve the moisture of the cork, but at the expense of disintegrating the labels. In these conditions, labels can be protected against damp by using clingfilm or by painting with clear varnish.)

Pulling a cork from a bottle of wine can be a smooth and slick operation or one inducing a hernia operation, depending on the efficiency of the corkscrew. Old-fashioned corkscrews can be things of beauty and ingenuity, but in practice difficult to use. The 'Screwpull' is perhaps the best corkscrew for ordinary use, though professionals prefer the 'Waiter's Friend'.

Gently twist the screw into the cork, using a good quality corkscrew. Try not to penetrate the cork all the way through as bits of cork may crumble into the wine. If the cork breaks before it is fully retrieved, it may be possible very gently to re-insert the screw and pull it out; otherwise you will do the wine no harm by gently pushing the remaining cork into the bottle, taking extreme care not to spray yourself or stain the carpet.

A wine whose cork has broken should be decanted. Indeed many not-so-brilliant wines benefit from the extra oxygenation resulting from the decanting process. Decanting can help if an immature wine is a little closed and tight and needs to be opened up on the nose and palate quickly. Finally, decanters are useful if you want to separate a wine from its sediment.

When opening potentially dangerous sparkling wine and Champagne bottles, remove the wire muzzle by untwisting the little wire loop, whilst keeping the other hand pressed firmly down on the mushroom-shaped cork. Hold the bottle at a 45^0 angle away from yourself and anyone else within firing range. The trick is to twist the *bottle* while holding the cork steady. Just before the cork is fully released tilt the cork slightly sideways to gently release the carbon dioxide gas. A soft sigh or gentle hiss should be heard and not a loud pop. It is better to keep the fizz in the wine than on the floor. This technique should be ignored by wine waiters for whom the size of their gratuity is often in direct relation to the number of decibels of the pop!

The most important aspect of serving wine is temperature. I suspect too many wines are not enjoyed to their full potential by being drunk at too cool or too warm a temperature. While most wines will perform well within a narrow range of temperatures a general guideline is 8^0–10^0C for sweet, sparkling, rosé and dull white wines. Coldness helps reduce any cloying taste in sweet wines while masking the acidity in very tart white wines and refreshing the flavour of low acidity wines. Overchilling can be a good thing in a bad wine. If a white wine is a bit brutish and you do not want to use it for cooking or for mulled wine, then chill it.

Some red wines with low tannin are structured similarly to white wines and may benefit from being cooled to 10^0–12^0C, e.g. Beaujolais, Valpolicella, Bardolino and reds from the Loire Valley.

More tannic red wines benefit from warmer temperatures of 15^0–18^0C as warmth counters the astringency of tannin. However, if tannic reds are served too warm, e.g. over 20^0C, the alcohol will begin to evaporate and dominate the wine's aroma and taste.

High quality dry whites and delicate wines show off all their subtleties and complexities at 12^0–16^0C.

The quickest way to chill a wine is to submerge it in water chilled with ice-cubes, as more surface area of the bottle is in direct contact with the coldness than using ice cubes alone. Unfortunately the result, though quick, leaves slippery bottles, often without labels. The refrigerator takes about four times longer to cool a wine. If you only wish to chill one bottle, a patent device, the 'Rapid Ice Vacu Vin', chills in minutes. It is a silver foil sleeve of liquid which slips over a bottle. It is kept frozen in the ice box until required.

To warm a wine quickly, pour it into a warmed jug or decanter. Let it rest for a few minutes before pouring back into the bottle. Alternatively pour the wine into glasses, cup your hands around the glass and gently swirl the wine. Ideally, time permitting, stand the wine in the room for several hours to gradually bring up the temperature.

Simply holding the bottle will indicate if a wine is too warm or too cold. It is better to serve a wine too cold than too warm as the wine will invariably warm up in the glass during the meal.

The order of serving wine

The order of serving wine is usually to start with the driest and lightest and finishing with the sweetest and fullest. White wines precede red wines which in turn precede sweet dessert wines or fortified liqueur wines. Exceptions exist. For instance, there are fewer more versatile aperitifs than a chilled fresh Fino Sherry (served correctly in a copita glass, of course). Or a sweet white wine partnering and contrasting with a salty starter—one defining and flattering the other. In such challenging circumstances, cleanse the palate with a piece of bread, water or a refreshing sorbet served between courses.

Editor's choice: new wines to try

Each year wines are included in The Best of Wine *for the first time. A number stand out this year as particularly exciting and worthy of special attention. Argentina and Greece are gaining in strength while Mexico has entered the market for the first time.*

L. A. Cetto Zinfandel 1998 (Mexico)

Milton Gisborne Chenin Blanc Te Arai Vineyard 1998 (New Zealand)

Casablanca Chardonnay 1998 (Chile)

Ptomaine des Blaguers Syrah VdP d'Oc 1996 (France-South)

Michel Picard Chardonnay VdP d'Oc 1997 (France-South)

Dom. des Lauriers Picpoul de Pinot AC Coteaux du Languedoc 1998 (France-South)

Finca Flichman Syrah 1996 (Argentina)

Catena Cabernet Sauvignon 1995 (Argentina)

Megas Oenos Skouras 1996 Peleponnes (Greece)

Fairview Zinfandel Carignan 1998 (South Africa)

The Wines

Argentina

In last year's *Best of Wine*, I wrote of Argentina as 'somewhere to watch in 1999'. Since that time, this newcomer has certainly found its feet in Ireland, and indeed in the export market in general. Its success is reflected in a thirty per cent increase in Argentinean wines listed this year.

However, Argentina is not just the current fashionable favourite. There are many serious reasons for its potential as a quality producer. First of all, Argentina produces quantity. It is the world's fourth largest producer, with declining home consumption and increasing commitment to quality winemaking. Reliable, large producers mean competitive prices and Argentina has shown its ability to produce quantities of inexpensive, easy-drinking reds with more character than often found at the price. The extra character often comes from different grape varieties. For Argentina has a range of grapes beyond the usual globetrotters. Italian varieties thrive, so do Rhône and Spanish grapes and the Malbec has long been made the country's own. Clever blends including Tempranillo or Sangiovese make very appealing party wines and offer something different.

Cooler-climate vineyards in the higher altitudes around Mendoza have improved the quality of white wines and more serious, long-lived reds especially Cabernet and Cabernet blends. Winemakers from all over Europe and the Americas are moving in to take advantage of Argentina's natural strengths and the country's wine is reaping the benefit.

The original leader in quality production in Argentina was Nicholas Catena who still produces some of the country's finest wines—see his starred Cabernet Sauvignon below. There are now a host of other good producers such as Flichman, Norton and Weinert, the latter producing some highly serious reds with considerable ability to age.

Undoubtedly Argentina is still a place to watch and may one day challenge Chile for South American supremacy.

White £5 - £6

Correas Torrontés/ Chardonnay 97   *Gilbeys*

Aromatic white, fruit-driven

Perfumed, slightly herbal nose. Ample ripe fruit flavours and just enough acidity, though generally mild. Delicate and quite attractive.
Asparagus rolls

Etchart Rio de Plata Torrontés 97   *Fitzgerald*

Aromatic white

Floral, boiled sweet aromas; light and floral in the mouth with lime cordial flavours. Light, clean finish.
Aperitif or party wine

Santa Isabel Chardonnay 98
Dunnes Stores

Full-bodied white, oak

Quite spicy nose with hints of vanilla. Lots of zingy fruit—grapefruit, pineapple and mango flavours with a thin layer of butter and crisp acidity. Nice length.
Monkfish with melon and ginger sauce

Trapiche Chardonnay 98
United Beverages

Light fruity white

Mineral nose. Rather grassy melon fruit; well-balanced with crisp acidity supported by highish alcohol. Nice young wine.
Guacamole with tortilla chips

White £6 - £8

Trapiche Chardonnay Oak Cask 97
United Beverages   C ££

Full-bodied white, oak

Lovely inviting aromas of ripe pineapple, lemon curd and melon. Similar fruit on the palate wrapped in an oak cloak. Tasty and satisfying and good value.
Christmas turkey

Etchart Cafayete Torrontés 97   *Fitzgerald*

Aromatic white

Rather honeyed nose. Light and clean on the palate with tropical fruit bowl flavours and very long finish.
Asparagus salad

Simonassi Lyon Chenin/ Tocai 98   *Gleeson*

Aromatic white

Wet wool on the nose with a floral touch. Clean fruit sorbet flavours, quite floral again with zippily fresh acidity and a crisp finish.
Guacamole

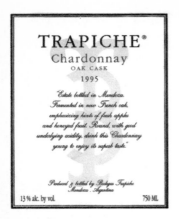

White £8 - £10

Etchart Cafayate Chardonnay 98
Fitzgerald

Full-bodied white, oak

Pineapple and butter on the nose. Round and ripe with balancing acidity and a warm, biscuity finish. Subtle it is not!
Grilled red snapper with ginger sauce

Red £5 or less

Parral Malbec/Merlot 98
United Beverages

Light fruity red

Fresh fruity nose; lively and fresh with berry fruit flavours and a bit of peppery spice in the finish. Great party stuff.
Pasta with bacon and tomatoes

Tesco Chimango Tempranillo/Malbec nv
Tesco

Light fruity red

Quite earthy touch to red fruit aromas. Intense flavour yet light, with good fruit and balanced structure. Slightly hard in the finish but good value.
Spicy pizza

Etchart Rio de Plata Malbec 96
Fitzgerald   C

Medium-bodied red

Ripe jam aromas with a hint of baked fruit. Plenty of plummy, fruitcake flavours and a nice bite of tannin. Good length too.
Lamb and bacon kebabs

Maranon Syrah 98
Barry & Fitzwilliam   ££

Medium-bodied red

Aromas of blackberries and pepper jumping out of the glass. Dry, well-balanced palate with plenty of rich, ripe berry fruit flavours. Holds up well as a great party wine.
Winter stew or a spicy bufffet casserole

Red £6 - £8

Finca Flichman Syrah 96
TDL   C

Full-bodied red, fruit-driven

Soft fruit and spice on the nose.

Ripe fig-type fruit with nicely balanced tannins. Round and smooth with a long finish.
Goulash

Trapiche Oak Cask Cabernet Sauvignon 95

United Beverages   C

Full-bodied red

Ripe bouquet of blackberry fruit. Good mix of black pepper and cassis flavours with firm tannins and balancing acidity. Long, dry finish. Very good value.
Needs meat, especially a good steak

Correas Syrah 96

Gilbeys

Full-bodied red, fruit-driven

Vanilla and spice on the nose. Rich, ripe and robust, full of mouthfilling baked fruit, almost like Port. Well-priced blockbuster.
Beef Stroganoff

Correas Syrah/Sangiovese 96   *Gilbeys*

Full-bodied red

Quite jammy on the nose with damson and bitter cherry fruit

Cabernet Sauvignon
—— 1993 ——

13% Vol.   75CL℮

flavours with a touch of spice. Quite firm and structured with a good finish.
Barbecued meat

Finca Flichman Cabernet Sauvignon 97   *TDL*

Full-bodied red, fruit-driven

Oaky cassis aromas with a touch of liquorice. Bramble fruit flavours with firm tannin and a warm finish.
Meatloaf

Norton Barbera 97

Oddbins

Medium-bodied red

Damp undergrowth and earthy fruit aromas. Very peppery to start followed by spicy, redcurrant fruit. Refreshing acidity and ripe friendly tannin. Pleasant, easy-going wine.
Spaghetti with meat sauce

Tesco's Monster Spicy Red Syrah nv   *Tesco*

Full-bodied red

Earthy blackberries on the nose with slightly floral hints. Well-balanced, firm structure with vegetal, earthy, spicy flavours. Lots going on and a long finish, too.
Venison casserole with redcurrant jelly sauce

TriVento Malbec 98

Findlater

Medium-bodied red

Tarry red fruit aromas and vegetal spicy fruit flavours. Nice touch of tannin and refreshing acidity. Clean, dry finish.
Grilled aubergine in pitta bread

Red £8 - £10

Alamos Ridge Cabernet Sauvignon 97
Searson   C

Full-bodied red, fruit-driven

Ripe blackcurrant aromas followed by mouthfilling velvet fruit. Very well-structured with good balance of fruit, tannin and acidity. Long and flavoursome finish.
Pot-roasted beef or steak

Arnaldo B. Etchart Cafayate 96
Fitzgerald   C

Full-bodied red, fruit-driven

Cassis and plums on the nose. Well-structured with a weight of blackberry and plum fruit well-supported by alcohol. Nice oaky backdrop and lingering finish.
Roast duck with beer

Red £10 - £12

Valentin Bianchi Cabernet Sauvignon 96
Oddbins   C

Full-bodied red

Good meaty nose, rich and savoury. Concentrated fruit with subtle oak. Very well-balanced with firm yet elegant structure. Good and getting better.
Roast game

Red £12 - £15

Catena Cabernet Sauvignon 95
Searson   I

Full-bodied red, fruit-driven

Elegant, most attractive aromas of blackcurrant and cigarbox.

Big velvety mouthfeel. Good intensity of fruit in a harmonious structure with well-integrated oak. Long and lovely in the finish.
Roast lamb with herbs

Weinert Carrascal 94
Molloy's

Full-bodied red, fruit-driven

Earthy fruit on the nose. Firm tannic structure with ripe yet restrained fruit nicely integrated with oak. Very traditional style.
Beef casserole

Weinert Carrascal 95
Woodford Bourne

Full-bodied red, fruit-driven

Earthy tobacco, fruitcake aromas. Firmly structured with stewed damson fruit and spice. Well-balanced:long spicy finish.
Grilled steaks

Red £15 - £20

Weinert Cabernet Sauvignon 91
Molloy's   C

Full-bodied red, fruit-driven

Forest fruit and rubber on the nose. Mature and well-structured with plenty of fruit; full bodied with ripe tannins. A complex wine with plenty of character and good value.
T-bone steak

Weinert Malbec 94
Woodford Bourne

Full-bodied red, fruit-driven

Earthy aromas with touches of barley sugar. Chunky— lots of oak and tannin and flavours of fruitcake and spice. Long finish.
Daube of beef or similar winter warmer

Australia

It might come as a surprise that the newest thing to come from Australia is Chardonnay! This is Australian Chardonnay as never before: cool, elegant, subtle, tightly-knit, restrained—are we in the right country? The original Australian Chardonnays were undoubtedly over the top. At the time these ripe, rich, monsters were a welcome relief from the then rather green offerings of lower-priced Burgundy. However, such popularity rapidly disappeared and the overblown Aussies acquired a very un-chic image. Now, all is changed. The peaches, butter and cream variety can still be found, but there are also many really delightful, perfectly balanced, moderately priced wines. Technology is in part responsible together with new experiments with old methods. But cooler climates have also made a difference with vineyards in Victoria, Western Australia and Tasmania, as well as regions such as Padthaway or the Adelaide Hills, really coming into their own.

Coolness, complexity, terroir are the new buzzwords of Australian winemaking. If varietals from all over the land formed the Australian wine revolution of the late twentieth century, then regional wines look set to take them into the twenty-first. Now we can no longer talk of 'Australian Shiraz' as we could ten years ago. Shiraz still makes some of the country's finest reds but in many different styles and different wines. While McLaren Shiraz is rich and powerful, Victoria makes a drier, spicy wine, Barossa is soft and full, Hunter Valley is all tar and leather. Cabernet Sauvignon is much the same with different wines emerging from Coonawarra, Western Australian, the Hunter Valley and so on.

Australia's discovery of cool climates has led to success with different grape varieties such as Riesling and Pinot Noir. Australian Riesling is full and rounded with ripe fruit flavour yet bracing lemon and lime acidity. Pinot Noir also tends towards the soft, fruity side of the grape but with increasing complexity of flavour and maturity.

Apart from the re-invention of Chardonnay, other white wine grapes are beginning to shine. Semillon is highly successful and may prove the best keeper in the long term, while Marsanne produces really lovely fragrant, fruity whites but with body and substance which are a perfect match for trendy Thai cuisine.

In the midst of such change and innovation, the consistency of many Australian wines is impressive. The big companies that dominate have an amazing ability to maintain quality across a range of styles and prices. Names such as Hardys, Lindemans, Penfold's, Rosemount, to mention a fe,w are a virtual assurance of good winemaking.

White £5 or less

Tesco Rhine-Riesling Australia White Wine nv
Tesco   ££

Light fruity white, off-dry

Intense fruit cocktail aromas. Off-dry with rich fruit and lime cordial flavours. Clean, fresh finish.
Chinese meals

Seppelt Moyston Colombard/Chardonnay 98
Dunnes Stores   ££

Light fruity white

Ripe, floral nose, nice fruit . Fresh and aromatic in the mouth with a slightly nutty influence in the background.
Summer salad

Seppelt Moyston Riesling 97
Dunnes Stores

Aromatic white, fruit-driven

Marzipan and chemical aromas, typical Riesling. Off-dry palate, oily with ripe red apple fruit and balancing acidity.
Spicy pastries of fish or vegetables

White £5 - £6

Moyston Seppelt Unoaked Chardonnay 98
Dunnes Stores   C

Light fruity white

Fat, buttery aromas. Plenty of tropical fruit on the palate. Flavoursome with an oily texture and dry finish.
Mussels in curry sauce

Angove's Butterfly Ridge Colombard/Chardonnay 98
O'Brien's

Light fruity white

Fresh and crisp with nice ripe fruit. Well-balanced with a clean finish.
Salad first course

Jacob's Creek Chardonnay 98
Fitzgerald

Full-bodied white

Lemon meringue pie jumping out of the glass. Very fresh with a creamy texture and loads of ripe orchard fruit. Not at all complex but really delicious!
Chicken satay

Jacob's Creek Semillon/ Chardonnay 98
Fitzgerald

Full-bodied white

Ripe fruit on the nose with

plenty of fruit flavour following through on the palate. Balanced acidity and crisp finish.

Creamy pork casserole

Lindemans Cawarra Semillon/Chardonnay 98
Gilbeys

Full-bodied white

Butterscotch and vanilla on the nose. Fruity with rounded texture and nice balancing acidity.

Chinese chicken with cashew nuts

Peter Lehmann Chenin Blanc 98
United Beverages

Light fruity white

Lanolin and a touch of honey on the nose. Lovely ripe peach fruit cut by green apple tartness. Smooth but very refreshing in the finish.

Pork satay

Seppelt Terrain Series Chardonnay 97
Dunnes Stores

Full-bodied white

Marzipan and honey on the nose, slightly floral. Lots of lemon and lime fruit with hints of butter and vanilla. Well-made wine.

Baked chicken with honey and lemon

Yaldara Semillon/ Chardonnay 98
Barry & Fitzwilliam

Medium to full-bodied white

Melon and mango fruit aromas with a touch of oiliness. Melon and lime fruit flavours with nicely balanced acidity and alcohol and a clean finish.

Stir-fried pork or chicken; seafood pasta

White £6 - £8

Penfold's Koonunga Hill Chardonnay 98
Findlater ☆

Full-bodied white

Stewed apples and pears on the nose with attractive spice. Lovely balance of acidity and ripe tropical fruit. Good weight and mouthfeel and a long spicy finish.

Stuffed turkey

Penfold's Rawson's Retreat Bin 21 Semillon/ Chardonnay/Colombard 98
Findlater C

Medium-bodied white

Honeyed tropical fruit with floral tones. Rounded palate with lovely tropical fruit and balancing acidity. Well-integrated hints of vanilla and a long smooth finish.

Stir-fried chicken or pork

Peter Lehmann The Barossa Semillon 97
United Beverages C

Full-bodied white

Ripe fruit and floral aromas with a touch of burnt toast. Concentrated with good weight —rich and mouthfilling right to the end.

Pork with cream sauce

Hardys Stamp of Australia Chardonnay/Semillon 98
Allied Drinks ££

Full-bodied white

Pronounced aromas of tropical fruit and warm hay! Lovely mix of ripe melon and zippy

gooseberry flavours which last well in the finish.
Seafood mayonnaise or rich salad; spicy fish casserole

Angove's Classic Reserve Chardonnay 98
O'Briens

Full-bodied white

Full and rich with lots of honeyed ripe fruit aromas. Buttery, tropical flavour cut through with crisp acidity; long, rich finish.
Grilled chicken in honey and lemon marinade

Carlyle Victoria Marsanne/ Semillon 96
Greenhills

Full-bodied white

Roasted nuts and honey on the nose. Dry, full and waxy with nutty, honeyed fruit. Punchy, intense wine with plenty of flavour and a long, hot finish.
Mildly spiced pork dishes

Cranswick Estate Semillon/ Chardonnay 97
MacCormaic

Full-bodied white

Ripe butterscotch aromas. Nice weight in the mouth with toasty flavours and citrus fruit. Full oily texture with lovely refreshing lemon all the way through.

Gnangara Chardonnay 98
United Beverages

Light fruity white

Well-made, relatively light wine with nice fruit and balance.
Creamy chicken curry

Houghton H. W. B. Dry White 97
Oddbins

Aromatic white, fruit-driven

Buttery melon aromas. Ripe dessert apple flavours with hints of spice and tart green apple finish.
Warm salad of fish or poultry

Lindemans Bin 65 Chardonnay 98
Gilbeys
Full-bodied white
Ripe, buttery apple aromas. Ripe melon and pineapple fruit with a touch of citrus flavour, slightly smoky especially in the finish.
Creamy smoked chicken pasta

McGuigan Bin 7000 Chardonnay 97
Barry & Fitzwilliam

Full-bodied white

Tropical fruit aromas mingle with butterscotch and vanilla. Similar palate, rich, almost creamy textured, shot through with bracing citrus acidity to the finish.
Barbecues or mixed salads, especially mayonnaise-based dishes

Oxford Landing Sauvignon Blanc 99
Cassidy

Aromatic white, fruit-driven

Grassy herbaceous aromas. Typical gooseberry fruit with balanced acidity and some length of finish.
Asparagus crostini

Rosemount Semillon/ Chardonnay 98
Grants

Full-bodied white

Lively, fresh citrusy nose. Plenty of fruit on the palate with lively fresh acidity and clean dry finish.
Barbecued chicken

Taltarni Victoria Sauvignon Blanc 98
Dunnes Stores

Aromatic white

Chalk and nettles on the nose. Very intense green fruit flavours. Highly extracted and ripe, almost sweet, with just balanced acidity. Sauvignon tamed in the Australian sun!
Prawns and asparagus with hollandaise sauce

Tatachilla McLaren Vale Chardonnay 98
O'Brien's

Full-bodied white, oak

Ripe melon fruit aromas. Toasty ripe fruit palate, rather oily and full with a long, white pepper finish.
Creamy chicken curry with almonds and coconut

Tatachilla McLaren Vale Clarendon Riesling 97
O'Briens

Aromatic white, fruit-driven

Forward petrol aromas with green apples. Ripe fruit--not too sharp. Quite rounded Riesling, well-balanced and easy-drinking.
Spicy fish

Tesco Hunter Valley Semillon 98
Tesco

Full-bodied white

Rich, toasty lanolin nose. Very elegant palate with barely ripe mouth-watering pineapple fruit and a cool citrus finish.
Spicy Chinese prawns

Tesco McLaren Vale Chardonnay 97
Tesco

Full-bodied white, oak

Oak aromas dominate on the nose. Exotic fruit is balanced by fresh acidity. Highish warming alcohol and new oak support the fruit. Really needs a year to mellow but nice now.
Pasta with cream

Tesco South-Eastern Australia Chardonnay nv
Tesco

Full-bodied white, oak

Warm sunny aromas of white pepper and vanilla. Rich ripe fruit--peaches, melons--spiced with pepper as in the bouquet. Warm alcohol in the finish.
Barbecued fish and chicken

Wakefield Clare Valley Promised Land Unwooded Chardonnay 97
Koala

Full-bodied white

Buttery tropical fruit aromas. Rounded mouthfeel with tropical fruit flavours. A pleasant wine.
Thai chicken curry

Wolf Blass White Label Semillon/Sauvignon Blanc 98

Dillon

slightly herbaceous twist. Broad apple-flavoured palate with bracing citrus acidity.
Escalopes of pork with cumin and lemon

White £8 - £10

Ch. Tahbilk Marsanne (Unwooded) 96

United Beverages ☆

Full-bodied white

Ripe pineapple aromas, slightly oily. Good weight and concentration of fruit with nicely balanced acidity. Should age well and gain complexity.
Pork or chicken in coconut milk

Peter Lehmann The Barossa Chardonnay 97

United Beverages ☆

Full-bodied white, oak

Complex aromas of toast, butter and honeyed tropical fruit. Full and robust yet with lovely fresh fruit flavour and toast and honey in the finish.
Chicken with a rich sauce

Evans & Tate Two Vineyards Chardonnay 98

United Beverages C

Full-bodied white, oak

Spicy fruit salad aromas, Full and creamy with plenty of rich fruit and vanilla flavours and zingy acidity.
Thai spiced prawns

Heggies Vineyard Riesling 98

Cassidy C

Aromatic white, fruit-driven

Lime and grapefruit aromas. Spritzy with green fruit and a clean zippy finish with a very limey edge.
Deep-fried spiced crab fritters

St Hallett Barossa Chardonnay 98

Dunnes Stores C

Full-bodied white, oak

Honeyed tropical fruit aromas. Broad mouthfeel with oaky backdrop and ripe fruit. Well-structured typical style with lots of ripe fruit appeal.
Monkfish with a lime and ginger cream

Angove's Mondiale Semillon/Verdelho/ Chardonnay 98

O'Briens

Light fruity white

Grapey, citrus nose; mellow soft fruit flavours, ripe and round with enough acidity to balance. Long, mellow finish.
Creamy chicken curry

Bethany Barossa Semillon 97

O'Briens

Full-bodied white

Buttery oaky spice on the nose. Waxy ripe fruit flavours with balancing lemon acidity. Well-made typical varietal.
Pork with spices

Brown Brothers Victoria Dry Muscat 98

Woodford Bourne

Aromatic white

Heady floral aromas; fresh and grapey with a creamy lemon mid-palate. Nice length of finish.
Grilled asparagus or similar vegetable salad

John James McWilliams Chardonnay 97
TDL

Full-bodied white, oak

Ripe and buttery with mineral notes in the background. Super-ripe fruit with oaky spice and rather low acidity.
Veal with orange sauce

Mount Pleasant Elizabeth Hunter Valley Semillon 94
TDL

Full-bodied white

Aromas of lemon meringue pie. Very waxy, nutty palate, showing quite a bit of age with a lemony finish.
Brill with cream and vanilla sauce

Penfold's Barossa Valley Semillon/Chardonnay 97
Findlater

Full-bodied white

Very full aromas of spring flowers with vanilla. Ripe melon and mango dominate a round, creamy, fat palate with balancing acidity.
Chinese chicken with cashew nuts

Pewsey Vale Eden Valley Riesling 98
Fields

Aromatic white, fruit-driven

Hints of oiliness on the nose with citrus fruit aromas; ripe fruit with citrus acidity, fresh and clean on the palate.
Gratin of fish

Rosemount Chardonnay 98
Grants

Full-bodied white, oak

Pineapple, spice and butter on the nose. Intense tropical fruit flavours. Fat and oily with warm spicy length.
Creamy pasta, say with mushrooms and bacon

Tatachilla Padthaway Chardonnay 98
O'Briens

Full-bodied white, oak

Restrained yet ripe, white peach aromas with oaky spice in the background. Red apple fruit and white pepper spice with balanced acidity. Still young and could develop more interest in time.
Turbot with hollandaise sauce

Tyrrell's Old Winery Chardonnay 98
Remy

Full-bodied white, oak

Big buttery aromas and ripe fruit. Fresh lively palate with lots of fruit. Sunny easy-drinking wine, though a bit pricey.
Swordfish kebabs

Wakefield Clare Valley Chardonnay 97
Koala

Full-bodied white, oak

Ripe apple, oak and butter on the nose. Well-balanced with a good weight of tropical fruit and nicely integrated oak. Pleasant, well-structured wine.
Smoked fish gratin

Yalumba Oxford Landing Viognier 96
Cassidy

Aromatic white, fruit-driven

Apricot and peach with nutty aromas. Rounded and quite fat with plenty of fruit. Fresh, slightly oily finish.
Carrot terrine with orange dressing

White £10 - £12

Basedow Barossa Semillon 96
MacCormaic ☆

Full-bodied white

Intriguing aromas of beeswax, roses and dried apricot. Ripe rich fruit--melon and peach in an oily, creamy texture. Good weight, perfectly balanced and very long-lasting.
Pork with ginger and coriander

Lindemans Padthaway Chardonnay 97
Gilbeys ☆

Full-bodied white, oak

Lovely ripe, balanced aromas. Full-bodied but very fresh and quite elegant with lovely ripe, honeyed fruit and a cool, subtly oaked structure. Long and lingering--a very stylish wine.
Scallops with pineapple salsa.

Mitchelton Goulburn Valley Marsanne 96
Cassidy ☆

Full-bodied white

Floral, citrus and honey aromas. Lovely balance of tropical fruit flavours with hints of honeysuckle and crisp acidity. Long, nutty finish.
Thai green curry

Yarra Ridge Chardonnay 96
Oddbins ☆

Full-bodied white, oak

Honey and buttered toast on the nose. Lots of fruit with structure and complexity. Very well-balanced with a long finish.
Roast poussin

CV (Capel Vale) Unwooded Chardonnay 97
Fields C

Full-bodied white

Tropical fruit with toffee and caramel aromas. Quite delicate and subtle with a glorious rich fruit character.
Scallops with ginger sauce

Rymill Coonawarra Sauvignon Blanc 96
Gleeson C

Aromatic white, fruit-driven

Enticing aromas of kiwi and mango, honeysuckle and ripe melon. Mouthfilling ripe fruit similar to the nose, balanced by mineral tones beneath and crisp acidity. Well-rounded fruit flavour lasts through a long finish.
Prawns with peppers

Sandalford Mount Barker/ Margaret River Chardonnay 97
Fitzgerald C

Full-bodied white, oak

Honey and butterscotch with ripe tropical fruit background. Nicely balanced oak and ripe buttery fruit with a long, dry finish.
Poussin with apricot and almond stuffing

Brown Brothers Victoria Semillon 96

Woodford Bourne

Full-bodied white

Ripe, even slightly burnt on the nose. Quite intense bittersweet citrus flavours and balanced acidity. Long finish.

Chinese chicken dishes or stir-fried pork

Driftwood Margaret River Semillon 97

Fields

Full-bodied white

Subdued nose, damp wool and candlewax. Richly textured palate of ripe tropical fruit in a waxy blanket. Clean, fresh finish with lasting fruit flavour.

Spiced monkfish with cream sauce

Ninth Island Tasmania Chardonnay 98

Fitzgerald

Medium-bodied white

Fresh zesty nose with a touch of grapefruit. Slightly oily apples and melons on the palate; ripe and well-balanced.

Avocado salad

Petaluma Riesling 96

Dunnes Stores

Aromatic white, fruit-driven

Distinct petrol aromas of mature Riesling. Quite typical varietal with crisp acidity and ripe, floral fruit with an oily background.

Spicy crabcakes with coriander and ginger

White £12 - £15

Rosemount Roxburgh Chardonnay 96

Grants ☆

Full-bodied white, oak

Complex aromas of toast, subdued tropical fruit and hazelnuts. Big, mouthfilling fruit in a buttery texture nicely balanced by acidity and spice. Long elegant finish. Refined and very stylish wine.

Lobster Thermidor

Rosemount Show Reserve Hunter Valley Chardonnay 97

Grants ☆

Full-bodied white, oak

Ripe melon and honey aromas with a citrus twist. Concentrated peach and melon fruit flavours in a classic, well-integrated style with excellent weight and balance and restrained elegant character. Long and impressive.

Stylish choice for Christmas turkey

Geoff Merrill Chardonnay 94

United Beverages

Full-bodied white, oak

Buttery creamy vanilla with toast and ripe fruit aromas. Nice rounded mellow wine with balanced flavours. Mature and long.

Monkfish with a rich sauce

Rothbury Estate Brokenback Semillon 97

Cassidy

Full-bodied white

Honey and lemon aromas which follow to the palate. Very

flavoursome wine with concentration of fruit and honeyed, spice complexity. Should age well.
Pork with lemon and coriander

Vasse Felix Semillon/ Sauvignon Blanc/ Chardonnay 96
Cassidy

Full-bodied white

Fruit salad aromas. Very concentrated, ripe, ripe fruit and tropical flavours. Quite developed with lots of interest. Drinking well now.
Breast of chicken with mango

Red £5 - £6

Geoff Merrill Owen's Estate Grenache/Shiraz 97
United Beverages   C

Full-bodied red, fruit-driven

White pepper and dark berry fruit aromas. Soft, ripe fruit, chewy weight with a dash of spice. Very appealing, good value wine.
Merguez sausages and kebabs

Angove's Butterfly Ridge Shiraz/Cabernet 98
O'Briens   ££

Full-bodied red, fruit-driven

Juicy fruit aromas. Soft, easy-drinking style with ripe fruit and spice to the fore. Well-made and very appealing.
Pizza with spicy sausage

Jacob's Creek Grenache/ Shiraz 98
Fitzgerald

Light fruity red

Simple aromas of ripe, jammy berries and similar fruits on the palate. Light and easy-drinking

with plenty of fruit.
Calazone pizza

Peter Lehmann Grenache 98
United Beverages

Full-bodied red, fruit-driven

Peppery fruit pastille aromas, touch of banana. Almost sweet on the palate, rich and chewy plum and cherry flavours. A robust wine yet soft and easy to drink.
Chunky sausages and barbecue food in general

Tesco Australian Shiraz nv
Tesco

Full-bodied red, fruit-driven

Red berry compote aromas. Juicy ripe berry fruit in a creamy texture with soft tannin and balanced acidity. Enjoyable, easy-drinking style.
Good party wine even with spicy food

Red £6 - £8

Rosemount GSM McLaren Vale Grenache/Syrah/ Mourvèdre 96
Grants   ☆

Full-bodied red, fruit-driven

Spicy, peppery nose. Silky palate with exuberant fruit and spice flavours cloaking the tannin. Nicely balanced oak and a long, flavoursome finish.
Venison medallions with a fruit and spice sauce

Aldridge Estate Shiraz/ Merlot 98
MacCormaic   C

Full-bodied red, fruit-driven

Immediate ripe fruit, plums and berries with a touch of

vanilla. Abundant fruit and quite youthful tannin. Juicy pastille flavours in the finish.
Spicy stir-fry of beef

Lindemans Bin 50 Shiraz 97
Gilbeys   C

Full-bodied red, fruit-driven

Intense ripe aromas of pears baked in red wine and spices. Good structure matched by ripe fruit. Well-balanced with a lingering flavoursome finish.
Spicy beef and chilli beans

Wakefield Clare Valley Shiraz/Cabernet 98
Koala   C

Full-bodied red, fruit-driven

Spicy baked soft fruits on the nose. Good weight of creamy fruit flavours with hints of spice. Lovely soft, easy-drinking wine with a long fruity finish.
Barbebcued meats and kebabs

Angove's Classic Reserve Cabernet 98
O'Briens

Full-bodied red, fruit-driven

Crushed fruit with a touch of spice on the nose. Plenty of rich fruit, blackcurrant wine gums, but not overblown. Soft but with tangy acidity and good length of flavour.
Lamb steaks

Angove's Classic Reserve Shiraz 97
O'Briens

Full-bodied red, fruit-driven

Dark fruit aromas with a touch of liquorice. Lovely ripe, creamy berry fruit flavours with nice bite of oak and chewy grip. Foodie stuff.

Barbecue steak and sausages

Black Rock Coonawarra Cabernet Sauvignon 96
Dunnes Stores

Full-bodied red, fruit-driven

Complex spice and wood aromas. Big and mouthfilling with baked fruit flavours; very intense with refreshing acidity and firm structure. A deep brooding wine with impressive impact.
Pigeon casseroled with grapes

Gnangara Shiraz 97
United Beverages

Full-bodied red, fruit-driven

Super-ripe plums and figs with a touch of leather on the nose. Flavours of spicy fruit crumble balanced by tannin and acidity and a warm finish.
Aubergine and red pepper casserole

Jacob's Creek Shiraz/ Cabernet 97
Fitzgerald

Medium-bodied red

Ripe, smoky blackberries on the nose. Uncomplicated and ripe on the palate with plenty of blackberry fruit and balanced acidity. Well-made.
Meatloaf

Lindemans Bin 45 Cabernet Sauvignon 97
Gilbeys

Full-bodied red, fruit-driven

Baked Christmas cake aromas. Jammy fruit flavours; big and mouthfilling with a clean dry finish.
Grilled hamburgers with relishes

McGuigan Cabernet Sauvignon Bin 4000 98
Barry & Fitzwilliam

Full-bodied red, fruit-driven

Ripe brambles on the nose with a touch of oak. Nice balance of tannin and acidity; good weight of ripe blackberry fruit with mint and herb overtones and a creamy, oaky texture.
Sunday lunch roast stuffed lamb

McGuigan Millennium Shiraz 2000 98
Barry & Fitzwilliam

Full-bodied red, fruit-driven

Fruit of the forest aromas, spicy and warm. Soft ripe plum and damson fruit with spicy, peppery flavours and balancing acidity.
Chilli con carne

Merrill Mount Hurtle Grenache/Shiraz 97
Oddbins

Full-bodied red, fruit-driven

Plum jam on the nose with a touch of spice. Ripe fruit flavours with spice and toffee and a bitter cherry twist in the finish. Firm and mouthfilling with plenty of interest.
Chorizo, ham and chicken casserole with red peppers

Oxford Landing Cabernet Sauvignon/Shiraz 98
Cassidy

Full-bodied red, fruit-driven

Ripe blackcurrants with a hint of chocolate on the nose. Quite firm tannin and high acidity which meld into a spicy dark fruit finish. Different and good value.
Kebabs of meat, onions and aubergines

Penfold's Rawson's Retreat Bin 35 Shiraz/Ruby Cabernet/Cabernet Sauvignon 98
Findlater

Full-bodied red, fruit-driven

Ripe fruit and pepper aromas. Very ripe, rather medicinal fruit with extremely crisp acidity and a warm finish.
Beef in beer

Rosemount Shiraz/ Cabernet 98
Grants

Full-bodied red, fruit-driven

Ripe fruit aromas of cassis, vanilla and pepper. Oodles of dark berry fruits balanced by mild tannins. Appealing spicy finish.
Chunky sausage casserole

Sacred Hill Shiraz/Cabernet 98
Febvre

Full-bodied red, fruit-driven

Hints of eucalyptus, tar and spice with bramble fruit aromas. Silky-textured and quite liquoricey in flavour with plenty of dark autumnal fruit and balancing tannin. Spice in the finish.
Spicy casseroles or soy-glazed lamb

Taltarni Fiddleback Terrace 97
Dunnes Stores

Full-bodied red, fruit-driven

Dark berry fruit with nuances of tar and rubber. Intense berry fruit again on the palate with a bitter twist. Soft, balanced tannin. Lots of flavour.
Winter stews

Tatachilla Partners Cabernet Sauvignon/Shiraz 98

O'Briens

Full-bodied red, fruit-driven

Spicy fruit aromas followed by a very fruit-driven palate with blackcurrant and berry flavours and a spicy finish.
Spicy dishes including nut roast and cutlets

Vine Vale Shiraz 97

United Beverages

Full-bodied red, fruit-driven

Jammy forest fruit aromas. Gorgeous ripe fruit with a hint of spice. Soft tannin and a pleasant streak of refreshing acidity to balance the rich fruit. Long and satisfying finish.
Chilli con carne

Wakefield Clare Valley Pinot Noir 98

Koala

Medium-bodied red

Rhubarb and tinned strawberries on the nose. Fresh and fruity with lots of strawberry flavours. Soft and easy to drink.
Pigeon with sweet and sour damson compote

Red £8 - £10

Tyrrell's Old Winery Pinot Noir 98

Remy ☆ ☆

Medium-bodied red

Lovely complexity of smoky toasted oak and nutty fruit. Beautifully balanced wine with strawberry fruit mingling with vanilla and toast. Very well-balanced with excellent use of oak. A delicious wine, full of

character and style.
Duck breast with mango

Tesco Coonawarra Cabernet Sauvignon 97

Tesco ☆

Full-bodied red, fruit-driven

Minty fruit and woodland undergrowth aromas. Good weight of fruit, quite cool and elegant, well-balanced by tannin and acidity with flavours carried through to the end.
Lamb noisettes with ratatouille

Wakefield Clare Valley Cabernet Sauvignon 97

Koala ☆

Full-bodied red, fruit-driven

Intense ripe bramble aromas with vanilla hints. Lovely balance of acid, tannin and ripe blackcurrant fruit, developing some chocolate richness. Long and lingering wine.
Lamb in whiskey and thyme marinade

Wolf Blass South Australia Shiraz 96

Dillon ☆

Full-bodied red, fruit-driven

Chocolate, spice and all things nice jumping out of the glass! A weight of fruit encased in chocolate and spice flavours. Well-rounded tannins and long lingering finish add even more pleasure.
Barbecued lamb with a spicy fruit relish

Ch. Tahbilk Cabernet Sauvignon 93

United Beverages C

Full-bodied red, fruit-driven

Concentrated fruit bouquet

with vanilla and cedar tones. Spicy palate with mature oaky flavours with mellow autumnal fruit. Lovely, long warm finish. Delicious!
Duck with apples

Evans & Tate Barrique 61 Cabernet/Merlot 98

United Beverages   C

Full-bodied red, fruit-driven

Blackcurrant and raisin aromas, quite spicy. Mellow spicy fruit with subtle oak, lots of flavour. Softening tannins and balanced acidity make a very appealing wine.
Loin of lamb

Hardys Bankside Shiraz 97

Allied Drinks   C

Full-bodied red, fruit-driven

Plum and damson fruit on the nose, attractively spicy. Complex flavours of ripe berry and plum fruit wrap around an oaky core. Long and spicy finish. Very appealing!
Teriyaki marinated beef

Hill of Hope Hunter Valley Cabernet Sauvignon 97

Mitchell   C

Full-bodied red, fruit-driven

Very warm, fruit-driven nose. Lovely rich fruits and soft tannin. Well-balanced fruit-driven style with a long creamy finish.
Grilled fillet of beef with orange and soy marinade

McGuigan Shareholders' Cabernet/Merlot 97

Barry & Fitzwilliam   C

Full-bodied red, fruit-driven

Eucalyptus and mint mingle with ripe blackcurrant aromas.

Mouthfilling wine, firmly structured with ripe blackcurrant, mint and vanilla tones. Big and beautiful but needs a bit more time.
Butterfly leg of lamb with plenty of herbs, cooked slightly rare

Yaldara Reserve Cabernet/ Merlot 95

Barry & Fitzwilliam   C

Full-bodied red, fruit-driven

Ripe blackcurrant and mint on the nose. Big and bold with loads of minty, ripe blackcurrant fruit and hints of dark chocolate in the long finish.
Marinated grilled lamb steaks with a herb relish

Yaldara Reserve Shiraz 98

Barry & Fitzwilliam   C

Full-bodied red, fruit-driven

Summer pudding aromas jump from the glass. Plenty of upfront fruity character with soft tannin and balanced acidity. Well-made wine, with long, lingering fruit flavours.
Spicy duck with ginger and plum

Brown Brothers Victoria Tarrango 98

Woodford Bourne

Light fruity red

Soft fruit aromas with rather medicinal overtones. Ripe juicy fruit, soft and easy-drinking with a dry finish. Quite expensive.
Spicy sausages from the barbecue

Deen de Bortoli Vat 9 Cabernet Sauvignon 97

Febvre

Full-bodied red, fruit-driven

Cedary blackcurrant with underlying vanilla aromas.

Lovely weight of fruit to balance a firm structure of tannin and acidity. Smooth, with nicely integrated toffee and vanilla flavours and finishing spice.
Stuffed shoulder or loin of lamb

Jamieson's Run Coonawarra Cabernet/ Shiraz/Cabernet Franc 95
Gilbeys

Full-bodied red, fruit-driven

Blackberry and vanilla aromas. Good weight of fruit with oaky backdrop. Nice spicy flavours in the finish and an appetising bite of tannin.
Robust lamb and sweet pepper casserole

John James McWilliams Cabernet Sauvignon 96
TDL

Full-bodied red, fruit-driven

Rich and spicy on the nose, hints of milk chocolate. Very ripe, mellow fruit with gentle tannins. Good weight and length of flavour.
Grilled lamb steaks with roasted red pepper relish

McGuigan Shareholders' Shiraz 97
Barry & Fitzwilliam

Full-bodied red, fruit-driven

Dark fruit aromas with hints of vanilla. Good weight of fruit, ripe and mouthfilling, though the acidity is rather marked. Leathery and spicy in the finish.
Robust beef casserole to tame the acidity and flatter the ripe fruit

Penfold's Bin 2, Shiraz/ Mourvedre 97
Findlater

Full-bodied red, fruit-driven

Bramble fruit and really peppery spice on the nose. A big mouthful of plum and damson fruit, soft tannin and peppery spice.
Beef casserole or pot roast

Penfold's Koonunga Hill Shiraz/Cabernet Sauvignon 96
Findlater

Full-bodied red, fruit-driven

Very ripe spicy blackcurrant aromas. Ripe and soft with hints of chocolate. Slightly chewy middle with spicy finish.
Braised lamb shanks or another hearty stew

Peter Lehman Clancy's 97
United Beverages

Full-bodied red, fruit-driven

Plummy fruit aromas with hints of mint and spice. Redcurrant and raspberry fruit with the mint coming through from the nose. Soft tannin and a peppery kick in the finish.
Lamb cooked like venison

Peter Lehmann The Barossa Shiraz 97
United Beverages

Full-bodied red, fruit-driven

Very ripe blackcurrant with a whiff of nutmeg. Lovely ripe plummy fruit with Christmas pudding spice. Big and warm with flavours lingering on.
Duck with plum sauce

Rosemount Cabernet Sauvignon 97
Grants

Full-bodied red, fruit-driven

Ripe soft fruit aromas. Plummy and smooth with good length of spice in the finish.
Marinated lamb chops

Rosemount Shiraz 98
Grants

Full-bodied red, fruit-driven

Aromas of spicy plums. Well-structured with a good weight of berry fruit to balance youthful tannins. Nice spicy, vanillin edge. Should continue to improve.
Venison steaks cooked rare

Rosemount Show Reserve Cabernet Sauvignon 96
Grants

Full-bodied red, fruit-driven

Very concentrated complex nose of spicy blackcurrant and earthy cedarwood tones. Full with silky smooth palate and plenty of fruit. Slightly stalky edge in the finish.
Robust casserole of beef or steaks with a sauce

Tatachilla McLaren Vale Langhorne Creek Cabernet Sauvignon 96
O'Briens

Full-bodied red, fruit-driven

Very minty blackcurrant fruit. Young with plenty of tannin underneath big, up-front fruit with cassis and blackberry flavours. Nice long finish with a touch of oak.
Bean casserole

Tesco McLaren Vale Shiraz 95
Tesco

Full-bodied red, fruit-driven

Concentrated aromas of ripe berry fruit. Big, flavoursome palate of spicy blackberries and ripe figs cloaking tannin. Enough refreshing acidity keeps the fruit in check right to the finish.
Roast turkey

Wakefield Clare Valley Shiraz 98
Koala

Full-bodied red, fruit-driven

Attractive nose of leather, spice and violets. Quite firm with mouthfilling ripe blackberry fruit. Robust and rich with warming alcohol and a long finish.
Steak with peppercorn sauce

Yaldara Whitmore Old Vineyard Reserve Grenache 97
Barry & Fitzwilliam

Full-bodied red, fruit-driven

Soft fruit, strawberry jam aromas. Ripe berry fruit flavours in abundance, with attractive spice. Full and warm with a balanced tannic edge.
Spicy lentil patties or a nut loaf

Yalumba Oxford Landing Black Grenache 97
Cassidy

Full-bodied red, fruit-driven

Pepper, spice and berries on the nose. Loaded with dark plummy fruit, spicy vanilla and a bite of tannin.
Beef and pepper casserole with beans

Five generations of winemaking in Australia,
and now for the third time
in the past four years,
International Red Winemaker of the Year.

Red £10 - £12

Wolf Blass President's Selection Cabernet Sauvignon 95

Dillon ☆ ☆

Full-bodied red, fruit-driven

Lots of ripe blackcurrant aromas with hints of pepper, mint and vanilla to add interest. A huge wine, soft and supple with ripe tannins and delicious blackcurrant fruit backed up by spice. Long velvety, fruity finish continues the charm.

Fillet of beef with Parma ham and mushrooms in filo pastry

Rymill Coonawarra Shiraz 93

Gleeson ☆

Full-bodied red, fruit-driven

Mature, developed nose with earthy fruit and spice. Rich chocolate-like texture with layers of complex flavour and a firm bite of tannin. Attractive, lingering finish.

Rich beef casserole

Wolf Blass President's Selection Shiraz 96

Dillon ☆

Full-bodied red, fruit-driven

Very chocolatey, spicy fruit aromas. Robust but well-balanced wine with lovely weight of chocolate and spice flavoured ripe fruit. All you would expect of Shiraz!

Beef fillet cooked with soy and garlic

Bethany Barossa Shiraz/ Cabernet 97

O'Brien's C

Full-bodied red, fruit-driven

Chocolate, spice and vanilla from the nose echoed on the palate. Rich and spicy with good balanced structure. Very appealing, harmonious style with a long finish.

Roast turkey or goose

Brown Brothers Victoria Shiraz 96

Woodford Bourne C

Full-bodied red, fruit-driven

Deep, complex aromas of oak and fruit. Big palate of ripe succulent fruit in firmly structured frame. Long, flavoursome finish. Still young.

Lamb steaks

Maglieri McLaren Vale Cabernet Sauvignon 96

Gleeson C

Full-bodied red, fruit-driven

Lovely aromas of blackcurrant jelly, vanilla and spice. Good intensity of ripe fruit spiked with pepper. Luscious and seductive more than complex with lingering ripe fruit and vanilla tones right through the finish.

Roast fillet of beef

Sandalford Mount Barker/ Margaret River Cabernet Sauvignon 97

Fitzgerald C

Full-bodied red, fruit-driven

Opulent ripe black fruits with tar and leather nuances. Layers of flavour unfold on the palate with bramble fruit giving way to black pepper, paprika and menthol. Well-cloaked, easy tannin and a long, warm finish. Drink now or keep.

Beef casserole with blackcurrant and herbs

Basedow Bush Vine Grenache 96
MacCormaic

Full-bodied red, fruit-driven

Very ripe caramel and fruit, slightly meaty nose. Baked fruit and spice flavours, a touch oaky. A big, chunky wine with ability to last.
Chorizo sausages

Brown Brothers King Valley Barbera 96
Woodford Bourne

Medium-bodied red

Summer pudding and vanilla on the nose. Full- bodied, big palate with luscious fruit and tobacco-like spice. Interesting and appealing.
Calf's liver with polenta

Brown Brothers Victoria Cabernet Sauvignon 96
Woodford Bourne

Full-bodied red, fruit-driven

Fruit and liquorice on the nose. Smooth and mouthfilling with fresh blackcurrant fruit, balanced tannin and a long finish.
Beef casserole with Parma ham and tomato

Knappstein Cabernet/ Merlot 95
Cassidy

Full-bodied red, fruit-driven

Meaty, gamey nose; juicy blackcurrant fruit with mint tones. Well-balanced and complex with lots of interest.
Butterfly lamb with rosemary

Maglieri McLaren Vale Shiraz 97
Gleeson

Full-bodied red, fruit-driven

Dark plummy fruit and spice on the nose. Lots of chewy fruit and spicy vanilla flavours. Concentrated with firm tannin and refreshing acidity.
Home-made sausages

Ninth Island Tasmania Pinot Noir 98
Fitzgerald

Medium-bodied red

Aromatic, earthy strawberry fruit. Elegant palate with ripe strawberry fruit, soft tannin and refreshing acidity. Attractive Pinot style.
Spiced quail with mango

Pewsey Vale Eden Valley Cabernet Sauvignon 95
Fields

Full-bodied red

Dusty blackcurrant and cedarwood aromas. Palate needs a bit of coaxing, firm tannins yielding to give hints of berry fruit to come. Refreshing acidity. Needs a bit more time.
Rare steak with shallots

Yalumba Barossa Bush Vine Grenache 96
Cassidy

Full-bodied red, fruit-driven

Plum, raspberry and redcurrant aromas, which follow through on the palate. Nice spicy tones and easy tannin. Appealing, robust style.
Pasta and chorizo

Yarra Valley Hills Pinot Noir 98
Oddbins

Medium-bodied red

Brambly aromas and similar fruit flavours expanding on the palate, well-balanced by acidity and tannin all tightly knit together. Big, beefy style of Pinot.

Sweet'n sour venison

Red £12 - £15

Ch. Reynella Basket-Pressed Cabernet/Merlot 96
Allied Drinks ☆

Full-bodied red, fruit-driven

Ripe blackcurrant with mint and vanilla aromas. A big wine with a huge weight of ripe blackcurrant fruit balanced by tannin and acidity. Very ripe and fruit-driven style but will hold and develop further. The finish is long and surprisingly elegant.

Venison and redcurrant casserole

Geoff Merrill Cabernet Sauvignon 92
United Beverages ☆

Full-bodied red, fruit-driven

Sandalwood, cassis, earth and spice aromas. Velvety palate with blackcurrant fruit and spicy oak, fresh acidity and a lovely long finish.

Lamb with apricots and couscous

Tatachilla Clarendon Merlot 97
O'Brien's ☆

Full-bodied red, fruit-driven

Summer fruit aromas emerge slowly from the glass. Concentrated chewy damson fruit, with chocolate, raisins and spice. Robust and flavoursome with plenty more to develop in the future.

Char-grilled lamb with beans

Bethany Barossa Shiraz 96
O'Brien's C

Full-bodied red, fruit-driven

Jammy fruit with youthful blackcurrant leaf aromas. Lovely rich, ripe fruit flavours shot through with mint, vanilla and cedar. Tannins are well-integrated and the whole wine is perfectly balanced with a warm lingering finish.

Sirloin steak with mustard glaze

Chatsfield Mount Barker Shiraz 96
Mitchell C

Full-bodied red, fruit-driven

Meaty, peppery plum aromas. Full-bodied and chocolatey with oodles of plum fruit and good concentration of flavour. Should develop very well.

Duck with apples

Hardys Coonawarra Cabernet Sauvignon 94
Allied Drinks C

Full-bodied red, fruit-driven

Complex aromas of baked plum with chocolate, spice and tobacco. Well-structured but rounded with almost Port-like flavours of spice, fruit and chocolate. Has developed beautifully in a year and will go further.

A lovely, different choice for roast pheasant

Maxwell Cabernet Merlot 97

Molloy's   C

Full-bodied red, fruit-driven

Slightly stalky blackcurrant aromas, blackcurrant leaves. Full and chewy on the palate with plenty of dark fruit flavours, balanced tannins and long liquorice finish.
Butterfly barbecued leg of lamb with herbs

Vasse Felix Cabernet/Merlot 97

Cassidy   C

Full-bodied red, fruit-driven

Cassis and chocolate on the nose. Spicy with lots of blackcurrant and blackberry fruit, balanced tannin and refreshing acidity. Attractive and smooth.
Roast pheasant

Basedow Barossa Shiraz 96

MacCormaic

Full-bodied red, fruit-driven

Minty jammy fruit aromas. Soft, very ripe fruit flavours with hints of mint and spice showing in the finish.
Spicy marinated kebabs from the barbecue

Best's Great Western Cabernet Sauvignon 95

Mitchell

Full-bodied red, fruit-driven

Seductive aromas of sugar-crusted blackberry pie. Firm but ripe tannins with subtle blackcurrant fruit still waiting to show. Restrained and suave but short on complexity.
Marinated ostrich fillets

Bethany Barossa Cabernet Sauvignon/Merlot 97

O'Brien's

Full-bodied red, fruit-driven

Meaty, berry fruit aromas. Well-structured with ripe fruit and subtle spicy oak. Long and flavoursome to the end.
Lamb hotpot and other such stews

Chatsfield Mount Barker Cabernet Franc 97

Mitchell

Light fruity red

Rather light red berry fruit on the nose, More intensity on the palate with sharp redcurrant and raspberry tones and a touch of oak spice. Fresh acidity and easy tannins. Enjoyable but seems expensive for the style.
Veal with ginger

Jim Barry McCrae Wood Shiraz 95

Dunnes Stores

Full-bodied red, fruit-driven

Very deep bouquet, with cigarbox, tar and eucalyptus aromas. Layers of baked fruit and spice flavours. A sturdy wine with plenty of extract and chewy intensity.
Barbecued beef

Penfold's Bin 128 Coonawarra Shiraz 96

Findlater

Full-bodied red, fruit-driven

Elegant aromas of ripe summer berries, smoke and spice. Great weight of ripe fruit, similar to the nose with balanced structure. Big yet elegant and very long.
Beef steak with pepper or another robust sauce

Rosemount Balmoral Syrah 95

Grants

Full-bodied red, fruit-driven, to keep

Smoky, spicy fruit, still a bit closed. Rich opulent palate with loads of dark smoky fruit and balancing ripe tannin. A big wine which will last.

Peppered steak

Seppelt Dorrien Vineyard Barossa Valley Cabernet Sauvignon 94

Dunnes Stores

Full-bodied red, fruit-driven

Impressive cedary blackcurrant nose. Real depth of flavour with dark fruit, herbs and spice and a balanced structure. Flavours last well. A good wine.

Roast shoulder of lamb with flavoursome stuffing

Seppelt Great Western Vineyard Shiraz 95

Dunnes Stores

Full-bodied red, fruit-driven

Blackberry, leather and spice aromas. Blackberry fruit with hints of chocolate and spice, nicely balanced tannin and acidity and good weight of alcohol. Delicious fruit-driven style which will also age.

Spicy beef--even a slightly tamed chili con carne!

Red £15 - £20

Ch. Reynella Basket-Pressed Shiraz 96

Allied Drinks ☆

Full-bodied red, fruit-driven

Plums, spice, oak and pepper waft from the glass. Well-structured with ripe, intense fruit balancing firm tannin and acidity. Leathery, oaky flavours lie beneath the jammy fruit showing plenty of complexity to come.

Peppered steak

Petaluma Coonawarra 95

Dunnes Stores ☆

Full-bodied red, fruit-driven

Ripe yet restrained blackcurrant fruit on the nose. Very rich fruit balanced by firm tannins on the palate. Full and intense with fruit and structure to match and a long flavoursome finish.

Steaks with a rich sauce

St Hallett Old Block Barossa Shiraz 95

Dunnes Stores C

Full-bodied red, fruit-driven

Baked fruit aromas with spicy chocolatey palate. Huge extract of ripe blackcurrant flavours. A real blockbuster with a long, flavoursome finish.

Venison casserole

Tyrrell's Winemaker Selection Vat 8 Shiraz/Cabernet Sauvignon 96

Remy C

Full-bodied red, fruit-driven

Complex smoky spicy fruit on the nose. Well-structured with full body and ripe fruit. A big wine with plenty of diverting flavours and a long satisfying finish.

Ostrich steaks with rice casserole and spicy fruit sauce

Best's Great Western Pinot Noir 95
Molloy's

Medium-bodied red

Very attractive vegetal strawberry fruit aromas. Earthy mineral fruit attack which mellows to ripe cherry fruit. Firm tannin and a long dry finish.

Pheasant with plum compote

De Bortoli Yarra Valley Shiraz 95
Febvre

Full-bodied red, fruit-driven

Soft and jammy on the nose with lots of warming spice. Plenty of smoky bramble fruit and firm tannin. Beginning to develop on the palate and reveal complex flavours behind the fruit and tannin. Long finish with a touch of bitter chocolate.

Steak au poivre

Lindemans Limestone Ridge Coonawarra Shiraz/Cabernet 93
Gilbeys

Full-bodied red, fruit-driven

Intense aromas of spicy, minty fruity with vanilla in the background. Rich and smooth with oodles of ripe fruit and a very long finish.

Grilled or roast lamb with plenty of herbs

Tatachilla Foundation Shiraz 97
O'Briens

Full-bodied red, fruit-driven

Slightly closed on the nose, some earthy fruit and spice coming through. Chewy damson and plum fruit with mocha and spice tones. Big and concentrated, needs time to really evolve but still attractive now.

Wild duck casserole

Red £20 - £25

Orlando St Hugo Cabernet Sauvignon 94
Fitzgerald ☆ ☆

Full-bodied red, fruit-driven

Intense aromas of smoky blackcurrant and mint. Soft dark chocolate and blackberry fruit on the palate with balancing acidity, friendly tannins and a long rich finish.

Grilled fillet of beef

Wolf Blass Black Label Cabernet/Shiraz/Merlot 94
Dillon

Full-bodied red, fruit-driven

Very ripe fruit with more mature aromas of spice and earthiness. Dense, very rich palate with concentrated fruit and hints of mint or eucalyptus. Well-balanced, long and delicious but expensive.

Grilled meat or ostrich or venison steaks

Red £25 - £30

Best's Great Western Pinot Meunier 93
Molloy's

Medium-bodied red

Figs and chocolate on the nose. Earthy, stony fruit with mild tannin and crisp acidity. Different and attractive.
Medallions of beef with shallot sauce

Ch. Tahbilk Cabernet Sauvignon Reserve 91
United Beverages

Full-bodied red

Slightly closed on the nose, delivers on the palate with concentrated berry fruit and spicy, oaky tones. A big, brooding wine, still dominated by firm tannins but lovely complex influences lurk in the fruit. Still a baby but with a good future!
Roast duck

Red £30 - £35

Peter Lehmann Stonewell Barossa Shiraz 92
United Beverages ☆ ☆

Full-bodied red, fruit-driven

Very complex and concentrated on the nose: earthy, sweet spicy fruit, smoky cherries and plums. Restrained power in a really stunning wine just entering its maturity.
Venison with blackberries

Peter Lehmann Stonewell Shiraz 91
Molloy's ☆ ☆

Full-bodied red, fruit-driven

Inky meaty nose with hints of mint and vanilla. Rich and smooth with ripe, ripe almost luscious dark fruits, well-balanced structure and good length. Lovely now but will get even better.
Venison with black pepper and blackcurrants

Jim Barry The Armagh Clare Valley Shiraz 96
Dunnes Stores

Full-bodied red, fruit-driven

Lots of fruit on the nose, ripe brambles and spice. Soft, berry fruit flavours with spice and smoky oak. Complex and balanced, very well-knit with a long, long finish.
Venison steaks with black pepper

Red £35 - £40

Barossa Valley Estate E & E Black Pepper Shiraz 95
Allied Drinks

Full-bodied red, fruit-driven, to keep

Super-ripe and intense on the nose but with complexity and elegance also. Powerful, concentrated palate, big in alcohol, fruit, extract and structure. One to keep--and should be wonderful.
Roast venison for a special meal

Rosé £5 - £6

Mount Hurtle Grenache Rosé 98
United Beverages

Rosé

Bubblegum and caramel with a touch of grassiness on the nose. Lively acidity and nice weight of berry fruit on the palate. Clean dry finish.
Goose terrine

Chile

Chile's main ambition in recent years has been to establish a reputation for fine wines as well as for the good value, well-made wines that made its name and market. This has been attempted through expansion and re-planting, especially of cooler vineyard regions; through outside expertise of flying winemakers and through the flagship reds released in the last two years: Sena from Errazuriz-Mondavi collaboration, Montes Alpha M from Montes and Almaviva from Concha Y Toro-Rothschild. It is too early to say if these super Chileans will merit their £30–£40 price tag; however, the quality drive is coming through in other price ranges.

The exploitation of cooler climate vineyards, high altitudes and microclimates has made a huge impact on the quality of Chilean white wines. Chilean Chardonnay between £6 and £10 is, for my money, some of the best value around. Investment in new winery equipment and sensitive use of oak, and much more French oak, is leading to some very subtle, complex, under-priced gems from makers such as Casa Lapostelle, Viña Casablanca etc.

Investment and commitment to quality has paid off at many wineries. M. Lurton from the Bordeaux family has transformed San Pedro, one of the country's largest vineyards, who are now producing some really cracking reds with great fruit and lots more. Villiard and Undurraga are also demonstrating new levels of quality especially with the reds, including Villiard's stunning Pinot Noir.

Expansion and investment apart, this was also Chile's year for making headlines. First the discovery that most Chilean Merlot was not Merlot at all but Carmenère. This was a cause for red faces all round especially among the wine press who for years had lauded Merlot as Chile's brightest star. Some wineries have responded by labelling wines as Carmenère and calling it Chile's own grape variety—which up to now the country lacked. Other producers claim that they have the true Merlot. Carmenère is an interesting grape in its own right, extensively planted pre-phylloxera in Bordeaux, which certainly has potential in Chile both as a varietal and in blends.

The other revelation was about flavonols. These are antioxidants present on grape skins, which help prevent heart disease. Apparently, Chilean red grapes have more than any other grape, as producers have been swift to point out.

Whatever about their benefit to health, Chilean reds vary widely in taste quality. There are many thoroughly inconsequential cheap Merlot/Carmenères and inexpensive Cabernets which are pretty unexciting. Above this level, however, there has been great improvement in Reserva Cabernet with good fruit extract, balance and well-used oak. Wines maintain their ripe fruit quality but have complexity and reserve which is most attractive.

The big question hovering over Chile at the turn of the century is the effect of Argentina, a much bigger producer now moving into the quality export market. Chile has had supply problems in recent years and the high volume, good value end of the market which it still needs may suffer from a more consistent competitor. Higher up the price scale, and especially for white wines, Chile should be secure. But now more than ever, commitment to quality is vital.

White £5 -£6

Viu Manent Sauvignon Blanc 97

Ecock C

Aromatic white, fruit-driven

Immediate tropical fruit aromas. Well-balanced with lots of green fruit flavour, crisp acidity and fresh finish.
Avocado and tomato salad with cheese

Las Casas del Toqui Chardonnay 97

Dunnes Stores ££

Full-bodied white

Aromatic nose of tropical fruit. Plenty of pineapple and guava fruit flavour with refreshing acidity and a long, crisp finish. Delicious and great value.
Fish in pastry with hollandaise sauce

San Pedro Chardonnay 97

Dunnes Stores

Full-bodied white

Ripe tropical fruit aromas. Ripe melon and pineapple palate with crisp citrus acidity. Clean dry finish.
Creamy pasta

Tesco Chilean Chardonnay nv

Tesco

Full-bodied white, oak

Quite oaky nose with ripe fruit beneath. Refreshing acidity right the way through with lively green fruit flavours.
Creamy chicken curry

Undurraga Sauvignon Blanc 98

United Beverages

Aromatic white, fruit-driven

Zippy citrus nose, clean and

fresh. Easy-drinking with lots of ripe fruit flavour.
Fish salad

Valdezaro Chardonnay 96
Barry & Fitzwilliam
Light dry white
Aromas of lime juice with a mineral touch on the nose. Light and bone-dry with a crisp citrus flavour. Clean and refreshing.
Seafood salad or fish kebabs

Viña Tarapaca Sauvignon Blanc 98
Gleeson
Aromatic white, fruit-driven
Green fruit and herbaceous aromas. Crisp and refreshing with plenty of ripe fruit on the palate.
Avocado and cheese salad

White £6 - £8

Casablanca Chardonnay 98
Oddbins I ££
Full-bodied white
Inviting aromas of exotic fruit with wealth of mango and pineapple flavours. Beautifully balanced with refreshing crisp acidity. Great value.

Casa Lapostolle Chardonnay 97
Oddbins I
Full-bodied white, oak
Lovely exotic fruit aromas. Full-bodied with ripe fruit and spice beautifully integrated. Round and balanced with a long finish.
Spicy fishcakes

Las Casas del Toqui Chardonnay Gr Réserve 97
Dunnes Stores I
Full-bodied white
Lovely nose of ripe tropical fruit and vanilla. Big and mouthfilling with a weight of tropical fruit flavours and spicy background. Lovely dry, crisp finish.
Roast monkfish with a rich sauce

Viña Tarapaca Chardonnay Reserva 97
Gleeson I
Full-bodied white, oak
Honeyed tropical fruit with a nice touch of oak. Nice round wine, perfectly balanced between ripe apple and peach fruit, vanillin oak and crisp acidity. Lovely fresh finish, too.
Duck with peach sauce

Undurraga Chardonnay Reserva 97
United Beverages C ££
Full-bodied white, oak
Peach, apricot and vanilla on the nose. Well-balanced with good structure, rich ripe fruit and honey with nicely judged oak. Long and complex.
Chicken or pork kebabs

Errazuriz Chardonnay 97
Allied Drinks C
Medium-bodied white
Attractive aromas of citrusy fruit and damp forest. A good weight of restrained fruit flavour with a slightly peppery edge and long finish.
Brill, sole or chunky cod with a light, cream-based sauce

Antu Mapu Sauvignon Blanc Reserva 98

Barry & Fitzwilliam   ££

Aromatic white

Herbal grassy nose with a flinty background. Dry with lovely lingering mineral tones. Classic style of Sauvignon and remarkable value.

Goat or feta cheese salad; lightly cooked salmon

Carmen Chardonnay 98

Dillon   ££

Full-bodied white

Smoky, flint aromas mixed with ripe fruit. Attractive palate with fruit and mineral flavours and citrus acidity, full and long in the finish. Quite classic in style.
Smoked fish pie or cakes; pasta with bacon and cream

Canepa Sauvignon Blanc 98

MacCormaic

Aromatic white, fruit-driven

Grassy nettle and elderflower aromas. Delicious gooseberry fruit with refreshing acidity and a clean sharp finish.
Spicy rice with prawns

Carmen Sauvignon Blanc 98

Dillon

Aromatic white, fruit-driven

Quite restrained on the nose but good weight of gooseberry and apple fruit on the palate. Clean, refreshing finish.
Pasta with tomato and courgette sauce or peppers, garlic and anchovies

Castillo de Molina Chardonnay 98
Cassidy
Full-bodied white, oak
Rather oaky, oily nose. Melon fruit on the palate, a touch over-ripe with crisp acidity. Dry and waxy mouthfeel and lots of oak in the finish.
Barbecued pork chops with pineapple salsa

Concha y Toro Casillero del Diablo Chardonnay 98
Findlater
Full-bodied white, oak
Buttery fat aromas with hints of marzipan. Dry with lots of tropical fruit offset by grapefruit acidity. Very long and lingering.
Spicy baked chicken

Concha y Toro Sunrise Chardonnay 98
Findlater
Full-bodied white
Ripe fruits on the nose, slightly lemony. Apple and citrus flavours with good rounded mouthfeel.
Chicken curry with coconut

Errazuriz Sauvignon Blanc 98
Allied Drinks
Aromatic white, fruit-driven
Green fruit aromas followed by citrus and gooseberry flavours. Refreshing style to drink young.
Tomato salad or a simple fish with tomato or pepper sauce

Millaman Chardonnay 97
Barry & Fitzwilliam
Light fruity white
Rather honeyed fruit on the nose. Dry palate with melon and peach fruit flavours enlivened by zippy acidity.
Chicken salad; light pasta; fish or chicken gratin

Montes Reserve Chardonnay 98
Grants
Full-bodied white, oak
Pronounced tropical fruit aromas with buttery hints. Fat, smooth texture and exuberant tropical fruit flavours. Plenty of weight and length.
Glazed chicken with honey and lemon

MontGras Sauvignon Blanc 98
Remy
Aromatic white, fruit-driven
Aromatic nettle and asparagus aromas. Plenty of fruit follows through on the palate with crisp acidity and some length.
Warm spicy chicken salad

San Pedro Barrel-fermented Chardonnay Reserva 97
Dunnes Stores
Full-bodied white
Tropical fruit, lemon and lime aromas. Ripe and buttery with a good weight of pineapple and melon fruit, butter and toast. Nice long, dry finish.
Thai-style chicken or noodles with coriander

San Pedro Sauvignon Blanc 98
Dunnes Stores
Aromatic white, fruit-driven

Aromatic elderflower nose. Very ripe palate with nice balance of acidity and alcohol. Good length.
Tomato and mozzarella salad

Santa Carolina Chardonnay 98
TDL
Light fruity white

Honey and tropical fruit on the nose and similar fruit on the palate. Quite buttery with balancing acidity. Dry warm finish.
Fried chicken and bananas

Santa Carolina Sauvignon Blanc 98
TDL
Aromatic white, fruit-driven

Ripe green fruits on the nose. Gooseberry and green apple flavours; balanced and with a good length of finish.
Pasta with prawns and sun-dried tomatoes

Santa Emiliana Palmeras Oak-aged Chardonnay 97
O'Briens
Full-bodied white, oak

Ripe tropical fruit and oak aromas. Melon and pineapple on the palate backed by subtle oak. Long flavoursome finish.
Scallops with avocado sauce

Santa Helena Seleccion del Directorio Chardonnay 97
Greenhills
Full-bodied white, oak

Vanilla custard with ripe melon and toast aromas. Fat, smooth texture with very ripe fruit and spice, balancing citrus acidity and a warm finish.
Good old fish pie

Santa Rita 120 Sauvignon Blanc 98
Gilbeys
Aromatic white, fruit-driven

Green fruit aromas and a touch of boiled sweets. Refreshing clean fruit flavours with zippy acidity. To drink young.
Avocado salad; salad lunch

Santa Rita Sauvignon Blanc Reserva 98
Gilbeys
Aromatic white, fruit-driven

Tropical smoky nose. Lots of very ripe fruit similar to the nose with balanced acidity just holding its own.
Salad of mozzarella cheese, peppers and aubergines

Torréon de Paredes Sauvignon Blanc 98
Ecock
Aromatic white, fruit-driven

Ripe green fruit on the nose. Similar palate with very fresh acidity and a citrus finish.
Rice salad or Chinese noodles

Valdivieso Chardonnay 98
Searson
Full-bodied white, oak

Deep and oily with restrained tropical fruit on the nose. Honeyed fruit with well-balanced acidity. Broad and long with citrus crispness in the finish.
Fish and shellfish pie

Villard Chardonnay 96
O'Briens

Full-bodied white

Buttery vanilla on the nose. Soft, buttery apple fruit with balanced acidity. Nice weight and length.
Roast chicken with leeks and grapes

Villard Sauvignon Blanc 97
O'Briens

Aromatic white, fruit-driven

Very ripe gooseberry aromas. Good weight of ripe tropical fruit flavour, nice balance and refreshing crisp acidity in the finish.
Grilled asparagus salad

White £8 - £10

Miguel Torres Santa Digna Chardonnay 97
Woodford Bourne   C

Full-bodied white, oak

Lemon meringue pie on the nose, with hints of vanilla. Creamy and smooth with tropical fruit flavours and lively acidity. Lovely.
Fish soufflé

Alto de Terra Andina Chardonnay Reserva 98
Fitzgerald

Full-bodied white, oak

Pungent aromas of ripe pineapple, mango and melon with vanilla spice. Similar palate with really assertive tropical fruit and a long dry finish.
Lobster with fresh pasta

Carmen Chardonnay Reserve 96
Dillon

Full-bodied white, oak

Ripe fruit aromas with honey and vanilla. Ripe apple and kiwi fruit flavours, quite tight and restrained in character with a nice touch of oak.
Creamy chicken or fish pie

Carmen Sauvignon Blanc Reserve 97
Dillon

Aromatic white, fruit-driven

Up-front gooseberry and citrus fruit tones. Fresh and crisp with gooseberry and lime flavours. Light and refreshing.
Stir-fried prawn with asparagus and snow peas

Santa Rita Chardonnay Reserva 97
Gilbeys

Full-bodied white, oak

Ripe apples and pineapple aromas. Ripe fruit in a creamy texture with hints of smoke. Well-balanced with a long finish.
Baked chicken with bacon and tomato sauce

Villard Premium Reserve Chardonnay 97
O'Briens

Full-bodied white, oak

Peppery melon fruit and vanilla icecream aromas. Smooth and well-balanced with plentiful fruit and a long finish.
Grilled halibut

Viu Manent Reserve Fumé Blanc 97

Ecock

Aromatic white, fruit-driven

Catty, kiwi aromas. Very dry with watermelon fruit and oily texture. Balanced wine with some length of flavour.
Chicken with feta and sun-dried tomatoes

White £10 - £12

Casa Lapostolle Cuvée Alexandre Chardonnay 96

Oddbins   C

Full-bodied white, oak

Tropical fruit laced with vanilla. Rich flavours but well-balanced and very much together.
Turbot or lobster with a cream sauce

Santa Rita Medalla Real Special Reserve Chardonnay 97

Gilbeys   C

Full-bodied white

Subtle ripe apple and vanilla aromas. Mouthfilling wine with excellent balance of ripe fruit and new oak. Well-made with a long elegant finish.
Roast chicken or turkey

Errazuriz Chardonnay Reserva 97

Allied Drinks

Full-bodied white, oak

Aromas of ripe melon with butter and mineral tones. Melon and citrus fruit with quite pronouced oak flavours. Nice balance and finish.
Roast chicken or turkey; turbot or monkfish with a cream sauce

Mondavi & Chadwick Caliterra Chardonnay Reserve 97

Febvre

Full-bodied white, oak

Ripe tropical fruit with honey and toast. Big and mouthfilling, quite toasty with creamy tropical fruit and a long, flavoursome finish.
Roast stuffed turkey or chicken

White £12 - £15

Santa Carolina Reserva De Familia Barrel-fermented Chardonnay 96

TDL

Full-bodied white, oak

Aromatic nose with restrained toast and melon fruit. Dry with well-concentrated ripe fruit and white pepper spice enriched with vanilla.
Veal cutlet with cream and ham sauce

Red £5 - £6

Santa Emiliana Andes Peak Merlot 98

O'Briens   C

Light fruity red

Complex mineral nose. Steely with ripe raspberry flavours and good structure. Well-made with plenty of rich fruit flavour.
Spicy sausages

Tesco Chilean Merlot Reserve nv

Tesco   C

Medium-bodied red

Ripe stewed plums and damsons on the nose. Lovely concentration of vanilla and blackcurrant flavours with rich black cherry tones coming

through. Rich and satisfying.
Grilled tuna with soy

San Pedro Cabernet Sauvignon 97

Dunnes Stores   ££

Medium-bodied red

Jammy blackcurrant aromas. Good ripe fruit flavours with a clean dry finish. Very decent wine at the price.
Barbecue meats and sausages

San Pedro Merlot 98

Dunnes Stores   ££

Light fruity red

Plummy aromas with ripe plum fruit on the palate, soft tannin and balanced acidity. Well-made, uncomplicated wine.
Pastries with mozzarella and Parma ham

Santa Emiliana Andes Peak Cabernet Sauvignon 98

O'Briens

Medium-bodied red

Ripe, fruit jelly aromas. Very soft, ripe and juicy though not excessively fruity. Good barbecue wine in an easy, popular style.
Char-grilled hamburgers

Santa Ines Carmenère 97

Molloy's

Medium-bodied red

Mellow fruit aromas with up-front fruit on the palate, creamy tannin and some length of flavour in the finish.
Mixed barbecue foods

Tesco Chilean Cabernet Sauvignon nv
Tesco

Medium-bodied red

Minty meaty aromas with jammy fruit. Nice balance between light tannin and fruit with good red berry flavours carried through.
Meatballs

Tesco Chilean Merlot 98
Tesco

Light fruity red

Nice ripe fruit aromas with a hint of blackcurrant leaf. Good concentration and ripeness of flavour with a nice bite of tannin and a long finish.
Spicy chicken wings

Undurraga Cabernet Sauvignon 98
United Beverages

Medium-bodied red

Rather smoky cassis aromas. Ripe blackberry fruit with soft tannin. Nicely balanced, well-made wine.
Meatballs with pitta bread

Viña Tarapaca Merlot 98
Gleeson

Light fruity red

Blackberries and plums with a hint of violet on the nose. Youthful, slightly stalky fruit with a touch of spice. Pleasant, soft tannin. Easy-drinking.
Pizza

Red £6 - £8

Viña Tarapaca Cabernet Sauvignon Reserva 95
Gleeson   I

Full-bodied red, fruit-driven

Complex aromas of cedar and bramble with earthy tones. Well-integrated flavours follow the bouquet with nicely balanced tannins and acidity. Good value for quite a classic style.
Roast rack of lamb

Canepa Merlot 98
MacCormaic   C

Medium-bodied red

Spicy capsicum tones on the nose. Classic style, young and stalky on the palate with shades of plum and spice and rich fruit emerging.
Marinated grilled tuna

Montes Alpha Cabernet Sauvignon 96
Grants   C

Full-bodied red, fruit-driven

Well-integrated, elegant nose followed by finely balanced palate with firm tannin and acidity offset by a weight of rich autumnal fruit. Spicy and mouthfilling with a very long finish. Will be even better in time.
Roast duck with a spicy stuffing

San Pedro Cabernet Sauvignon Reserva 97
Dunnes Stores   C

Full-bodied red, fruit-driven

Quite complex mingling of blackcurrant and smoky vanilla aromas. Very appealing ripe, rich fruit of the forest flavours with easy tannins and rounded texture.
Lamb steaks with grilled peppers

Undurraga Cabernet Sauvignon Reserva 96
United Beverages   C

Full-bodied red, fruit-driven

Elegant aromas of pencil

shavings. Full-flavoured palate with dark ripe fruit and a tarry edge, also a touch of pepper. Ripe tannins beginning to mellow with the wine.
Pheasant with lentils

Carmen Merlot 97
Dillon   ££
Medium-bodied red

Quite complex aromas of plums and spice. Mouthfilling flavours of summer fruits. Well-balanced, with spice tones just beginning to show and a long finish.
Lighter meats and offal, or meatier fish: e.g. calf's liver and onions or baked tuna

Errazuriz Cabernet Sauvignon 98
Allied Drinks   ££
Medium-bodied red

Ripe cassis-type aromas with a touch of earthiness. Richly textured layers of ripe fruit with a touch of spice and nice long finish.
Roast lamb with mustard and soy or marinated chops

Las Casas del Toqui Cabernet Sauvignon Réserve 97
Dunnes Stores   ££
Full-bodied red, fruit-driven

Intense ripe blackcurrant aromas and similar weight of fruit on the palate with nice spicy tones, warming alcohol and good length. Great value.
Grilled lamb with Merguez and couscous

Santa Emiliana Palmeras Merlot 97
O'Brien's   ££
Medium-bodied red

Herbaceous aromas with fresh, juicy blackberry fruit flavours. Soft tannin and fresh acidity give a pleasant structure. Good value.
Grilled tuna or swordfish

Canepa Cabernet Sauvignon/Malbec 97
MacCormaic
Full-bodied red, fruit-driven

Cassis and mint aromas; earthy palate with cherry and black-berry fruit, balancing acidity and a nice bite of tannin offering some complexity for the price.
Grilled lamb chops

Carmen Cabernet Sauvignon 97
Dillon
Medium-bodied red

Slightly smoky, earthy black-currant fruit aromas; much riper and softer on the palate with rich chocolatey fruit heightened by high alcohol. Concentrated, rather warm finish.
Stir-fried beef, including Chinese spices; also steaks or medallions of meat with punchy relish or sauce

Concha y Toro Sunrise Cabernet Sauvignon 98
Findlater
Medium-bodied red

Slightly earthy palate. Chewy blackcurrant fruit flavours with refreshing acidity.
Rich meaty pasta with tomato sauce

Concha y Toro Sunrise Pinot Noir 98
Findlater

Medium-bodied red

Quite intense nose with farmyard touches to ripe berry fruit. Very ripe plummy fruit with hints of liquorice flavour. Soft tannin and crisp acidity with spicy kick in the finish.
Mushroom pastries or kidneys

Cousiño Macul Cabernet Sauvignon 97
Ecock

Medium-bodied red

Clean soft berry and currant fruit aromas. Very approachable ripe fruit palate; flavoursome, with a dry finish.
Grilled lamb chops

Errazuriz Merlot 98
Allied Drinks

Medium-bodied red

Attractive summer pudding aromas, raspberries and strawberries. Dry and firm with good weight of spicy fruit well-supported by alcohol. Good length and finish.
Mixed salamis

Miguel Torres Santa Digna Cabernet Sauvignon 98
Woodford Bourne

Medium-bodied red

Spicy cooked fruit aromas, raspberry jam. Very ripe blackberry fruit, soft and easy-drinking but with enough supporting tannins to balance.
Lasagne or shepherd's pie

Millaman Merlot 97
Barry & Fitzwilliam

Medium-bodied red

Typical Merlot aromas of plums and blackberries mixed with vegetal overtones. Rather jammy intensity on the palate, enlivened by peppery spice and lively acidity. Soft, easy drinking.
Flavoursome pasta and pizza

Mondavi & Chadwick Caliterra Cabernet Sauvignon 98
Febvre

Full-bodied red, fruit-driven

Lots of wood hiding blackcurrant and plum fruit on the nose. More fruit-driven palate with spicy plums and underlying smoky tones. Nicely balanced tannins and good finish.
Lamb in pastry and similar dishes

Montes Reserve Merlot 98
Grants

Medium-bodied red

Very fruity aromas of raspberry and cherry fruit. Similar palate with nice spicy touch to exuberant fruit. Easy-drinking.
Minute steak or chops

MontGras Merlot 97
Remy

Medium-bodied red

Lots of blackcurrant and damson fruit on the nose. Mouthfilling wine with ripe jammy blackcurrants. Big and rich with lingering flavours.
Grilled tuna or swordfish steaks

Santa Carolina Cabernet Sauvignon Reservado 97
TDL

Medium to full-bodied red, fruit-driven

Nice berry fruit aromas. Easy-drinking style with slightly spicy berry fruit and soft tannin.
Grilled lamb with pineapple salsa

The Viña MontGras range of great wines

'A warm, faintly spicy nose presages a palate that is soft and very approachable. This wine is as impressive for what it lacks (overdone jammy fruit) as for what it possesses.'

Raymond Blake *on the MontGras Merlot Reserva 1997*

'Deliciously dense and soft, packed with fruit and so deeply-coloured that it's almost black. MontGras is a young producer and this Carmenere is certainly one of the more interesting things it currently produces.'

Tom Doorley *on the MontGras Carmenere Reserva 1997, Wine of the Week*

Wines widely available in SuperValu/ Centra, Superquinn, Londis, O'Brien's Fine Wines and Independent Off Licences Nationwide: Merlot, Cabernet Sauvignon, Chardonnay, Sauvignon Blanc, Merlot Reserva, Cabernet Sauvignon Reserva, Carmenere Reserva, Chardonnay Reserva, Ninquén Chardonnay, Ninquén Cabernet-Merlot

Viña MontGras is distributed by Remy Ireland, Ltd.

Santa Carolina Merlot Reservado 97
TDL

Medium-bodied red

Damsons and plums on the nose. Quite tough tannins for a Merlot but balanced by ripe plummy fruit and a long warm finish.
Calf's liver with a red onion confit

Santa Carolina Merlot/ Cabernet Sauvignon 98
TDL

Medium-bodied red

Fruit of the forest nose and similar direct fruit appeal on the palate. Firm ripe tannin and balanced acidity well-knit through the fruit. Attractive spicy finish.
Pasta with tomato, olive and aubergine sauce

Santa Emiliana Palmeras Cabernet Sauvignon 97
O'Briens

Medium-bodied red

Blackcurrant and mint on the nose. Plenty of fruit; smooth and well-balanced with highish alcohol kicking in at the end.
Chunky terrine or meatloaf

Santa Helena Selección del Directorio Reserve Cabernet Sauvignon 97
Greenhills

Full-bodied red, fruit-driven

Blackcurrant with stalky cedarwood aromas. Spicy blackcurrant fruit with a touch of smoke. Balanced acidity and firm, ripe tannin.
Lamb chops with a herb crust

Santa Rita 120 Cabernet Sauvignon 97
Gilbeys

Medium-bodied red

Compote of berries on the nose. Lovely ripe blackcurrant palate with herbaceous background and a touch of black pepper in the finish. Soft and supple with nice length.
Pitta bread with kebabs

Torréon de Paredes Cabernet Sauvignon 97
Ecock

Medium-bodied red

Good varietal nose, fruit-driven style. Plenty of juicy blackcurrant fruit. Well-made, nicely balanced wine.
Spicy stir-fry of lamb or beef

Torréon de Paredes Merlot 98
Ecock

Light fruity red

Ripe soft fruit aroma with a touch of something herbal. Similar palate with plenty of ripe juicy fruit.
Zesty pizza or pasta

Undurraga Pinot Noir Reserva 97
United Beverages

Medium-bodied red

Fruit jelly aromas, raspberry, cream and vanilla. Quite oaky palate, fruit not as pronounced as on the nose, but still nice.
Teriyaki chicken

Villard Cabernet Sauvignon 97
O'Briens

Full-bodied red, fruit-driven

Minty nose with nice vegetal complexity. Well-balanced,

rounded soft fruit flavours with nice underlying spice. Should develop a bit more.
Lamb in pastry

Red £8 - £10

Villard Casablanca Valley Pinot Noir 97

O'Briens   I I

Medium-bodied red

Upfront raspberry fruit aromas which follow to the palate. Complex yet appealing with lovely blend of fruit and spice and elegant structure with finely balanced tannin and bright acidity.
Richly cooked red mullet

Veramonte Merlot 97

Oddbins   I

Full-bodied red, fruit-driven

Wonderful dark fruit aromas with a really meaty tone. The palate echoes the nose with spicy, savoury fruit, balanced tannins and a long finish. What a classic at the price!
Beef fillet with a herb crust

Carmen Cabernet Sauvignon Reserve 96

Dillon   C

Medium to full-bodied red, fruit-driven

Brambles and toffee on the nose with herbal tones. Lots of ripe, summer pudding fruit flavours with hints of mint, vanilla and chocolate. Full, with firm tannin and balancing acidity and long finish. Still young and will gain complexity.
Roast guinea-fowl with bacon and rosemary

Alto de Terra Andina Cabernet Sauvignon Reserva 97

Fitzgerald

Full-bodied red, fruit-driven

Peppery blackcurrants on the nose. Ripe soft fruit flavours with mild tannin, vanilla and spice flavours. Well-made, pleasing wine.
Lamb with cumin, ginger and coriander marinade

Canepa Private Reserve Cabernet Sauvignon 96

MacCormaic

Full-bodied red, fruit-driven

Rather subdued on the nose with a burst of rich, ripe blackcurrant fruit and black pepper. Good length and still developing.
Irish stew

Cousiño Macul Antiguas Reservas Cabernet Sauvignon 96

Ecock

Full-bodied red

Appealing blackcurrant fruit on the nose, almost baked, with a hint of spice. Good weight of fruit and balanced tannin. Quite oaky with decent length of finish.
Rack of lamb with herbs

Las Casas del Toqui Cabernet Sauvignon Reserve Prestige 97

Dunnes Stores

Full-bodied red, fruit-driven

Baked plummy fruit aromas and good weight of ripe, baked fruit flavours. A big wine with a lovely long finish.
Beef ribs with corncakes and garlic sauce

Santa Rita Reserva Merlot 97

Gilbeys

Medium-bodied red

Spicy plum and cherry aromas with a touch of damp wood. Quite meaty palate with hints of liquorice. Savoury, traditional style.

Home-made lasagne

Valdivieso Pinot Noir 97

Searson

Medium-bodied red

Fruit pastilles on the nose. Very ripe fruity style with lots of juicy strawberry and fresh acidity.

Stir-fried chicken with Chinese spices

Viña San Pedro Castillo de Molina Cabernet Sauvignon Reserva 97

Cassidy

Full-bodied red, fruit-driven

Enticingly complex nose--leathery cigar tones with the blackcurrant fruit. Firm structure and well-integrated layers of fruit. Long finish.

Loin of lamb in pastry

Viña Tarapaca Gran Reserva Cabernet Sauvignon 94

Gleeson

Full-bodied red, fruit-driven

Brambles and a touch of wood on the nose. Ripe spicy fruit with firm tannin and good concentration. A bit green in the finish.

Lamb pie

Red £10 - £12

Carmen Grande Vidure Cabernet Reserve 94

Dillon I

Full-bodied red, fruit-driven

Stewed plums and damsons with herbal aromas. Ripe, ripe fruit with vanilla and herbs, earthy tones developing. Firmly structured with plenty of time to go.

Magret of duck with glazed shallots for an impressive dinner party!

Bodega de Familia Undurraga Santa Ana Cabernet Sauvignon 95

Tesco C

Full-bodied red, fruit-driven

Sandalwood and pencil box aromas--quite classic and complex. Ripe but well-structured palate with blackcurrant fruit, firm tannin and good length. Drinks now but should improve.

Stuffed shoulder of lamb

Errazuriz Cabernet Sauvignon Reserva 97

Allied Drinks C

Full-bodied red, fruit-driven

Complex aromas of vanilla, strawberry and blackcurrant. Firmly structured with ripe blackcurrant fruit, mint and spice influences and a long finish tinged with dark chocolate.

Lamb or beef in pastry

CHILE

Red £12 -£15

Undurraga Bodega de Familia Cabernet Sauvignon 95

United Beverages　　C

Full-bodied red, fruit-driven

Pencil shavings with floral hints on the nose. Elegant fruit with spicy earthy tones. Tannins are mellow and flavours are maturing to promising complexity. Reserved and stylish.

Roast pheasant with game sauce

Santa Carolina Reserva de Familia Cabernet Sauvignon 95

TDL

Full-bodied red, fruit-driven

Brambles and rosehips on the nose. Firm, ripe dusty tannins and elegant blackcurrant fruit with hints of menthol. Peppery, even fiery finish—needs time.

Lamb with couscous

Red £15 - £20

Miguel Torres Manso de Velasco 95

Woodford Bourne

Full-bodied red, fruit-driven

Farmyard aromas mix with blackcurrant jam and spice. Full

and velvet-like palate with complex flavours of spice, eucalyptus and baked fruit. A real delight for those willing to pay!

Rack of lamb with herbs

Santa Rita Casa Real Cabernet Sauvignon 95

Gilbeys

Full-bodied red, fruit-driven

Cassis and cedar with hints of chocolate give an intense opulent nose. Very ripe fruit yet quite elegant with blackcurrant and spice flavours and firm, yet balanced tannins. Perhaps at a slightly closed stage, should develop very well.

Roast duck for a special dinner party

Rosé £6 - £8

Miguel Torres Santa Digna Cabernet Sauvignon Rosé 98

Woodford Bourne　　C

Rosé

Very aromatic nose—floral, cherry fruit aromas. Delicious burst of lively fruit on the palate with a clean, refreshing finish.

Warm grilled vegetable salad

Eastern and Central Europe

When a Dublin wine merchant comments that one of his bestselling wines is an Austrian Merlot at close to £20 a bottle, there has clearly been a striking change in the Irish wine market. Austria had an up-hill struggle after the scandals of the eighties. The strength of the Austrian economy and small scale of its wine industry made the wine expensive. It is difficult for such an environment to compete. The light aromatic style of the whites and cool, northern reds, also have a limited market. Most frustrating of all, many consumers still confuse Austrian wines with cheap German wines and assume they are sweet.

In spite of the obstacles, Austria is slowly beginning to find a niche for its high quality, distinctive wines. Look especially for the properly sweet Beerenauslese category. The Austrian climate allows such wines to be produced more frequently and consistently than the German and at a lower price. Austrian Riesling is also top quality and the new-wave reds, especially from the Wachau, region are intriguing.

There is a lot of interest and quality coming from Austria today. Prices are high but are intrinsic to the country. Anyone prepared to pay is likely to be rewarded.

For the majority of countries of the former Eastern bloc, the wine industry is still described in terms of potential rather than reality. Right across this part of Europe, from the German borders to the Balkans, there are fine conditions for growing grapes and making wine and a long tradition of viticulture. Yet economic instability, insecurity of land tenure, war and lack of investment, have meant a very slow, uneven start.

Hungary has fared best—a combination of a head start from an already Westernised economy and some very pragmatic decisions about land has enabled large-scale investment from home and abroad. Hungary also had Tokay, a magnet of attraction for dollars and pounds, as one of the very few noble wines exploited to date on today's market. Tokay is a wonderful dessert wine of complexity and highly individual style. Although prices have risen in the last two or three years, it is still extremely good value and cellars very well. Tokay apart, Hungary is producing a range of light whites and red, many through the expertise of flying winemakers and international consultants. Many of the whites show good ripe fruit and careful use of oak. There are also interesting results with local grape varieties like the Irsay Oliver and Tokay's Furmint, as well as Muscats.

Bulgaria has been surprisingly slow to re-emerge, given its already established market through the state-run wine company of Communist times. It made Bulgarian red the great party plonk of the seventies partnered by white Laski Risling of Yugoslavia. Bulgaria's problem has been land ownership, recently resolved. Until July 1999 nobody had been able to securely buy or hold land as the state endeavoured to trace the original owners and restore their properties. Now 80 per cent has been returned and the remainder put up for sale on the open market. This should give the necessary security to encourage planting of suitable grapes in suitable sites and to bring foreign investment in technology and expertise.

Romania is also a country with great potential and is beginning to re-vitalise its industry in spite of considerable difficulties. The chief problems have been inconsistency, bottle variation due to outdated equipment and insufficiently trained and motivated staff. When you taste a really delicious Pinot Noir or earthy, complex Cabernet at a bargain price, it may take many bottles to find similar quality. However, within the country this is changing; there is greater commitment to quality and better standards all round which should soon come through to the market.

The whole of Eastern Europe has a lot to offer in wine, which will most certainly become apparent as the twenty-first century unfolds.

Austria

Dom. Müller Sauvignon Blanc 97
Mitchell

Aromatic white

Aromatic gooseberry fruit and grassy tones. Fresh and crisp with lovely weight of green apple and citrus fruit, good length and a clean finish.
Spinach soufflé

Red £15 - £20

Dom. Müller Cabernet Sauvignon 95
Mitchell

Medium-bodied red

Restrained blackcurrant fruit aromas. Lovely balanced wine with good weight of cool fruit merged with cedary spice and lasting through the finish. Fine structure holds the wine elegantly. Good but expensive.
Medallions of fillet steak with herb sauce

Bulgaria

White £5 or less

Bulgarian Vintners' Rousse Reserve Chardonnay 95
Fitzgerald   ££

Full-bodied white, oak

Ripe tropical bouquet. Full and flavoursome with fruit cocktail ripeness. Nicely balanced, good value wine.
Escalope of chicken with cream sauce

Red £5 or less

Bulgarian Vintners' Rousse Reserve Cabernet Sauvignon 94
Fitzgerald

Full-bodied red

Clean, ripe fruit on the nose which follows to the palate. Well-made and fine at the price.
Meat pie

Red £5 - £6

Bulgarian Cabernet Sauvignon Reserve 93
Tesco

Medium-bodied red

Blackberries with a hint of rubber on the nose. Ripe cassis flavours with a touch of oak. Alcohol shows in the finish with nice fruit flavour.
Lasagne

Red £6 - £8

Dom. Boyar Oriachovitza Cabernet Sauvignon Reserve 94
Woodford Bourne

Medium-bodied red

Quite complex and characterful nose, cassis, tobacco and vanilla. Ripe mellow fruit on the palate balanced by a firm bite of tannin. Some peppery spice in the finish.
Steak pie

Hungary

White £5 - £6

Chapel Hill Balatonboglár Irsai Oliver 97
Barry & Fitzwilliam   C
Aromatic white
Very floral and aromatic. Fresh and zippy with spicy fruit and nice weight. Long finish with lively spice to the end.
Chinese noodles or vegetable pastries

White £6 - £8

Oremus Mandulás Tokaji Dry Furmint 97
Mitchell   C
Light fruity white
Clean, fruity aromas with a mineral streak. Ripe apple fruit with balanced acidity finishing with a sour apple and peppermint flavour. Something different.
Green vegetable mousse

Red £5 or less

Tesco Reka Valley Merlot nv
Tesco
Medium-bodied red
Plummy nose. Soft, slightly earthy fruit flavours, well-defined with a balanced structure. Easy-drinking, approachable wine.
Liver and bacon

Red £5 - £6

Volcanic Hills Merlot 96
Gleeson
Medium-bodied red
Soft fruit aromas with a touch of old wood. Nice fruit flavours with slightly dusty wood and a decent finish.
Sausages

Romania

White £5 - £6

Posta Romana Tarnave Valley Gewürtztraminer 96
Barry & Fitzwilliam   C ££
Aromatic white
Spicy lychee fruit aromas. Nice balance of honeyed exotic fruit flavours and lively acidity. Oily and full with a gorgeous finish of warm ripe fruit and spice. Quality way ahead of its price!
Peking duck and other Oriental dishes

Posta Romana Classic Chardonnay 98
Barry & Fitzwilliam
Light fruity white
Apples and pear drops on the nose. Apple and pear flavours with balanced acidity and weight and some length. Good, modern winemaking.
Creamy chicken and rice

Red £5 or less

Tesco Reka Valley Pinot Noir nv
Tesco
Medium-bodied red
Soft earthy fruit on the nose. Similar palate with slight Pinot

gaminess. Balanced and good value.

Kidneys and mushrooms

Prahova Valley Pinot Noir Reserve 96

Barry & Fitzwilliam

Medium-bodied red

Nice intensity of ripe strawberry fruit aromas with a touch of the farmyard. Well-structured palate with silky smooth berry fruit, moderate tannin and balanced acidity. Well-made with a touch of complexity.

Chicken in red wine with mushrooms or cheese and mushroom tart or pasta

Dealul Viilor Vineyards Special Reserve Cabernet Sauvignon 96

Barry & Fitzwilliam   ££

Medium-bodied red

Interesting aromas of cassis and vanilla with a touch of liquorice. Claret-like style with blackcurrant fruit, spice and herb flavours, well-rounded tannins and some length of finish.

Steak and kidney pie

Rovit Vineyards Pinot Noir Special Reserve 93

Barry & Fitzwilliam   ££

Medium-bodied red

Really ripe berry fruit aromas. Very well-balanced on the palate showing good, concentrated ripe fruit with a touch of vanilla. A classic at a small price.

Home-made game pie

France

Editor's choice: lesser-known French wines

The classic wine appellations of France continue to produce some of the world's finest wines. But throughout the country exciting and different regional wines can be found. Some areas, such as Madiran and the Cornas appellation of the northern Rhône, produce very traditional, individual wines. Others have benefited greatly from improved techniques and the wines have jumped in quality while maintaining traditional character; the reds of the Loire are a good example. Here is my selection from this edition's crop.

Ch. d'Aydie AC Madiran 1994

Cave de Tain l'Hermitage Les Nobles Rives AC Cornas 1995

Dom. Filliatreau AC Saumur-Champigny 1997

Alain Graillot AC Crozes-Hermitage 1997

Ch. Jolys 1996 AC Jurançon sec 1996

Excellence AC Touraine 1997

Rasteau Dom. Martin Rasteau AC Côtes du Rhône Villages 1995

Ch. de Fesles Vieilles Vignes AC Anjou 1997

Albert Mann Sylvaner AC Alsace 1997

Dom. du Rey VdP Côtes de Gascogne 1998

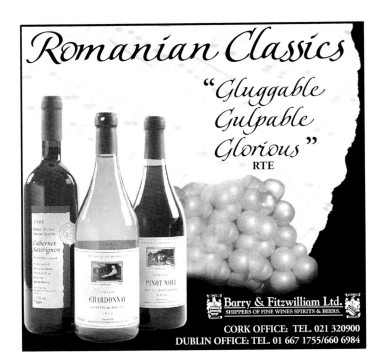

Alsace

It is strange that in an age of varietal wines, France's only wines traditionally labelled by grape variety, those of Alsace, are rather neglected by consumers. In fact the simplicity of Alsace labelling—AC Alsace with a name of the grape variety plus a Grand Cru if appropriate—might be copied across the Rhine or in neighbouring Burgundy. The grape is everything in Alsacien wine-making. Oak is not used, vinification tends to be traditional, non-interventionist. A house like Hugel is very traditional indeed, while Domaine Zind-Humbrecht takes a more innovative line. Although domaines are increasing, Alsace is still dominated by co-ops and negociants such as Hugel, Trimbach and Leon Beyer.

Most of the wine is white, made from six major grape varieties. Pinot Blanc is traditionally a lesser varietal but planting has greatly increased. Well-made in a ripe vintage it is the perfect aperitif wine: rounded, discreet and elegant. Gewürztraminer, one of the best known grapes outside Alsace, is heady and perfumed, the best of all wines for Oriental food, but also excellent with the local Munster cheese. Tokay Pinot Gris is rich and full, lightly spicy and highly versatile with food. It is a great restaurant wine, that can match meat, fish and vegetable dishes.

Muscat is usually dry with lighter fruit than Gewürztraminer but also heady and perfumed. Riesling is king: dry, even austere with very refined steely fruit. It is best of all from a Grand Cru vineyard. Vendange Tardives, lightly sweet wines from late picked grapes, and Selection de Grain Nobles, luscious dessert wines of great complexity, are now more readily available and highly distinctive.

White £5 - £6

Kientzheim-Kayserberg Kaefferkopf Riesling AC Alsace 96
Febvre

Aromatic white, classic

Hints of petrol and floral tones. Dry and oily with very lemony fruit. Fresh and well-priced but rather tart on the finish.
Fish in cream sauce

Tesco AC Alsace nv
Tesco

Light dry white

Lovely subtle but ripe aromas. Big weight of ripe green fruits,

nicely balanced with refreshing acidity and a clean finish.
Aperitif with tiny savoury quiches

White £6 - £8

Dietrich Pinot Blanc AC Alsace 98
TDL ££

Light dry white

Aromatic and ripe on the nose—apples and a touch of honey. Quite steely palate with crisp acidity cutting through the fruit. Good weight and well-balanced—an excellent example of Pinot Blanc at this price.
Courgette quiche

Albert Mann Pinot Blanc Auxerrois AC Alsace 96
Oddbins

Aromatic white, classic

Apple-like aromas. Dry with nice weight of peaches and cream fruit. Balanced and broad with a good long finish.
Warm chicken salad

Dopff & Irion Pinot Blanc AC Alsace 97
Bacchus

Aromatic white, classic

Crisp, aromatic nose with hints of peach and mineral. Almost creamy palate with peach fruit flavours and crisp clean finish.
Light fish or cheese soufflé

Hugel Cuvée Les Amours Pinot Blanc de Blancs AC Alsace 96
Grants

Aromatic white

Fresh aromatic nose, citrus fruit with a touch of honey. Nice weight of crunchy green apple fruit with zippy acidity and a crisp finish.
Omelette

Trimbach Pinot Blanc AC Alsace 97
Gilbeys

Light dry white

Ripe apple aromas, a touch earthy. Dry and simple with mineral fruit and balanced acidity.
Leek tartlets

White £8 - £10

Charles Koehly & Fils Saint-Hippolyte Gewürtztraminer AC Alsace 97
Fitzgerald C

Aromatic white

Tropical fruit with rose petals and spice on the nose. Dry and full with honey, raisin and tropical fruit flavours. Well-structured and balanced.
Goose pâté

Sipp Mack Tokay Pinot Gris Réserve AC Alsace 97
Mitchell C

Aromatic white

Complex aromas of stewed apple, mineral and honey. Mouthfilling texture; very ripe apple and custard flavours and a lingering finish.
Pork with cumin

Albert Mann Sylvaner AC Alsace 97
MacCormaic

Aromatic white, classic

Light smoke aromas with almond and honey nuances. Red apple and nectarine flavours, balanced acidity and good length.
Noodles with prawns

Charles Koehly & Fils Pinot Blanc AC Alsace 97
Fitzgerald

Light dry white

Floral, citrus nose. Lots of crunchy green apple fruit and racy acidity. Good long finish.
Light pasta tossed with butter and cheese

Charles Koehly & Fils Saint-Hippolyte Riesling AC Alsace 97
Fitzgerald

Aromatic white, classic

Flowery, mineral aromas with shades of petrol beginning to show. Bone-dry with very crisp acidity and excellent weight of green fruit. Long and lingering.
Crab gratin

Dietrich Gewürztraminer AC Alsace 98
TDL

Aromatic white

Lychees and spices from the nose.Quite oily, spicy palate with a modest weight of fruit.
Spicy wontons

Dopff & Irion Riesling AC Alsace 97
Bacchus

Aromatic white, classic

Fragrant wild honey with a touch of oiliness. Concentrated and long flavour with nicely balanced acidity.
Brill or sole in a cream and shellfish sauce

Dopff au Moulin Pinot Blanc AC Alsace 96
Woodford Bourne

Aromatic white, classic

Ripe candied orange aromas. Fresh and quite creamy palate with good concentration and a clean finish.
Aperitif

Dopff au Moulin Riesling AC Alsace 97
Woodford Bourne

Aromatic white, classic

Fresh, fresh aromas of green apple and lemon. Good weight of ripe fruit with bracing acidity. Attractive and flavoursome with good length.
Typically with a creamy quiche

Sipp Mack Riesling AC Alsace 97
Mitchell

Aromatic white, classic

Apple and citrus aromas with quite pronounced honey and a mineral streak. Steely apple fruit on the palate with very crisp acidity and good length.
Mousseline of fish with butter sauce

White £10 -£12

Sipp Mack Gewürztraminer Réserve AC Alsace 97
Mitchell   C

Aromatic white

Intense aromas of roses and lychees. Similar intensity of ripe, rich fruit and spice on the palate with nicely balanced acidity and an excellent finish.
Munster cheese

Albert Mann Tokay Pinot Gris AC Alsace 96
MacCormaic
Aromatic white, classic
Multi-dimensional bouquet with orange zest, almonds and a whiff of diesel! Juicy citrus flavours and lively acidity with

a touch of honey. Lovely balance and lingering honey and lemon finish.
Glazed quail salad

Dietrich Gewürztraminer Cuvée Exceptionelle AC Alsace 98
TDL

Aromatic white

Tropical fruit and rosewater aromas. Huge weight of ripe fruit and spices giving great richness. Long and full.
Chinese duck

Dopff au Moulin Gewürztraminer AC Alsace 96
Woodford Bourne

Aromatic white, classic

Aromas of dessert apples and Turkish Delight. Dry palate with spicy lychee fruit. Concentrated and lingering.
Greek hummous

Hugel Gewürztraminer AC Alsace 96
Grants

Aromatic white

Lively aromas of rose petals and watermelon. Medium weight with plenty of ripe exotic fruit notes and a long, dry finish.
Salad of red peppers

Trimbach Gewürztraminer AC Alsace 96
Gilbeys

Aromatic white

Floral musky nose followed by flavours of tropical fruit. Full and round with touches of honey and a dry finish.
Chinese meals, especially crispy duck

Trimbach Pinot Gris Réserve AC Alsace 96
Gilbeys

Aromatic white

Muted aromas of apple skin; really opens up on the palate with concentrated oily, smoky fruit. Richly textured and long.
Pasta with grilled vegetables

White £12 - £15

Sipp Mack Riesling Rosacker AC Alsace Grand Cru 97
Mitchell   C

Aromatic white, classic

Steely, mineral aromas. Perfectly balanced wine with layers of green fruit cut through with crisp acidity. An understated wine which should develop very well in time.
Brill with cream sauce

Albert Mann Schlossberg Riesling AC Alsace Grand Cru 96
MacCormaic

Aromatic white, classic

Elegant restrained aromas, floral, citrus fruit with mineral tones. Youthful palate with good intensity of rather tart fruit which should develop very nicely.
Fish terrine

White £15 - £20

Albert Mann Steingrubler Gewürztraminer AC Alsace Grand Cru 97
MacCormaic   ☆ ☆

Aromatic white, classic

Aromas of fresh Cox's Pippins undercut with new-mown hay

and diesel. Slight spritz on the palate cuts the rich intensity. Broad and creamy with layers of flavour: apples, nectarines, honey and spice in great length.
Duck cooked with apples and choucroute

Dom. Zind Humbrecht Riesling Wintzenheim AC Alsace 97

United Beverages   ☆

Aromatic white, classic

Flinty smoky nose with apple fruit underneath. Rich mouthfilling fruit and complex flavours, honey, lime and smoke. Rich and oily with a lovely finish.
Traditional, freshly-cooked quiche lorraine

Trimbach Cuvée des Seigneurs de Ribeaupierre AC Alsace 88

Gilbeys

Aromatic white

Lovely rosewater and cinnamon bouquet. Richly assertive palate but without agression; eloquently expressed spicy floral fruit with balanced acidity.
Warm salad of spiced honey glazed quail

White £20 -£25

Dom. Zind Humbrecht Herrenweg de Turckheim Gewürztraminer AC Alsace 97

United Beverages   ☆

Aromatic white, classic

Lychee and tangerine aromas with honey and spice. Broad, spicy, complex palate just balanced by acidity. Fruity

mineral flavours, slightly smoky and wonderfully rich with good supporting alcohol and an endless finish.
Spiced guinea-fowl

White £30 -£35

Dom. Zind Humbrecht Clos St Urbain Riesling AC Alsace Grand Cru 97

United Beverages   C

Aromatic white, classic

Elegant green fruit aromas with a touch of kerosene. Opens up beautifully in the glass with smoky, flinty touches to offset ripe apple fruit. Young but well-balanced and with a way to go.
Crab gratin

Dom. Zind Humbrecht Clos Jebsal Pinot Gris AC Alsace 97

United Beverages

Aromatic white, classic

Elegant, youthful nose. Rich honey and lemon style on the palate, broad and creamy and just beginning to open up.
Chicken fillets in pastry

Dom. Zind Humbrecht Pinot Gris Clos St Urbain AC Alsace Grand Cru 96

United Beverages

Aromatic white, classic

Developed aromas, smoky vegetal tones creeping in. Broad, rich and intense palate develops greater delicacy and complexity with restrained mineral flavours coming in. Probably at its peak this year.
Red mullet cooked with white wine

Beaujolais

The darling wine of the seventies, especially in Nouveau form, Beaujolais has had some bad press in recent years. Its popularity was partly responsible for subsequent problems as it caused prices and expectations of what was a fundamentally simple wine to rise too high. Beaujolais became bad value.

Youth and lively fruit are everything in Beaujolais. At its best, like a good Muscadet, Beaujolais has a special place: a light fruity red with character to drink with simple flavoursome food like olives and salami. Carbonic maceration, the special enclosed fermentation process by which most Beaujolais is made, which brings out colour and fruit but not tannin, has led to a decline in character or at least individual style. Now even the Cru wines can be hard to distinguish. Some traditionally-made Beaujolais is still available and is quite a revelation.

The Crus, the ten named Villages, Fleurie, Morgon etc., offer more sophistication and polish, though rarely much complexity. Moulin à Vent can age for five or even ten years depending on its producer and vintage. However, the general rule in Beaujolais is to find a reliable producer at a tolerable price and drink the wine young and fresh and cool.

Red £6 - £8

Boisset AC Beaujolais-Villages 96
Gleeson   C
Light fruity red
Raspberry fruit aromas with some developed savoury notes. Raspberry follows through on the palate with some liquorice and spice flavours.
Baked ham

Faiveley AC Fleurie98
Remy
Light fruity red
Fresh ripe raspberry aromas with a touch of violets. Light and delicate with lively scented fruit and silky tannin. Easy-drinking and very attractive.
Chicken and mustard

Ch. du Bourg AC Beaujolais-Villages 98
Wine Warehouse
Light fruity red
Lots of jammy strawberry fruit on the nose and similar flavours follow. Soft and fruity with balanced acidity.
Mushroom pastries

J. P. Brun Dom. des Terres Dorées Cuvée à l'Ancienne AC Beaujolais 97
Wines Direct

Light fruity red

Very ripe/sweet fruit on the nose with a touch of steeliness underneath. Less on the palate—light, simple fruit in an easy-drinking style.
Steak sandwich or on its own

Michel Brugne Le Vivier AC Moulin-à-Vent 98
Dunnes Stores

Light fruity red

Earthy, meaty aromas with the fruit; nice strawberry fruit and good length of flavour.
Proper salami

Dom. André Pelletier Les Envaux AC Juliénas 98
Dunnes Stores

Light fruity red

Straightforward jammy red berries on the nose. The flavours follow on the palate with a rather hot finish.
Chinese dishes

Red £8 - £10

Anne Delaroche AC Fleurie 98
Gleeson

Light fruity red

Summer berry aromas. Young, lively fruit with nice balance of acidity and mild tannin. Well-made and should develop over the next year.
Peking duck

Louis Max AC Beaujolais-Villages 97
United Beverages

Light fruity red

Slightly smoky red berry and cherry fruit. Soft and light with lively raspberry fruit and nice balance.
Pan-fried kidneys

Louis Jadot AC Beaujolais-Villages 98
Grants

Light fruity red

Boiled sweets on the nose. Berry fruit character with a touch of rhubarb. Soft and lively with good length of fruit flavour.
Spicy meatballs

Bouchard Ainé & Fils La Vigneronne AC Beaujolais-Villages 97
Cassidy

Light fruity red

Smoke and strawberries on the nose. Nice vegetal touch to the ripe fruit on the palate with balanced acidity. Good easy-drinking style.
Sausages

Red £10 - £12

Jaffelin AC Fleurie 97
Fields   C

Light fruity red

Summer pudding with spice and caramel on the nose. Good structure behind ripe berry fruit. Nicely balanced alcohol and acidity and altogether rather delicious.
Roast veal

Louis Jadot Ch. des Jacques AC Moulin-à-Vent 96
Grants

Medium-bodied red

Rich, soft fruit aromas with a spicy twist. Rather stalky berry fruit with balanced tannin and acidity. Long finish with fruit flavours carrying through well.
Carpaccio beef salad

Ch. du Bourg AC Fleurie 97
Wine Warehouse

Light fruity red

Ripe berry aromas and hints of spice. Silky berry fruit on the palate with balanced acidity and mild tannin. Lovely and rounded with quite a creamy finish.
Chicken breast with mustard

Alain Coudert Clos de la Roilette AC Fleurie 98
Wines Direct

Light fruity red

Cherries and raspberries on the nose. Great burst of fruit flavour nicely balanced by acidity and a bite of tannin.
Roast salmon

Dom. Maurice Gaget Côte du Py AC Morgon 97
Fields

Medium-bodied red

Meaty blackberries and chocolate on the nose. Young but with lovely weight of dark fruit and spice flavour. Well-balanced and should drink well beyond 2000.
Good charcuterie

J-P & H Gauthier Dom. de la Treille AC Fleurie 97
Wines Direct

Light fruity red

Violets and spice on the nose. Ripe cherry fruit flavours with a touch of tannin. Good dry finish.
Grilled or baked chicken

Louis Jadot Dom. de Poncereau AC Fleurie98
Grants

Light fruity red

Aromas of fresh raspberries with a floral note. Dry with a good weight of soft, ripe red berry fruit. Appetising, long dry finish.
Chinese duck

Bouchard Père & Fils Dom. Estienne de Lagrange AC Moulin-à-Vent 96
Findlater

Medium-bodied red

Ripe berry fruit and vanilla on the nose. A bit young with soft tannins showing but nice balancing strawberry fruit with a touch of spice.
Veal casserole

Paul Beaudet Dom. Vert-Pré AC Fleurie 97
Bacchus

Light fruity red

Slightly stalky mineral nose. Intense fruit with light, integrated tannins and balanced acidity.
Mixed charcuterie or roast chicken

Red £12 - £15

Louis Max AC Fleurie 97
United Beverages   C

Light fruity red

Red fruit and caramel aromas. Quite developed savoury tones mingle with fruit flavours. Nice supporting alcohol and a long finish.

Pork and chestnuts

Reine Pédauque Cuvée Étiennette Courtieux AC Fleurie 98
Barry & Fitzwilliam

Light fruity red

Aromas of boiled sweets and cherries with floral notes. Good weight of ripe fruit—raspberries, fruit pastilles. Balancing mild tannin and lively acidity. Long, fruity and dry at the finish.

Spicy baked chicken

P. Ferrand & Fils Dom. du Clos des Garands AC Fleurie 98
Febvre

Light fruity red

Blackberry and spice aromas. Silky, velvet palate with nice weight of fruit. Well-balanced, polished wine but expensive.

Chinese duck

What the awards mean

☆☆☆ —exceptional wines of considerable complexity with classic balance from a very good vintage.

☆☆—elegant wines with character and complexity above expectations, showing balance, subtlety and 'typicité'.

☆—wines with character and style that are particularly good examples of their region and winemaking.

C—commendation: good, interesting wines that merit attention but not quite a star, including wines which are good examples of particular regional styles and wines which are a little young but show good potential.

££—value: wines offering exceptional value for money in their type/region; mainly lower-priced wines but including well-priced classics.

Bordeaux

Bordeaux makes headlines for the prices fetched by its top wines. This year the first-growth châteaux 1998 vintages, a good-ish year, came on offer at over £1,000 a case, still in their cellars and a good ten years off approachable drinking. They will change hands many times between now and into the future, and at ever increasing cost.

In the real world, however, Bordeaux still provides good wine for drinking rather than investment. The less fashionable Crus Classés and Crus Bourgeois can still provide good value in the £20 price range. They offer complexity and the ability to age and may well be out of reach in a few years time. Châteaux D'Angludet, Phélan-Segur, Grand Puy Ducasse and Fourcas Hosten are good examples from current vintages.

At a simpler level, AC Médoc and the minor Bordeaux appellations have improved in quality and consistency and some very stylish wines are available for around £10 a bottle. Some are the lesser labels or properties of the large producers, others are from small, quality-driven estates in less established appellations.

Dry white wine from Graves and especially Pessac-Léognan is another affordable (just) classic, while Bordeaux sec is increasingly well-made with a more sauvignon, fresh flavour and often a touch of new oak.

For this year's *Best of Wine* we tasted only the 1995 and 1996 vintages for Bordeaux red wines. These are the youngest good vintages and are readily available. The best wines will age well and should be stored, while lesser wines, especially from 1995 are drinking well now. In general, 1995 is a riper, warmer more forward year, 1996 more reserved and classically structured but it may prove best in time.

White £5 - £6

Tesco AC Graves 97
Tesco
Medium-bodied white
Gooseberry and floral notes on the nose. Very dry, stewed apple and kiwi fruit flavours. Young and crisp.
Plaice with cream and mussel sauce

White £6 - £8

Ch. Haut Rian AC Bordeaux 98   *Wines Direct*
Aromatic white
Clean, fresh citrus aromas. Nice weight of ripe fruit and balancing acidity sustained through the finish.
Fish and rice salad as a first course

Sirius AC Bordeaux 96
Fitzgerald
Aromatic white
Ripe melon fruit with a hint of caramel. Dry and fresh with good weight of pear and citrus fruit flavour and a long, smooth finish.
Warm salad with smoked haddock

White £8 -£10

Dom. de Sours AC Bordeaux 96
Woodford Bourne
Aromatic white
Lovely ripe fruit on the nose. Green apple and lemon zest dominate the palate. Good weight and dry crisp finish.
Seafood pancakes

White £10 -£12

Ch. de Sours AC Bordeaux 96
Woodford Bourne   C
Aromatic white
Honeyed citrus fruit aromas. Abundance of ripe fruit— lemons, apples and pears with crisp zingy acidity. Floral hints in a long mellow finish.
Scallops with cream sauce

White £12 - £15

Ch. de Rochemorin AC Pessac-Léognan 97
Febvre   C
Full-bodied white
Slightly herbal nose, fennel and thyme. Rather grassy palate with mellow fruit and citrus freshness. Long and attractive finish but needs more time.
Salmon en croûte with butter sauce

Red £5 - £6

Tesco's Vintage Claret AC Bordeaux Supérieur 96
Tesco
Medium-bodied red, classic
Plenty of blackcurrant fruit on the nose. Dry with rather stalky fruit and green tannin but still good value.
Beef stew

Red £6 - £8

Ch. Bertinerie AC 1ères Côtes de Blaye 97
Wines Direct   C ££
Full-bodied red
Punchy aromas of cough medicine, eucalyptus and pepper. Plenty of ripe blackcurrant fruit balanced by tannin

and acidity. Well-made, decent Bordeaux.
Irish stew

Sirius AC Bordeaux 95
Fitzgerald   C
Medium-bodied red, classic

Soft brambly aromas with subtle cedarwood. Mellow tannin nicely integrated into the fruit. Excellent value Bordeaux.
Lamb with herb sauce

Ch l'Ombrière AC 1ères Côtes de Bordeaux 95
Dunnes Stores
Medium-bodied red

Interesting quite complex vegetal aromas. Lots of ripe fruit balanced by firm tannin. Berry fruit flavours persist with nice green pepper twist in the finish.
Noisettes of lamb with herb sauce

Marquis de Chasse AC Bordeaux 96
Bacchus
Medium-bodied red, classic

Fruit first on the nose. Palate supported by modest tannin and acidity. Nice weight and balance--a typical AC Bordeaux.
Rare beef sandwiches

Red £8 - £10

Ch. Beauséjour AC Fronsac 95
Grants   C
Full-bodied red, classic

Aromas of blackberries, butter and vanilla. Warm, spicy and inviting. Rich fruitcake flavours with a backbone of firm tannin and a stalky, appetising finish. Well-polished but definitely Fronsac!
Guinea-fowl pot roast

Ch. Cadillac Lesgourgues AC Bordeaux Supérieur 96
Mitchell   C
Medium to full-bodied red, classic

Ripe berry fruit aromas with hints of spice and mint. Firm tannic structure offset by ripe blackcurrant fruit. Nicely rounded in the finish.
Rack of lamb

Ch. Béchereau AC Bordeaux Supérieur 95
MacCormaic
Medium-bodied red, classic

Lots of blackcurrant fruit on the nose, well-sustained on the palate. Flavours just beginning to develop and backed by firm tannin.
Grilled meat, chops or steak

Ch. de la Vieille Tour AC Bordeaux Supérieur 95
Barry & Fitzwilliam
Medium-bodied red, classic

Berry fruit aromas with flavours of forest fruit to follow. Quite firmly structured with a good weight of fruit in the finish.
Traditional mixed grill

Ch. Haut Bertinerie AC 1ères Côtes de Blaye 95
Wines Direct
Full-bodied red

Earthy, soft fruit aromas with a touch of oakiness. Slightly stalky blackcurrant fruit with nice supporting tannins and creamy texture. Easy-drinking and appealing style.
Duck breast with a fruity sauce

Ch. La Prade AC Bordeaux Côtes de Franc 96

Wines Direct

Full-bodied red

Fresh, slightly jammy berry fruit aromas. Light, elegant style with ripe plum and berry fruit, pleasant tannin and a dry finish.

Beef medallions with mushroom sauce

Ch. Livran Cru Bourgeois AC Médoc 95

Grants

Full-bodied red, classic

Rather vegetal fruit aromas. Well-structured with dry, rather chewy fruit and oak and a long, satisfying finish. Very traditional.

Casseroled duck legs with wine and shallots

Ch. Méaume AC Bordeaux Supérieur 95

Findlater

Medium-bodied red, classic

Subtle fruit on the nose; quite closed and tannic on the palate. A keeper which should prove rewarding in a year or so.

Rare roast beef or lamb

Ch. Tanesse AC 1ères Côtes de Bordeaux 96

United Beverages

Medium-bodied red, classic

Developed and quite vegetal on the nose. Lots of blackcurrant fruit balanced by firm tannin in the background. Good length of flavour and interest which should evolve further.

Loin of lamb with herb and shallot sauce

Dom. de Sours AC Bordeaux 97

Woodford Bourne

Medium-bodied red, classic

Complex fruit with hints of vanilla and smoke. Firm tannin and bramble fruit flavours with hints of spice in the finish.

Lamb cutlets with shallot sauce

Michel Lynch AC Bordeaux 96

Barry & Fitzwilliam

Medium-bodied red, classic

Spicy fruit aromas with hints of vanilla. Soft ripe fruit flavours, blackberries and vanilla pod. Well-balanced and smooth with attractive fruit at the finish.

Stuffed shoulder of lamb

Red £10 - £12

Ch. Larrivaux Cru Bourgeois AC Haut-Médoc 95

Wine Warehouse ☆

Full-bodied red, classic

Subtle aromas of autumn berries, quite mature with hints of cedar and spice. Perfect harmony between mellow tannins and mature fruit. A wine at its peak—enjoy!

Rare roast beef with its own jus

B & G Roi Chevalier AC St Émilion 97

Dillon C

Full-bodied red, classic

Unusual violet and toffee aromas, very inviting. Good weight of fruit--strawberries and plums. Soft and velvety structure with good length and delicious fruit in the finish.

Roast turkey

Frank Phélan AC St Estèphe 96

Barry & Fitzwilliam   C

Full-bodied red, classic

Deep cassis and spice aromas. Mouthfilling soft fruit flavours, berries with a touch of damsons, and oaky backdrop. Long fruit and spice finish.

Fillet of venison with blackberries for a special dinner party

Ch. Bonnet Réserve AC Bordeaux 97

Febvre

Full-bodied red, classic

Quite deep and complex on the nose. Ripe fruit flavours—blackcurrant, brambles, plums—balanced structure and longlasting finish.

Lamb noisettes in pastry

Ch. de Camensac AC Bordeaux 98

Dalton

Medium-bodied red, classic

Light blackcurrant aromas and a floral background. Much riper, more intense palate with slightly jammy, juicy fruit.

Mixed grill

Ch. de Sours AC Bordeaux 95

Woodford Bourne

Full-bodied red, classic

Ripe complex aromas of bramble fruit with vanilla and toffee. Well-structured tannins and excellent weight of mouthfilling bramble fruit. Balanced, well-made wine with flavours that linger on and on.

Pigeon with wine and bacon sauce with green cabbage leaves

Ch. La Fleur St Georges AC Lalande de Pomerol 96

Wines Direct

Full-bodied red

Blackcurrant and fruitcake on the nose. Good mouthfeel with firm but balanced tannin, savoury fruit and long finish with definite bite.

Pork with prunes or lamb chops

Ch. le Chêne AC Haut-Médoc 96

MacCormaic

Full-bodied red, classic

Cedarwood nose, slightly spicy, old-style Bordeaux. Firm structure and intense blackberry and blackcurrant fruit with a good long spicy finish.

Roast lamb with flageolet beans

Ch. Tour du Pas St Georges AC St Georges St Émilion 96

Wines Direct

Full-bodied red

Quite rich and ripe, though not especially distinctive on the nose. Needs a bit of time: tannins show at present but should be nice.

Confit of duck usually softens tannins in this style of wine

Tesco AC Margaux 96

Tesco

Medium-bodied red, classic

Nice complexity on the nose with coffee and mocha aromas and hints of vanilla against a background of ripe berries. Lovely rich mocha flavours with herbal touches and ripe autumn fruit. Well-balanced structure and finish.

Braised guinea-fowl

Red £12 - £15

Ch. Patache d'Aux Cru Bourgeois AC Médoc 95

Grants ☆

Full-bodied red, classic

Oaky, spicy bramble fruit aromas. Ripe, mouthfilling fruit with spice and hints of caramel. Tightly-knit with firm tannins and a great lasting finish of spice and fruit.

Braised pheasant

Ch. Rocheyron AC St Émilion Grand Cru 96

Remy ☆

Full-bodied red, classic

Plum and damson fruit with cedar tones. Firm tannins off-set by a big weight of ripe fruit. Good wine, potentially excellent but with time to go.

Duck casserole with herbs

Ch. Coufran Cru Bourgeois AC Haut-Médoc 95

Gilbeys C

Full-bodied red, classic

Soft berry fruit aromas with vegetal hints. Ripe fruit with warm, spicy vanilla flavours. Firm and appetising with a bite of tannin in the finish.

Navarin of lamb

Don't forget to explore Sandy O'Byrne's *Editor's Choices*—see the mini-index on page 6

Ch. de la Tour AC Bordeaux Supérieur 96

Woodford Bourne C

Full-bodied red, classic

Brambly, herbaceous fruit. Rich velvety wine with intense fruit flavour. Quite classic and well-made beyond expectations of the AC.

Beef in pastry

Ch. Fourcas Hosten Cru Bourgeois AC Listrac-Médoc 95

Remy/O'Briens C

Full-bodied red, classic

Earthy blackberry, damson and cassis with spicy tones. Firm and well-structured young wine with a good weight of fruit which should evolve very well.

Roast pork with garlic

Ch. Loudenne Cru Bourgeois AC Médoc 95

Gilbeys C

Medium-bodied red, classic

Spicy cassis aromas with vegetal hints. Soft, peppery fruits with backdrop of oak. Firmly structured and well-balanced with a lovely spicy, oaked fruit finish.

Loin of late spring lamb

Ch. Magnol Cru Bourgeois AC Haut-Médoc 96

Dillon C

Full-bodied red, classic

Rather vegetal aromas. Good weight of fruit mixed with caraway and pepper flavours. Firm and tightly-knit with a long, lingering finish of fruit and spice. Still young.

Pheasant with game sauce

Ch. Moncets AC Lalande de Pomerol 95

Searson   C

Full-bodied red, classic

Stalky blackcurrant with hints of mint and eucalyptus. Tightly-knit structure integrated with plentiful fruit with some mature development. Lovely length and balance. Very stylish.
Mallard with mushrooms

Ch. Vieux Gueyrot AC St Émilion Grand Cru 96

Wine Warehouse   C

Full-bodied red, classic

Developed aromas of mature blackberry and damson fruit. Firm tannins are softening into the fruit. Needs a bit more time to achieve full complexity.
Duck with Calvados

B & G Tradition AC St Julien 95

Dillon

Full-bodied red, classic

Fruit and spicy oak on the nose. Dry and firm with nicely balanced oak and fruit, and good length of stalky fruit and spice.
Casserole of pheasant or guinea-fowl

Ch. de la Cour AC St Émilion 95

Mitchell

Full-bodied red, classic

Subtle aromas of blackberries, cedar and smoke. Full-bodied with richer fruit than the 96, already showing some development but with plenty of time to go.
Chicken with truffles

Ch. de la Cour AC St Émilion 96

Mitchell

Full-bodied red, classic

Bramble, plum and black cherry aromas. Good weight of autumn berry fruit and firm tannins; nice oaky frame. A lovely wine which should evolve with age.
Sunday roast beef with all the trimmings, if drinking now

Ch. Faizeau AC Montagne St Emilion 96

Wines Direct

Full-bodied red

Intense brambly fruit on the nose. Nice balance of fruit and tannin. Ripe fruit flavours with a touch of green pepper and a dry finish.
Chicken with a rich mushroom or similar sauce

Ch. Magnol Cru Bourgeois AC Haut-Médoc 95

Dillon

Full-bodied red, classic

Cassis, plum and pepper aromas. Well-balanced with a firm structure and excellent weight of ripe fruit, nicely blended with oak and spice flavours. Long finish. Still a touch hard but will develop well.
Casserole or even confit of duck would soften the remaining edges of youth

Ch. Maison Blanche AC St Émilion 96

Wines Direct

Full-bodied red

Summer berries with a touch of medicinal herbaceous aromas. Fruit-driven and quite light but

with a nice finish.
Veal sweetbreads with a cream sauce

Ch. Tour du Haut Moulin Cru Bourgeois AC Haut-Médoc 96

Wines Direct

Full-bodied red

Grassy herbal nose with a whiff of tar. Red berries and liquorice on the palate. Full and velvety with nicely oaky backdrop and a long finish.
Navarin of lamb or cold pheasant

Dom. du Milan AC Pessac-Léognan 95

Dalton

Full-bodied red, classic

Aromas of baked plum and cherry. Very ripe fruit on the palate initially with big structure coming in. Firm tannin but ripe and well-cloaked with fruit and flavour. Classic long finish.
Steak and kidney pie

Red £15 - £20

Ch. d'Armailhac AC Pauillac Grand Cru 96

Oddbins ☆

Medium-bodied red, classic

Intense aromas of ripe bramble fruit on the nose. Lovely integration of blackcurrant fruit, vanilla and spicy oak. Beginning to develop rich plummy tones and layers of complexity.
Saddle of lamb

Ch. de la Cour AC St Émilion Grand Cru 95

Mitchell ☆

Full-bodied red, classic

Mature blackberry, mint and cassis aromas. Great intensity of fruit and soft mellow tannins. Refined and elegant and more forward than the 96.
Chateaubriand

Ch. de la Cour AC St Émilion Grand Cru 96

Mitchell ☆

Full-bodied red, classic

Seductive aromas of mature dark fruits, plums and black cherries. Tannins yield beautifully into the mature fruit to give a classic complex palate. A young wine with a lot of potential.
Pot-au-feu

Frank Phélan AC St Estèphe 96

Gilbeys C ££

Full-bodied red, classic

Ripe blackcurrant aromas with typically earthy character. Elegant, refined palate with concentrated, chocolatey fruit and well-structured tannins. Drinking well now but will improve. Good value.
Shoulder of lamb

Ch. de Lamarque Cru Bourgeois AC Haut-Médoc 95

Woodford Bourne C

Medium-bodied red, classic

Aromatic bramble fruit aromas. Well-balanced with ripe juicy blackcurrant fruit and cigar-like spice. Forward and agreeable now but will hold and develop well.
Rack of lamb or roast pheasant

Ch. Meyney Cru Bourgeois AC St Estèphe 95

United Beverages C

Medium-bodied red, classic

Blackcurrant, chocolate, cedar

and spice all emerge from the nose. Rich and intense flavours with softening tannins. Very finely balanced with already considerable complexity which should gain more with time.
Fillet of beef in pastry

Ch. Rollan de By Cru Bourgeois AC Médoc 95

Wines Direct   C

Full-bodied red, classic

Abundant cassis aromas with a touch of new oak. A weight of ripe, up-front fruit, but concentrated enough to last and with balanced structure. New-wave Bordeaux but very attractive.
Guinea-fowl cooked with mushrooms or leeks

Ch. Arnauld AC Haut-Médoc 95

Febvre

Medium-bodied red, classic

Autumnal fruit on the nose with pronounced earthiness. Youthful palate but with plenty of promise; ripe fruit with nice spicy tones, very firm tannin. Slightly rustic but should mellow and develop subtlety.
Medallions of venison

Ch. Clarke AC Listrac-Médoc 96

Mitchell

Full-bodied red, classic

Subtle nose with soft bramble fruit, cedarwood and spice. Mellow tannins blend harmoniously with the fruit. Lovely forward development and a long lingering finish.
Lamb cutlets

Ch. Lanessan AC Haut-Médoc 95

Grants

Full-bodied red, classic

Rather closed on the nose, youthful. Firm tannins with spicy fruit underneath. Plenty of potential but needs two to three years.
Rare roast beef

Ch. Teyssier AC St Émilion Grand Cru 96

Grants

Full-bodied red, classic

Damson and plum aromas with a touch of spice. Broad, ripe palate with damson and plums again. Spicy, with a long flavoursome finish.
Fillet of beef with a shallot sauce

Red £20 - £25

Ch. La Tourette AC Pauillac 95

Wines Direct   ☆ ☆

Full-bodied red, classic

Fragrant summer berries and ripe blackcurrant aromas. Mouthfilling flavours of ripe, intense fruit and spicy oak with a firm structure. Young but well-integrated and delicious, a keeper with a great future.
Casserole of pheasant with wine

Ch. Gloria AC St Julien 95

Grants   ☆

Full-bodied red, classic

Beguiling aromas of fruit and chocolate slowly unfolding. Highly complex wine with layers of flavour and superbly balanced. Mouthfilling and delicious. Lovely now, potentially great.
Loin of lamb roasted with herbs

Ch. Yon-Figeac AC St Émilion Grand Cru 95

Febvre ☆

Medium-bodied red, classic

Rich raspberry and strawberry aromas with layers of similar fruit flavours. Beginning to develop complex spice and richness with a nice balance and long, lingering finish.

Quail with mushrooms

Ch. Berliquet AC St Émilion Grand Cru 96

Wines Direct C

Full-bodied red, classic

Pronounced, rich nose with plum and black cherry aromas. Round and supple in spite of its youth with an abundance of fruit in a creamy texture. Full-bodied with firm tannin and a long finish.

Roast pheasant, hot or cold

Ch. Camensac AC Haut-Médoc Grand Cru 95

Grants C

Full-bodied red, classic

Blackcurrant, plum, cedar and tobacco aromas. Great depth of fruit with balanced structure of tannins and acidity and full-bodied weight. Classic claret to drink now or keep.

Magret of duck with a wine and cassis sauce

Ch. La Tour de Mons Cru Bourgeois AC Margaux 95

Gilbeys

Full-bodied red, classic

Super-ripe blackcurrant fruit on the nose. A big, quite chunky wine with firm tannin and rich fruit character. Approachable but will improve significantly.

Rib of beef with wine sauce

Ch. Labégorce AC Margaux 96 *Grants*

Full-bodied red, classic

Almost perfumed nose of vanilla and plum. Firm with very spicy, chocolatey fruit. Complex but young: needs time to show its true character.
Roast goose or duck

Red £25 - £30

Ch. Phélan Segur AC St Estèphe 96

Grants ☆ ☆

Full-bodied red, classic

Intense aromas of blackcurrant and violets with a rustic touch. Very concentrated, slightly earthy fruit with a sturdy structure. Ripe, mouthfilling flavours that seem endless. One for the hedonist!
Medallions of venison

Ch. Roc des Cambes AC Côtes de Bourg 96

Wines Direct ☆

Full-bodied red, classic

Deep complex aromas of fruit and spice. Concentrated with a big firm structure and mouthfilling flavours of fruit, oak and spice. A bold, flavoursome wine with a long finish for the AC, stunningly impressive.
Fine, carefully cooked, game casserole

Ch. Grand-Puy Ducasse AC Pauillac Grand Cru 95

Grants

Full-bodied red, classic

Perfumed and spicy on the nose. A good weight of ripe fruit with chocolate and gamey flavours underneath. Youthful but well-integrated, not to drink now but will repay keeping.
For now, rare beef or venison steaks

Red £30 - £35

Ch. La Rose Figeac AC Pomerol 95

Wines Direct ☆ ☆ ☆

Full-bodied red, classic

Complex nose with concentrated chocolatey fruit scented with vanilla and freshly-cut meadow flowers. Rich and layered palate with concentrated fruit and spice. Still young but with impressive balance and finesse.
Roast pheasant with truffles or morel mushrooms

Ch. Bourgneuf AC Pomerol 95 *Febvre*

Medium-bodied red, classic

Aromatic summer pudding aromas. Excellent weight of ripe blackcurrant fruit with flavours of chocolate and spice. Young and delicious, worth storing for at least ten years!
Very good Camembert

Les Fiefs de Lagrange AC St Julien 95
Grants

Full-bodied red, classic

Elegant, refined aromas of plums and chocolate. Good intensity of fruit with spice and chocolate overtones but lacks some complexity at this level.
Pheasant pie

Red £35 - £40

Ch. Branaire Duluc-Ducru AC St Julien Grand Cru 95
Grants ☆ ☆

Full-bodied red, classic

Complex, gamey nose. Excellent balance of suavely cloaked tannin and ripe fruit. Wonderfully integrated and appealing at such a young age--the flavours linger for ever.
Magret of duck with a rich sauce.

Red £40 and over

Ch. Tertre Rôteboeuf AC St Émilion Grand Cru 96
Wines Direct ☆ ☆

Full-bodied red, classic

Dark autumnal fruit aromas with spicy, smoky oak underneath. Great concentration of ripe fruit with well-integrated oak offsetting firm tannins to give a silky effect. Very young and with great potential—unfortunately it may be drunk too soon.
Roast or casseroled pheasant

Ch. Montrose AC St Estèphe 2ème Cru Classé 95
Grants ☆

Full-bodied red, classic

A big, bold wine with great concentration of fruit but also subtle and elegant. Ripe complex fruit is balanced by firm tannins. Harmonious but very young with a long promising finish.
Roast fillet of beef

Rosé £6 - £8

Ch. Thieuley AC Bordeaux-Clairet 98
Wines Direct

Rosé

Berry fruit and boiled sweet aromas. Good weight of subtle fruit and balanced acidity. Dry finish.
Charcuterie and terrines, picnic fare

Rosé £10 - £12

Ch. de Sours AC Bordeaux 98
Woodford Bourne C

Rosé

Very lively nose with red gooseberry and raspberry leaf aromas jumping from the glass. Zippily fresh with bursts of raspberry fruit dancing over the palate. Pleasantly stalky long finish. Definitely OTT but lovely!
Thai fish soup

Burgundy

Much that is written about Burgundy tells a story of high prices and inconsistency, of big vintage variation and unreliable grapes. There is also a very positive side and in many ways, the nineties were Burgundy's decade.

Burgundy is a small region that has for generations produced some of the world's finest red and white wines. With such a reputation, demand will always exceed supply and prices will always be subject to market pressure. However, in Chablis and the Côte de Beaune, for white Burgundy, prices have stabilised and become more realistic and quality, especially in Chablis, is a lot more consistent. If in any doubt of Chablis' greatness as a wine, try one from someone like William Fèvre or Louis Michel from the fabulous 1996 vintage. The Côte de Beaune itself has had some excellent vintages in the nineties and quality is high. These wines are Chardonnay at its best : powerful yet restrained, elegant and complex, slow to emerge but endlessly rewarding. The quality of Village wines from the big negociants such as Latour, Jadot and Lupé Cholet really impressed in this year's tastings.

However, the real excitement in white Burgundy is not in the classic areas so much as further south in the Côte Chalonnaise and Mâcon. These were the regions really challenged by New World Chardonnays and the response has been impressive. More new oak, better vinification, riper fruit, selected yeasts, in fact a successful blend of the best of new and traditional winemaking has had stunning results. Just try the Mâcon Clessé from the small property of René Michel. With eyes closed it tastes a lot further north.

It must be said that red Burgundy is still something of a tease, largely due to the Pinot Noir grape. Admittedly, the prices fetched by the classed growths of Bordeaux these days are beginning to make top Burgundy look like good value, but moderate prices are sstill hard to find. A small number of producer/negoçiants manage a good compromise between price and quality and the simpler level of Burgundy. Pierre Ponnelle and Pierre André are worth considering.

White £6 - £8

Tesco's White Burgundy AC Bourgogne 98

Tesco ££

Medium-bodied white

Pear and apple aromas with a hint of honey. Dry and fresh with nice clean fruit—ripe melon and pear—and clearly defined structure. Good value.
Pasta with spinach, chicken and cream

Pierre Ponnelle AC Mâcon-Villages 97

Dunnes Stores

Full-bodied white

Clean, fresh melon fruit aromas. Quite round with balanced acidity and tart green fruit. Reasonable length and good value.
Gratin of fish or chicken

Louis Latour VdP des Coteaux de l'Ardèche 97

Gilbeys

Medium-bodied white

Peach and mineral aromas make an inviting nose; dry with balanced acidity and a nice depth of fruit flavour. Good at the price.
Creamy pasta with ham and cheese

Louis Latour Chardonnay AC Bourgogne 97

Gilbeys

Full-bodied white

Ripe apple aromas. Fresh palate of similar green and red apple fruit with balanced acidity and alcohol. Well-integrated flavours. A decent wine at a good value price.
Chicken galantine

White £8 - £10

Dom. René Michel AC Mâcon-Clessé 97

Searson ☆

Full-bodied white, classic

Quite developed nose with honeyed tones, soft vanilla and tropical fruit. Excellent weight of ripe fruit with fresh acidity and a long finish.
Roast farm chicken with courgettes and rosemary

Edouard de la Brevière AC Chablis 97

Gleeson ££

Medium-bodied white

Green apple fruit with mineral and chalk influences. Bone-dry with initial attack of grapefruit acidity which evolves into stony, mineral-like fruit. Well-balanced typical Chablis, excellent value.
Oysters

Joseph Drouhin AC St Véran 97

Gilbeys C

Full-bodied white

Slightly earthy nose. Smooth oily palate with smoky pear fruit and a long mineral and woodsmoke finish. Good value with classic style.
Blanquette of veal

Louis Jadot Couvent des Jacobins AC Bourgogne 97

Grants C

Full-bodied white

Lovely mix of citrus fruit, honey and vanilla on the nose. Good weight of buttery fruit and vanilla with balanced acidity and creamy texture. Nice length in the finish.
Light fish or cheese soufflé

Lupé Cholet AC Mâcon-Lugny 97
Dillon

Medium-bodied white

Hints of pears and almond on the nose. A touch green with understated apple and melon fruit and crisp acidity. Good, long finish.
Seafood lasagne

Dom. Grand Roche AC Chablis 97
Wines Direct

Medium-bodied white

Elegant nose with pronounced aromas of ripe fruit and a hint of vanilla. Good weight of warm buttery fruit with nicely balanced acidity and a long finish.
Chicken pancakes with cheese sauce

Pierre Ponnelle AC Chablis 97
Dunnes Stores

Medium-bodied white

Clean and crisp with lemon and melon flavours. Quite round for a Chablis, with some length.
Deep-fried fish

Cuvée Claude Dominique AC Chablis 97
Tesco

Medium-bodied white

Steely, subtle nose, hints of green apple and citrus. Fresh acidity and firm structure with good balance and nice length of finish.
Mussel soup

Prosper Maufoux Dom. les Combelières AC Mâcon-Clessé 97
Woodford Bourne

Medium-bodied white

Melon and hints of citrus on the nose. Delivers more on the palate with a good mouthful of ripe fruit, balancing acidity and mineral tastes in the finish.
Fricassé of veal or chicken

Roger & Christine Saumaize Dom. Saumaize-Michelin AC St Véran 97
Wines Direct

Light dry white

Floral, slightly tropical aromas. Mellow, fruit cocktail flavours with balancing acidity and a clean crisp finish. Easy to drink.
Omelette or creamy fish soup

Louis Latour Les Genièvres AC Mâcon-Lugny 97
Gilbeys

Medium-bodied white

Citrus fruit aromas with mineral overtones. Green fruit flavours with lively acidty and some length in the finish.
Creamy fish gratin or fricassé

Bouchard Père & Fils Mâcon Lugny St Pierre AC Mâcon-Lugny 97
Findlater

Medium-bodied white

Nice green apple aromas. Ripe melon and peach flavours in a nicely balanced wine with pleasant length.
Fish with Mornay sauce

White £10 -£12

Dom. Léger-Plumet AC St Véran 96

Fields   C

Full-bodied white

Ripe limes and butterscotch with an earthy twist on the nose. Spicy, minerally flavour with background of peach fruit and refreshing acidity. Well-balanced and mature style.
Asparagus quiche

Louis Latour La Grande Roche AC Montagny 1er Cru 97

Gilbeys   C

Full-bodied white

Ripe, slightly tropical aromas, with a touch of butter. Full and broad with ripe fruit flavours and a long finish.
Roast poussin with a herb stuffing

Dom. Henri Naudin-Ferrand AC Bourgogne Haute-Côte de Nuits 97

Wines Direct

Medium-bodied white

Sweet-jar, lemon and honey aromas. Ripe melon fruit with a hint of spice. Well-balanced acidity and nice length of finish.
Brill with butter sauce

Reine Pédauque Coupées AC Mâcon-Villages 96

Barry & Fitzwilliam

Medium-bodied white

Ripe apple aromas with citrus tones beneath. Mellow palate--flavours of spice and brioche with a citrus twist in quite a mouthfilling style. Crisp acidity and nice length.
Traditional chicken pie

White £12 - £15

Dom. Saumaize-Michelin Clos sur la Roche AC Pouilly-Fuissé 97

Wines Direct   ☆

Full-bodied white

Buttery, tropical fruit aromas. Great weight of warm buttery fruit, honey and vanilla beautifully balanced to give an elegant wine with a lingering finish.
Scallops in a cream sauce

Pierre André Les Reforts AC Montagny 1er Cru 93

TDL   C

Full-bodied white, classic

Ripe honeyed fruit and subtle vanilla aromas. Dry and full with excellent weight of ripe tropical fruit. Long and elegant.
Breast of chicken in pastry

Joseph Drouhin AC Chablis 97

Gilbeys

Light dry white

Chalky, slightly green aromas. Initially very dry but broader fruit emerges creating quite a soft Chablis. Good weight and length of finish.
Brill or sole, simply cooked, with butter sauce

Laroche AC Chablis 98

Allied Drinks

Light dry white

Unusual aromas of tropical fruit and boiled sweets! Very youthful with pleasant fruity palate and some length in the finish.
Chicken escalopes with a light sauce

Jaffelin AC Chablis 98
Cassidy

Medium-bodied white

Tropical fruit, honey and vanilla on the nose. Firm fruit structure with fresh acidity and a long rounded finish.
Trout with almonds

Bouchard Ainé & Fils AC Chablis 98
Cassidy

Light dry white

Honeyed, tropical fruit aromas with a steely side. Youthful, fresh and vibrant with a good weight of ripe fruit and fresh acidity. Well-balanced wine.
Kedgeree

Ropiteau AC Chablis 98
TDL

Medium-bodied white

Subtle melon fruit aromas with steely tones. Firmly structured with nice ripe fruit, smooth and balanced.
Deep-fried plaice

Lupé Cholet Ch. de Viviers AC Chablis 97
Dillon

Light dry white

Mineral and chalk aromas. Dry with bracing acidity and citrus/green fruit flavours. Well-balanced, typical Chablis.
Simply cooked mussels

William Fèvre Champs Royaux AC Chablis 97
Febvre

Medium-bodied white

Lovely nose; firm and crisp palate with hints of lemon zest, quince and mineral. Long finish.
Mussel stew

Guy Mothe & Fils Dom. du Colombier AC Chablis 97
Fields

Medium-bodied white

Concentrated green fruit with underlying mineral tones. Plenty of rather young, minerally fruit and clean, zippy acidity. Young, refreshing wine which should evolve further.
Kedgeree

Jean Thévenet & Fils Dom. Emilian Gillet AC Mâcon-Viré 96
Wines Direct

Full-bodied white

Lemon and lime aromas. Good concentration of fruit, citrus fruit and spice, with balanced acidity and a crisp long finish.
John Dory with a rich sauce

Alain Geoffroy Dom. Le Verger AC Chablis 98
Febvre

Medium-bodied white

Crisp fresh fruit on the nose; tart, citrusy palate with mineral tones in the background. Firm and lean to finish.
Oysters

Dom. de la Paulière Fourchaume AC Chablis 1er Cru 97
Ecock

Full-bodied white

Good nose; rather tart in the mouth with moderate intensity and length.
Mixed fish and shellfish casserole

Faiveley Les Joncs AC Montagny 97

Remy

Full-bodied white

Quite woody, oaky nose. Orchard fruits in a woody, walnut shell, needs time to integrate. Good intensity but very young. Should show well in two to three years.
Deep dish chicken pie

Dom. Bart Les Tavières AC Marsannay 97

Wines Direct

Full-bodied white

Vanilla and citrus fruit aromas. Plenty of fruit with butter and vanilla flavours. Crisp acidity and long flavoursome finish with a citrus twist.
Chicken sauté

White £15 -£20

Joseph Drouhin AC Chablis 1er Cru 97

Gilbeys ☆

Full-bodied white, classic

Tightly-knit, rather unyielding nose—yields more on the palate. Dry with intensity and structure; green apple fruit with buttery hints. Traditional-style Chablis. Long and elegant and will get even better.
Mixed shellfish or brill with a prawn sauce

Jaffelin Côte de Léchet AC Chablis 1er Cru 97

Cassidy ☆

Full-bodied white, classic

Very elegant nose, pears and honey with subtle oak. Broad and fleshy with ripe fruit and classic style.
Salmon with hollandaise sauce

Bouchard Père & Fils Fourchaume AC Chablis 1er Cru 96

Findlater ☆

Full-bodied white

Ripe tart fruit aromas with touches of wet wool on the nose. Full and firm with tightly-knit flavours of fruit and oak. Plenty of character and complexity at a good price.
Dover sole

Joseph Drouhin AC Pouilly-Fuissé 97

Gilbeys C

Full-bodied white

Elegant aromas of ripe melon and buttery oak. Beautifully integrated flavours of subtle toasted oak and creamy, buttery fruit. Big and full with a long rich finish.
Chicken with truffle oil noodles

Ropiteau Chablis-Montmains AC Chablis 1er Cru 97

TDL C

Full-bodied white, classic

Mature tropical fruit and honey aromas. Clean and flinty with well-balanced fruit structure and a long smooth finish.
Oysters

Dom. La Marche Les Rochelles AC Mercurey 95

United Beverages

Full-bodied white

Heady aromas of honey, lemon and peach fruit. Mature flavours of rather earthy fruit with citrus acidity in the finish.
Creamy pasta

Louis Max Les Vaillons AC Chablis 1er Cru 96

United Beverages

Full-bodied white

Floral, lemon curd aromas with underlying spice. Lots of ripe melon and peach fruit well-sustained and balanced by acidity. Long finish. A big wine, needs time.

Grilled Dover sole

Dom. Long-Depaquit Les Vaillons AC Chablis 1er Cru 97

Fitzgerald

Full-bodied white, classic

Mature honeyed fruit and vanilla aromas. Full-bodied with a weight of ripe melon and dessert apple fruit, fresh acidity and a smooth finish.

Brill with prawn sauce

White £20 - £25

Louis Latour AC Meursault 97

Gilbeys   C

Full-bodied white, classic

Lovely aromas of buttery hazelnuts, toast and lemon. Creamy and full with flavours of green apple and mellow spice with balancing acidity. Full and long, a good Meursault.

Turbot and hollandaise—the perfect match

Louis Jadot AC Meursault 95

Grants   C

Full-bodied white

Complex, elegant aromas of citrus fruit, honey and vanilla. Full and mellow with buttery melon fruit. Smooth and creamy in the mouth with well-integrated oak and a refreshing touch of citrus in a long finish.

Simply-cooked lobster

Ch. de Meursault AC Meursault 94

Gleeson   C

Full-bodied white

Intense aromas of lightly roasted nuts and ripe fruit. Lovely balance of ripe fruit, spicy oak and clean acidity. Classic and well-made.

Coquilles St Jacques

Dom. Jacques Thevenot-Machal AC Meursault 96

Wines Direct

Full-bodied white

Rich and quite mature on the nose, with a caramel and toffee edge to the fruit. A big wine with plenty of ripe fruit and buttery oak, well-judged acidity and a refreshing finish.

Chicken with Madeira sauce

Prosper Maufoux Mont de Milieu AC Chablis 1er Cru 97

Woodford Bourne

Full-bodied white

Nice fruit on the nose. Tightly-knit, well-structured with good balance of acidity and fruit and a long finish.

Warm oysters

White £25 - £30

Louis Jadot AC Chassagne-Montrachet 96

Grants   C

Full-bodied white

Honey-rich aromas with lemon and vanilla. Ripe fruit flavours of mango, melon and lemon mix with oak and spice in a

buttery warm texture. Delightfully complicated in true Burgundian fashion!
Truffle risotto

Lupé Cholet AC Puligny-Montrachet 96

Dillon   C

Full-bodied white, classic

Assertive, complex nose. Melon and lychee fruit flavours with underlying spice and butter. Long, flavoursome finish.
Roast chicken with morels

Louis Max Les Champs Gains AC Puligny-Montrachet 1er Cru 90

United Beverages   C

Full-bodied white

Intriguing aromas of melon, peach and hazelnuts. Flavours spread across the palate with lovely mix of fruit and mineral tones. Well-balanced and long with classic style.
Roast farm chicken

Dom. Jacques Thevenot-Machal AC Mersault-Charmes 1er cru 96

Wines Direct

Full-bodied white

Mature aromas of toffee and caramel. Good complexity of flavour slowly evolves through the wine. Buttery fruit, spice and honey all mix and mingle right through to the finish.
Chicken with mushroom sauce

White £30 -£35

Faiveley Les Champs Gains AC Puligny-Montrachet 1er Cru 97

Remy   C

Full-bodied white

Oak dominates the nose with vanilla and clove. Very minerally fruit spiced with ginger and subtly woven honey and lemon flavours. Lovely now but it is a pity to drink it so young.
Roast monkfish

Red £8 - £10

F. Chauvenet AC Côte de Beaune-Villages 94

United Beverages

Medium-bodied red, classic

Ripe red fruit--plums and strawberries--with earthy tones. Firm tannin well-knit with concentrated fruit, strawberries and red fruit again. Good weight of flavour right to the end.
Chicken in red wine

Pierre Ponnelle AC Côte de Nuits-Villages 96

Dunnes Stores

Medium-bodied red, classic

Summer berries on the nose with a nice earthy Pinot touch. Lively juicy quality and a clean finish. A well-made, well-priced wine.
Typically with chicken Dijonnaise

Louis Jadot Couvent des Jacobins AC Bourgogne 96

Grants

Medium-bodied red, classic

Ripe cherry fruit aromas with medium weight of ripe berry

fruit to follow and some length in the finish.
Typically a gougère

Red £10 -£12

Jaffelin AC Haute-Côte de Beaune 97
Cassidy
Medium-bodied red
Ripe berry fruit on the nose with a touch of tar. Plenty of similar fruit on the palate with softening tannin and balanced acidity.
Pheasant and mushroom pie

Lupé Cholet AC Côte de Beaune-Villages 95
Dillon
Medium-bodied red, classic
Mature, attractive nose with brambly fruit. Dry with good balance of tannin and acidity and vegetal fruit character. Very ripe flavours though a bit short in the finish.
Gougère or cheese tart

Louis Jadot AC Côte de Beaune-Villages 94
Grants
Medium-bodied red, classic
Complex vegetal aromas, like a country lane! Relatively light but with good balance of tannin, alcohol and slightly green fruit with some length in the finish.
Veal chop with a mushroom sauce

Pierre Ducret Les Grands Pretans AC Givry 1er Cru 96
Wines Direct
Medium-bodied red, classic
Typical Pinot nose of vegetal fruit aromas with hints of rubber in the background. Nice

balance of earthy fruit, tannin and alcohol.
Cold pheasant pie

Antonin Rodet Pinot Noir Vieilles Vignes AC Bourgogne 96
Febvre
Medium-bodied red
Typical vegetal aromas; rather tart berry fruit flavours and dry, spicy finish.
Richly sauced mushroom pasta

Red £12 - £15

Dom. Chandon de Briailles Comte et Comtesse A. C. de Nicolay AC Savigny-lès-Beaune 97
Wines Direct   C
Medium-bodied red, classic
Elegant nose with rich cherry fruit in the background. Full and intense in the mouth with good weight of fruit and lingering finish. Lovely wine at the price.
Spatchcocked quail or a rich chicken casserole

Joseph Drouhin AC Maranges 1er Cru 96
Gilbeys
Medium-bodied red, classic
Brambly, farmyard aromas. Very sweet, intense berry fruit and nice length in the finish.
Mushroom pasta or beef stew

Red £15 -£20

Dom. Chandon de Briailles Comte et Comtesse A. C. de Nicolay Ile des Vergelesses AC Pernand-Vergelesses 1er Cru 97
Wines Direct   ☆
Medium-bodied red, classic

Elegant, complex aromas. Big, intense wine with an abundance of bramble fruit and a bold structure. Very long, classic finish.
Beef en croûte with a wine sauce

Louis Max Dom. La Marche Les Vasées AC Mercurey 1er Cru 96

United Beverages ☆

Medium-bodied red, classic

Complex aromas of ripe strawberry fruit with smoke and vegetal tones. Mellow tannins harmonise with developed, fragrant fruit and spice. Plenty of concentration and length of flavour.
Magret of duck with mushrooms

Louis Jadot AC Vosne-Romanée 95

Grants C

Medium-bodied red, classic

A punchy nose with a mélange of aromas: cough syrup, brambles, cedarwood and smoke. Complex, concentrated palate with rich fruit and spice and firm structure. Flavours develop all the time and last well.
Wild duck with Port sauce

Pierre André Clos des Guettes AC Savigny-lès-Beaune 1er Cru 96

TDL C

Medium-bodied red

Smoky red fruits on the nose. Really ripe fruit tightly woven with acidity and tannin and supporting alcohol. Lovely warm finish.
Duck with bitter cherry sauce

Dom. de Montmain Les Genevrières AC Bourgogne Haute-Côte de Nuits 88

Wines Direct C

Medium-bodied red, classic

Typical 'Nuits' nose, vegetal and smoky. Lovely complexity of rich fruit, spice and earth flavours with balanced acidity and tannin and a long, long finish.
Winey beef or game casserole

Bouchard Père & Fils AC Beaune 1er Cru 95

Findlater

Medium-bodied red

Slightly dumb on the nose but with a weight of ripe summer fruit flavour, berries and bitter cherries. Lean but classic and with a good finish.
Quail with a rich sauce

Dom. Bart AC Fixin 95

Wines Direct

Medium-bodied red, classic

Jammy nose with earthy tones. Quite jammy fruit with a bitter twist and green tannins showing through. Light structure with medium length in the finish.
Beef medallions with Parma ham

Louis Latour Dom. Latour AC Aloxe-Corton 96

Gilbeys

Medium-bodied red, classic

Mature vegetal nose with farmyard tones. Vanilla-scented strawberry fruit with refreshing acidity and mellow tannins. Well-rounded wine, nicely forward.
Sweetbreads with mushrooms and cream

Red £20 - £25

Dufouleur Père & Fils Clos du Chapitre AC Fixin 1er Cru 96
Bacchus ☆

Medium-bodied red, classic

Lovely compote of fruit aromas with scents of cigar and wood. Tightly-knit rich dark fruit—everything Burgundy should be.
Wild duck or other such game

Louis Jadot Clos des Couchereaux AC Beaune 1er Cru 96
Grants C

Medium-bodied red, classic

Rich fruit aromas with notes of tar and rubber. A big, highly-concentrated wine with rewarding summer fruit flavours.
Duck with a rich wine sauce

Dom. David Duband Les Procès AC Nuits-St-Georges 1er Cru 96
Wines Direct C

Medium-bodied red, classic

Curious burnt rubber and caramel on the nose. Lovely velvety mouthfeel with ripe cherry fruit and a harmonious blend of spice and earth flavours. Big structure and firm tannin with a long lingering finish.
Medallions of venison with a rich sauce

Joseph Drouhin AC Gevrey-Chambertin 97
Gilbeys

Medium-bodied red, classic

Complex nose with ripe fruit, smoke and vegetal elements. Soft and mellow with intense sweet berry flavours and underlying earthiness.
Wild duck cooked with wine

Louis Max La Justice AC Gevrey-Chambertin 96
United Beverages

Medium-bodied red, classic

Lovely ripe strawberry fruit with smoky earthy tones. Dry and firm with plenty of fruit to support the tannins. Needs time to evolve, potentially a classic.
Casserole of beef and wine

Red £25 - £30

Ropiteau AC Meursault 93
TDL C

Medium-bodied red

Complex earthy fruit aromas. Very well-balanced with lovely spicy, complex fruit and a balanced structure. Flavours develop well on the palate and last endlessly. Seductive stuff.
Fillet of beef with morel mushrooms

Lupé Cholet Ch. Gris AC Nuits-St-Georges 1er Cru 95
Dillon C

Medium-bodied red, classic

Quite mature on the nose, rich and earthy. Bold structure with layers of ripe fruit and mellow hints of cloves and cinnamon. Long, flavoursome finish. Should improve further.
Roast or casseroled pheasant or a mature fillet of beef

Dufouleur Père & Fils Les St George AC Nuits-St-Georges 1er Cru 94
Bacchus
Medium-bodied red, classic

Plenty of fruit showing on the nose and an interesting mature palate. A nice wine to drink this year.
Fillet of beef

Mommessin La Forge AC Morey St Denis 1er Cru 95
Woodford Bourne   C
Medium-bodied red, classic

Farmyard aromas with a touch of cigarbox spice. Finely-wrought elegant wine, very smooth with lovely spicy tobacco and complex flavours gradually emerging and expanding through to the finish.
Roast teal with ceps

Editor's choice: dinner party reds

Wines for formal entertaining do not have to be classics. Here are some ideas to complement good food—why not try the suggested dish in the entry?

Vasse Felix Cabernet/Merlot 1997

Wolf Blass President's Selection Shiraz 1996

Ch. Cadillac Lesgourgues 1996 AC Bordeaux Supérieur

Ch. de Sours 1995 AC Bordeaux

Ch. de Gourgazeaud Réserve 1997 AC Minervois

Réserve des Voconces Cairanne 1995 AC Côtes du Rhône-Villages

Faustino 1 DOC Rioja Gran Reserva 1992

Undurraga Cabernet Sauvignon Reserva 1996

Castello di Volpaia DOCG Chianti 1997

Plaisir de Merle Cabernet Sauvignon 1996

Loire

I always return from the Loire inspired by the quality and variety of its wines, and the innovation and dedication of its producers. Yet this is rarely reflected at home; too often Loire wine means Muscadet, Sancerre and Pouilly Fumé, which may be very good wines (though not inevitably so) but are not at all the whole story.

The Loire is a very long river with parcels of vineyard areas all along its banks from the shores of the Atlantic to the heart of France. There is obvious variation in style, but also in quality, and local knowledge is still the key to finding the best. The wines, both white and red, are also at their best with food. The acidity is too high and the fruit too elegant and lean to be enjoyable without food. Local dishes provide the best possible foil.

Although the Sauvignon Blanc is the best known grape, the Chenin Blanc is more widely planted. It is a highly impressive grape variety capable of producing high quality wines in a number of different styles, from bone-dry to sweet, both impressively long-lived, and from sparkling to commercial off-dry. Savennières is the classic source of dry Chenin. It is a majestic wine which needs ageing to bring out its real quality. However, Anjou and Saumur Blanc, wines from the broader appellation are increasingly better made and good value.

Vouvray has a bad name based on poor quality commercial, off-dry, off-sweet varieties which in the past were greatly over-sulphured. Dry, mousseux or moelleux, real Vouvray is a different and very fine wine. From a good maker, it will last for years and improve.

Loire reds are also gaining ground and are subtle, light and savoury. Chinon, Bourgueil and St Nicholas de Bourgueil and Saumur-Champigny are the major appellations. The more concentrated wines from good vintages, especially those of Chinon, have an ability to age over five or even ten years to delightful complexity

White £5 or less

Grand Fiacre Grande Réserve AC Muscadet de Sèvre et Maine sur lie 97
Dunnes Stores

Light dry white

Firm dry wine with crisp acidity and a touch of yeast. Good concentration of citrus and green apple fruit. To drink now.

Mussels in garlic butter

Tesco AC Vouvray nv
Tesco

Light fruity white

Floral, sorbet-like nose. Off-dry style, ripe grapey fruit with zippy fresh acidity and a good length of finish. Very good value.

Cheese and pear salad

Tesco AC Muscadet de Sèvre et Maine sur lie 98
Tesco

Light dry white

Light green apple aromas. Crisp and refreshing with crunchy green apple fruit and light yeast undertones. Fresh and simple.

Mussels vinaigrette

White £5 - £6

Goulaine Sauvignon VdP Jardin de France 97
Gilbeys

Aromatic white

Lemon peel and apple blossom aromas. Very fresh attack with high acidity and simple lemony fruit. Drink young and fresh and cold.

Fish and chips

White £6 - £8

Excellence AC Touraine 97
River Wines   C

Aromatic white

Very minerally fruit aromas with lemon backdrop. Lovely palate-hugging flavours of yellow plums, green apples and lemons. Very well-balanced and concentrated with a long finish.

Herb omelette

Ch. de Rochefort AC Muscadet de Sèvre et Maine sur lie 98
Fields

Light dry white

Subtle nose of citrus fruit, flint and yeast. Crisp and very fresh with nice apple and melon fruit and a citrus twist in the finish.

Shellfish mousse

Ch. La Noë AC Muscadet de Sèvre et Maine sur lie 98
O'Briens/Remy

Light dry white

Stony, mineral aromas with green fruit. Bone-dry with slightly lactic apple fruit character and spritz in the finish.

Moules marinières

Clos de Nouys AC Vouvray 98
United Beverages

Light fruity white

Pears and boiled sweet aromas. Off-dry with lots of honeyed pear fruit and a crisp, clean finish.

On its own or with mildly spicy food

Pineau de Sauvignon la Loire AC Touraine 98

River Wines

Aromatic white

Grassy, sappy green fruit aromas. Fresh and very crisp with crunchy green orchard fruit finishing with a grapefruit tang.

Asparagus quiche

Tesco AC Sancerre 98

Tesco

Aromatic white, classic

Blackcurrant leaves and greengage aromas. Fresh and juicy with lots of under-ripe green fruit. A wine to be drunk young and fresh.

Sashimi and other Japanese fish

White £8 - £10

Goulaine AC Vouvray 98

Gilbeys

Aromatic white

Chalk and earth aromas, restrained and understated nose. Very rich palate with ripe fruit and balanced acidity. Red apple flavours persist right through the long finish.

Cheese tart

La Croix au Garde AC Sancerre 98

Oddbins

Aromatic white, classic

Citrus and gooseberry fruit aromas with grassy tones. Plenty of green apple fruit with balanced acidity. Well-made wine.

Goat's cheese salad

Le Master de Donatien AC Muscadet de Sèvre et Maine sur lie 96

Woodford Bourne

Light fruity white

Citrus aromas with apple and pear. Very crisp and fresh and quite broad with apple fruit flavour and some length.

Simply-cooked mussels

Marquise de Goulaine Cuvée du Millénaire AC Muscadet de Sèvre et Maine sur lie 98

Gilbeys

Light dry white

Chalk and mineral fruit aromas, with a touch of yeast in the background. Bone-dry with good breadth of tongue-tingling mineral flavours. Clean, fresh finish with green apple acidity.

Warm fish mousse with beurre blanc

White £10 - £12

Fournier AC Sancerre 96

Wine Warehouse   C

Aromatic white, classic

Concentrated green fruit aromas. Good intensity of green, grassy fruit and mineral flavours. Long finish. Typical Sancerre.

Sashimi or smoked salmon

Ch. de Chasseloir AC Muscadet de Sèvre et Maine sur lie 97

Febvre   Light dry white

Citrus fruit, biscuit and a hint of yeast on the nose. Crisp acidity balanced by ripe fruit; clean and fresh finish.

Seafood

Chatelain AC Pouilly-Fumé 98
Findlater

Aromatic white, classic

Apple aromas with hints of gooseberry. Fresh acidity with citrus and melon fruit; firm and well-structured with a long finish.
Fish and herb terrine

Dom. du Petit Soumard AC Pouilly-Fumé 97
Fitzgerald

Aromatic white

Very typical flinty, smoky aromas. Green apple and citrus fruit in a mineral shell with fresh but balanced acidity and nice length.
Trout cooked in butter

Dom. Masson-Blondelet Villa Paulus AC Pouilly-Fumé 98
Wines Direct

Aromatic white, classic

Very fresh elderflower aromas with mineral background. Crisp with lean, green—very young—fruit but promising length of flavour. Wait six months.
Grilled crottin or other firm goat's cheese

Dom. Michel Brock Le Coteau AC Sancerre 98
Fitzgerald

Aromatic white

Earthy mineral aromas. Lively lemon and nettle flavours in good concentration with balanced acidity. Intensity of flavour lasts right through the finish.
Avocado mousse

Jean Max Roger Cuvée C. M. AC Sancerre 98
Findlater

Aromatic white, classic

Tropical fruit and mineral aromas. Flinty gooseberry fruit flavours with crisp acidity and a refreshing finish.
Zesty pasta with shellfish, herbs etc.

Le Chailloux AC Sancerre 98
Gleeson

Aromatic white, classic

Interesting mix of citrus, honey and smoke aromas. Very fresh crisp acidity nicely offset by ripe fruit with long flavoursome finish.
Smoked fish and walnut salad

Les Pierres Plates AC Pouilly-Fumé 97
Gleeson

Aromatic white, classic

Developed aromas of ripe peaches. Good weight of ripe fruit with a citrus twist and refreshing acidity.
Cheese soufflé

White £12 - £15

Fournier Vieilles Vignes AC Sancerre 96
TDL ☆ ☆

Aromatic white, classic

Very pronounced aromas of slightly honeyed, oily fruit. Green fruit and lemons on the palate--really intense explosive flavours with a firm mineral backdrop. Beautifully balanced harmonious wine which should hold. Good value.
River fish with a rich herb sauce

Fournier AC Pouilly-Fumé 98

TDL ☆

Aromatic white, classic

Flinty mineral bouquet with a touch of grapefruit. Very intense with concentrated green fruit, mineral and grassy tones. Crisp and well-knit with a long finish.
Salmon trout in pastry with herb butter sauce

Pascal Jolivet AC Sancerre 98

Remy ☆

Aromatic white

Heady aromas of floral gooseberry fruit, minerals, nettle and chalk. Delicious and mouthfilling with tangerine fruit, mineral and citrus tones. Very intense but balanced and refined. Long and satisfying finish.
Goat's cheese soufflé

Pascal Jolivet AC Pouilly-Fumé 97

Remy C

Aromatic white

Restrained citrus aromas with a touch of flint. Quite full and rounded with fruit slowly evolving on the palate. Elegant mineral tones and a long lemony finish.
Smoked salmon

Comte Lafond AC Sancerre 97

Gilbeys

Aromatic white, classic

Slightly tropical, super-ripe fruit aromas. Lots of fruit on the palate, Granny Smith apples and greengages in good concentration with lively acidity.
Trout and herb sauce

Dom. Champeau AC Pouilly-Fumé 98

Fields

Aromatic white, classic

Complex aromas of ripe melon, herbs and apple fruit. Fresh with subtle hints of vanilla and smoke with the fruit. Clean citrus twist in the finish. Elegant, well-made wine.
Poached salmon

Dom. Vacheron AC Sancerre 98

Febvre

Aromatic white, classic

Flinty aromas with citrus hints. Nicely balanced, elegant wine with good concentration of gooseberry and citrus flavours.
Monkfish and bacon kebabs

Fournier AC Sancerre 97

TDL

Aromatic white, classic

Concentrated lime and green apple aromas. Lean greengage and unripe mango fruit with a mineral side. Complex and fresh with excellent weight of flavour.
Baked feta cheese

La Chatellenie AC Sancerre 98

Allied Drinks

Aromatic white, classic

Really opulent gooseberry jam aromas with leaner blackcurrant leaf and chalk in the background. Similar green fruit and mineral hints come through on the palate with well-balanced acidity and a long finish.
Nothing beats the regional combination of Sancerre and goat's cheese

Pascal Jolivet Les Caillottes AC Sancerre 97 *Remy*

Aromatic white

Concentrated aromas of earthy apple fruit. Orchard flavours with ripe citrus notes. A well-balanced wine with character and style.
Poached trout with dill cream

White £15 - £20

Pascal Jolivet Les Griottes AC Pouilly-Fumé 96
Remy C

Aromatic white

Intensely aromatic. Oily and well-integrated palate with mineral and gooseberry fruit and just a touch of asparagus. Good concentration of mineral, gravel flavours and a very long finish. Will develop further.
Raw salmon salad

Ch. de Tracy AC Pouilly-Fumé 98 *Febvre*

Aromatic white, classic

Gooseberry and nettle on the nose followed by gooseberry and green apple flavours, well-integrated and developed. Nice balancing acidity and long finish.
Brill or turbot with a herb sauce

De Ladoucette AC Pouilly-Fumé 97 *Gilbeys*

Aromatic white, classic

Light aromas of citrus fruit and nettles. Good concentration of gooseberry flavour. Quite full with balancing acidity and length.
Smoked salmon

Red £5 - £6

Manoir de la Tête Rouge Bagatelle AC Saumur 98
Dunnes Stores

Light fruity red

Berries with a touch of violet on the nose. Ripe fruit flavours with a light, balanced structure. Dry and appetising with nice length in the finish.
Cheese and herb tart

Red £6 - £8

Dom. du Ruault AC Saumur-Champigny 96
Dunnes Stores

Light fruity red

Intense leafy herbaceous nose with stalky blackcurrant fruit. Lovely weight of blackcurrant fruit with balanced fresh acidity and firm tannin. Lovely, balanced wine.
Spring lamb with herb sauce

Red £8 - £10

Dom. Filliatreau AC Saumur-Champigny 97
Searson C

Light fruity red

Lots of stalky herbaceous fruit aromas. Firm but well-integrated tannins with excellent ripe fruit and a long impressive finish.
Rack of spring lamb with garlic crust

Ch. de Fesles Vieilles Vignes AC Anjou 97
Febvre

Light fruity red

Earthy herbaceous nose; rather stalky berry fruit, mellow and appealing with well-balanced structure. Nice fruit sustained

through the finish.
Baked salmon trout or other river fish.

Red £10 - £12

Fournier AC Menetou-Salon 96

Wine Warehouse   C

Light fruity red

Steel and mineral from the nose, very Pinot Noir. Light in body but with lots of flavour of bitter cherry fruit with an earthy tone. Balanced and long with plenty of character.
Brandade of salt fish

Red £15 - £20

Ch. de Varrains AC Saumur-Champigny 96

Woodford Bourne   ☆

Light fruity red

Lovely aromas of blackcurrant and wild flowers, complex, inviting. Delicious mouthfilling

flavours of fruit and spice in a velvet texture. Perfect balance between light tannins and refreshing acidity. Good long finish.
Rack of very young spring lamb

Ch. de Fontaine-Audon AC Sancerre 97

Woodford Bourne

Light fruity red

Quite vegetal, mineral aromas. Light on the palate, without the intensity of the nose but still elegant.
Baked salmon

Rosé £5 or less

Tesco AC Rosé d'Anjou nv

Tesco

Rosé, off-dry

Boiled sweets and strawberries on the nose are echoed on the palate. Slightly sweet finish.
Good choice in a Chinese restaurant

Rhône

The Rhône Valley divides into two very distinctive wine regions, entirely different in geography and viticulture. Although the north claims more prestige the south is better known, mainly through Châteauneuf-du-pape, its big name, and through the generic Côtes du Rhône.

As prices have risen so much in the other classic regions of France, the Northern Rhône is a good investment. Although the best wines are expensive, notably the cult single vineyard Côte Rôties of Guigal and the Hermitage of Jaboulet, longevity is more or less assured and mature vintages are always in demand. For the cellar, Côte Rôtie and Hermitage are the most obvious choices. Côte Rôtie is made from Syrah and a tiny portion of Viognier to create a powerful though elegant wine from the 'roasted slopes'. Hermitage, once shamefully used as a blending wine to beef up thinner years in Bordeaux, is now recognised as one of the great wines of the world. It is made entirely from the Syrah grape and is majestic in style. The best examples are from Jaboulet and rather better value, from Chavet.

Cornas is the big secret of the North, a fabulous, long lasting wine that develops extraordinary complexity through its long lifespan. Currently less fashionable but a good option for the future, the wines of St Joseph and Crozes Hermitage are less structured and long lived, at least by Northern Rhône standards, but are generally undervalued and excellent with robust, flavoursome food. Chapoutier and Graillot produce superb examples.

In the south, Châteauneuf-du-pape is going through a period of change. Many producers have lightened the style of the traditional wine to achieve more elegance, more forward fruit appeal. A few, such as Château de Beaucastel, remain resolutely traditional and the wines age well.

The Villages of the Côtes are also changing and quality has risen. Gigondas, Vacqueyras and Cairanne in particular are now producing some serious, intriguing and quite complex wines with plenty of terroir and individual character.

Rhône (North)

Louis Latour Grand Ardèche Chardonnay VdP Coteaux de l'Ardèche 96
Gilbeys

Full-bodied white

Buttered toast aromas followed by quite butter, toasty flavours on the palate nicely tempered by crisp acidity. Lingering finish.
Chicken with tagliatelle

White £10 - £12

M. Chapoutier Les Meysonniers AC Crozes-Hermitage 97
Grants

Full-bodied white

Floral exciting nose with lavender and herb aromas. Round and full with ripe fruit flavours and just enough acidity.
Typical southern fish stew

Red £6 - £8

Cave de Tain l'Hermitage AC Crozes-Hermitage 97
Tesco   C

Full-bodied red

Aromas of fruit, tar and chocolate. Full and satisfying on the palate with a touch of peppery spice and smooth balanced tannin.
Beef casserole

Cave de Tain l'Hermitage Les Nobles Rives AC Crozes-Hermitage 96
Dunnes Stores

Full-bodied red

Stewed blackberry fruit with spice and cassis, quite developed aromas. Warm autumn berry fruit with yielding tannins. Well-balanced wine with nice length of flavour.
Raised pie

Red £8 - £10

Cave de Tain l'Hermitage Les Nobles Rives AC St Joseph 96
Dunnes Stores   ☆

Full-bodied red

Aromas of damson and mint with a touch of pepper. A big wine with lovely mature complex fruit, spicy and full-flavoured. Great value.
Beef Stroganoff

Louis Max AC Crozes-Hermitage 93
United Beverages   C

Full-bodied red

Quite vegetal aromas with bramble fruit. Smooth palate with a mature mix of fruit and spice, mellow tannin and a very long finish.
Pot-roasted pheasant

Dom. des Remizières Cuveé Particulière AC Crozes-Hermitage 96
Wines Direct

Full-bodied red

Spicy autumn fruits, slightly baked. Quite firm tannins but well-sustained by fruit: spicy blackberries and damsons.

Warm spicy finish.
Steak and mushrooms

Red £10 - £12

Delas Frères Les Launes AC Crozes-Hermitage 97
Febvre   C

Full-bodied red

Big concentration of berry fruit with spice and liquorice. Full weighty wine with firm tannins offset by dark baked fruit. Big and chunky but very well-balanced.
Beef or game casserole with a wine sauce

Cave de Tain l'Hermitage Les Nobles Rives AC Cornas 95
Dunnes Stores

Full-bodied red

Rather muted nose, baked blackberry aromas. Firm and earthy with softening tannin and blackberry and plum fruit. Mature and well-rounded.
Wild duck with damsons

Gabriel Meffre Laurus AC Crozes-Hermitage 96
Dillon

Full-bodied red

Forest floor aromas and ripe soft fruit flavours with good weight and softening tannins.
Chunky home-made hamburgers

M. Chapoutier Les Meysonniers AC Crozes-Hermitage 96
Grants

Full-bodied red

Spicy fruit and coffee bean aromas. Firm tannins with summer berry fruit behind and crisp acidity. Full with notice-able alcohol and a ripe, rasp-berry fruit finish.
Hearty pot roast

Paul Jaboulet Ainé Le Grand Pompée AC St Joseph 96
Gilbeys

Full-bodied red

Attractive summer pudding aromas. Good weight of ripe fruit similar to the nose; well-balanced with a warm spicy finish.
Steak and kidney pie

Red £12 - £15

Alain Graillot AC Crozes-Hermitage 97
Syrah Wines   ☆

Full-bodied red

Mature complex nose with ripe sweet fruit, cedar and mint aromas. Huge fruit concentra-tion, blackberry, damson, and earthy tones with firm tannic structure. Manages power and elegance at the same time.
Pheasant casserole

Cave de Tain l'Hermitage Les Nobles Rives AC Hermitage 92
Dunnes Stores   C

Full-bodied red

Mature combination of black cherries, cedar and spice on the nose. Mellow tannins tightly-knit with mature flavours of baked autumn fruit. Lingering and attractive flavours: a refined elegant wine.
Rib of beef

Gabriel Liogier Le Ribier AC St Joseph 95
TDL

Medium-bodied red

Ripe dark fruits and plenty of

spice on the nose. Lots of berry fruit flavours and spice backed by firm tannin and a long finish.
Toulouse sausages

Red £20 - £25

Delas Seigneur de Maugiron AC Côte Rôtie 94
Febvre ☆

Full-bodied red

Mature complex nose with rich autumn berry fruit, blackberries, cassis and cedar. Mellow tannins in perfect harmony with the fruit. Lovely combination of fruit flavours and vegetal earthy tones which go on and on. Really excellent.
Wild duck or pheasant

M. Chapoutier La Sizeranne AC Hermitage 96
Grants C

Full-bodied red

Obvious farmyard aromas with nice touches of violet and roses. Full and earth-flavoured with balanced supporting tannin and acidity. Big but elegant with a good finish.
Steak or saddle of venison

Red £25 - £30

Guigal AC Côte Rôtie 95
Syrah Wines ☆

Full-bodied red

Elegant, refined nose with violet tones. A big, beefy Côte Rôtie with generous flavours, rounded, earthy fruit and spice and a long, robust finish.
Good beef fillet, cooked rare

Red £40 - £50

Paul Jaboulet Aîné La Chapelle AC Hermitage 97
Gilbeys C

Full-bodied red, to keep

Dark fruit and violets on the nose. Tight compact structure of a very young wine with a long way to go. Perfect structure and depth of fruit suggest real quality as yet immature.
If drinking now, a game casserole would be a good match

Rhône (South)

White £6 - £8

Dom. la Réméjeanne Les Arboisiers AC Côtes du Rhône 98
River Wines

Full-bodied white

Lemon and citrus aromas with riper fruit beneath. Well-structured with lots of youthful fruit and good balancing acidity. Full and well-made.
Marinated raw salmon

Gabriel Liogier Dom. de la Taladette AC Côtes du Rhône 98
TDL

Full-bodied white

Floral, slightly candied aromas. Fresh with tangy citrus flavours. Round and full with quite a fat texture but clean and fresh in the finish.
Grilled salmon

La Vieille Ferme AC Côtes du Luberon 97

Allied Drinks

Medium-bodied dry white

Apple and citrus fruit aromas with a touch of lavender. Medium weight with apple and pear fruit similar to the nose. Nicely balanced, pleasant wine.
Simply-cooked salmon

White £8 - £10

Guigal AC Côtes du Rhône 97

Syrah Wines

Full-bodied white

Ripe, slightly floral fruit aromas. Good weight of fruit with balanced acidity. Peach and melon flavours with light, elusive spice. Full and creamy with a clean finish.
Suitably delicate choice for sushi or raw salmon salad

White £10 -£12

Ch. du Trignon AC Côtes du Rhône 97

River Wines   C

Full-bodied white

Very floral with tropical fruit aromas. Rich and weighty with ripe peach fruit, nicely balanced acidity and alcohol and a warm finish.
Mullet with rosemary

Red £5 - £6

Anne Delaroche AC Côtes du Rhône 98

Gleeson

Medium-bodied red

Strawberry fruit aromas. Slightly jammy raspberry fruit off-set by a touch of tannin.

Easy, supple style.
Ratatouille casserole

Barton & Guestier AC Côtes du Rhône 97

Dillon

Light fruity red

Slightly vegetal fruit aromas. Plenty of red berry fruit flavour with light tannins. Well-balanced, easy fruity style.
Good party wine for buffet food: cold meats, chunky terrines and the like

Les Peyrières Rasteau AC Côtes du Rhône-Villages 97

Dunnes Stores

Medium-bodied red

Strong earthy aromas with dried fruit and a touch of rubber. Good berry fruit with an earthy, stalky background to provide interest. Good taste for the price.
Moussaka or meat-filled vegetables

Tesco AC Côtes du Rhône-Villages 98

Tesco

Light fruity red

Ripe raspberries on the nose. Fresh, fruity summer wine with clean, fruity finish.
Nut loaf or shepherds' pie

Red £6 - £8

Dom. des Anges AC Côtes du Ventoux 94

Bacchus   C

Full-bodied red

Rich, roasted and smoky on the nose, jammy spicy fruit. Full-bodied with gripping tannins but softening into bramble fruit flavours. Now at its best.
Goulash

Ch. de Ruth AC Côtes du Rhône 97

Dillon

Medium-bodied red

Earthy fruit nose, cherries and leather. Flavours of fruit and spice with balanced acidity and some length.

Lasagne or moussaka

Dom. des Ameleraies AC Vacqueyras 96

Dunnes Stores

Medium-bodied red

Subtle aromas of cherry fruit and forest floor earthiness. Good intense fruit with a touch of green pepper and firm tannin. Nice weight and length.

Steaks of beef or lamb

Dom. Didier Charavin AC Côtes du Rhône 98

Wines Direct

Medium-bodied red

Ripe brambly fruit on the nose. Easy-drinking with plenty of fruit. Well-balanced style.

Kebabs

La Chasse du Pape AC Côtes du Rhône 97

Dillon

Medium-bodied red

Slightly jammy bramble and cherry fruit on the nose. Good weight of similar fruit on the palate and a long dry finish.

Hearty daube de boeuf

Paul Jaboulet Ainé Parallèle '45' AC Côtes du Rhône 97

Gilbeys

Medium-bodied red

Aromas of ripe chocolatey fruit with earthy backdrop. Smooth, well-rounded wine with nice

supporting tannins for the spicy fruit. A sound finish.

Beef and red pepper casserole

Red £8 - £10

Dom. Brusset Cairanne AC Côtes du Rhône-Villages 97

Woodford Bourne ☆

Medium-bodied red

Dense aromas of bramble fruit and tar. Fruit follows through on the palate with layers of dark autumn berry flavour, supple tannin and fine length.

Pigeon with confit of garlic

Réserve des Voconces Cairanne AC Côtes du Rhône-Villages 95

Molloy's C ££

Medium-bodied red

Wonderful rich aromas of dark autumn fruit. Beautifully balanced with soft tannins, firm acidity and superb length. Great bargain too!

Moussaka

Dom. de Grangeneuve AC Coteaux du Tricastin 97

Fields C

Medium-bodied red

Ripe fruit aromas, full of promise. Very fruit-driven with plum, damson and fig flavours, nicely balanced by tarry spicy tones. Delicious chocolate finish.

Moussaka

Dom. Grand Romane AC Gigondas 95

United Beverages C

Full-bodied red

Attractive meatiness on the nose. Rich, ripe and robust with mouthfilling aromas of baked plums, spice and pepper.

Delicious to drink now but worth keeping.
Venison steaks

Dom. Martin Rasteau AC Côtes du Rhône-Villages 95
River Wines   C
Medium-bodied red

Dominant pepper spice on the nose. Some finesse on the palate and very attractive fruit. Well-balanced and restrained style.
Pigeon

Perrin Reserve AC Côtes du Rhône 96
Allied Drinks   C
Medium-bodied red

Concentrated fruit aromas with touches of chocolate and herbs. Plenty of punchy fruit and spice flavours, bold and forward though balanced by tannin. Smooth, lingering finish.
Marinated lamb steaks

Guigal AC Côtes du Rhône 96
Syrah Wines
Medium-bodied red

Very aromatic fruit and spice on the nose. Plummy fruit with plenty of spice. Quite firm tannin, good weight and length.
Grilled meat or a hearty casserole

J. Vidal-Fleury AC Côtes du Rhône 95
Fitzgerald
Medium-bodied red

Elegant aromas with good concentration of fruit. Quite polished and smooth on the palate with fruit rather than spice to the fore.
Moussaka

La Beulière Rasteau AC Côtes du Rhône 97
Dalton
Medium-bodied red

Nice ripe fruit on the nose. Well-balanced with soft, chewy fruit flavours and easy-drinking style.
Lasagne or other meaty pasta

Red £10 -£12

J. Vidal-Fleury AC Vacqueyras 97
Fitzgerald   ☆
Medium-bodied red

Ripe fruit with some complexity on the nose. Lovely palate of black and red fruits with excellent balance and roundness. Very well-made with charm and character.
Beef in red wine

Dom. des Anges Clos de la Tour AC Côtes du Ventoux 97
Bacchus
Medium-bodied red

Ripe jammy fruit with a touch of mint. Plenty of ripe meaty fruit flavours—damsons and mince pies! Round and smooth with a touch of tannin.
Grilled rabbit with herbs or mustard

Dom. Roger Perrin AC Châteauneuf-du-pape 96
Dunnes Stores
Full-bodied red

Ripe fruit with tobacco and spice tones. A big wine with liquoricey, spicy fruit and firm tannin. Good weight of dark, flavoursome fruit; full-bodied with a long, spicy finish.
Game pie or casserole

Red £12 - £15

Dom. Jérome Quiot AC Châteauneuf-du-pape 97

Searson ☆

Full-bodied red

Lighter style of Châteauneuf, fruit first rather than power. Slightly floral, elegant touches. Lovely, refined fruit, accessible and subtle. A modern side of the AC.

Roast goose

Le Grand Montmirail AC Gigondas 97

Woodford Bourne ☆

Full-bodied red

Rich and complex aromas with ripe autumn fruit and hints of tar. Smooth palate with a touch of gripping tannin nicely balanced by the depth of fruit flavour. Will improve further.

Roast goose

Ch. des Fines Roches AC Châteauneuf-du-pape 94

O'Briens C

Full-bodied red

Ripe fruit with tobacco and spice scents. Well-developed mature palate with good fruit quality. Complex and mellow with the richness of age.

Roast pheasant

Innocent VI AC Châteauneuf-du-pape 97

Gleeson

Full-bodied red

Intense ripe bramble aromas with similar weight of fruit on the palate backed up by tarry spice and pepper. Big and mouthfilling with a long finish.

Roast goose

J. Vidal-Fleury AC Gigondas 93 *Fitzgerald*

Full-bodied red

Attractive mature nose with just a touch of volatility. Mature fruit just beginning to dry on the mid-palate but with lovely mellow character.

Lamb casserole

Red £15 - £20

Clos des Papes AC Châteauneuf-du-pape 97

Syrah Wines C

Full-bodied red

Very complex intriguing nose of baked fruit, spice and warm earth. Big structure yet with finesse and elegance. Great weight of rich fruit and spice— fruitcake flavours. Well-balanced with a long complex finish.

Christmas goose

Dom. de Montpertuis AC Châteauneuf-du-pape 95

United Beverages C

Full-bodied red

Ripe concentrated blackcurrant and figs on the nose. Dark inky palate with blackcurrant flavours and warm alcohol. Nice touch of spice in the finish.

Game with lentils

Dom. Duclaux AC Châteauneuf-du-pape 96

Febvre C

Full-bodied red

Punchy aromas of toffee and figs. Complex earthy palate, smoky, spicy fruit; intense and mouthfilling with a long, hot finish.

Pheasant and lentils

Gabriel Meffre Laurus AC Châteauneuf-du-pape 96

Dillon   C

Full-bodied red

Dark fruit aromas with cedar overtones, complex and impressive. Very well-balanced wine with concentrated fruit and underlying earthy flavours and mellow tannins. Good long finish, too.

Venison casserole

Guigal AC Gigondas 96

Syrah Wines   C

Full-bodied red

Toffee, leather and tar all feature on the nose. A big wine with lovely balance of cherry fruit, acidity and firm tannins. Smoky nuances add to the interest. Expensive but offers a lot.

Ideal with pigeon and most game

M. Chapoutier La Bernardine AC Châteauneuf-du-pape 96

Grants   C

Full-bodied red

Baked fruit with earthy, tobacco leaf aromas. Mouthfilling intensity of flavours. Warm and spicy with balanced, well-cloaked tannins and a long finish.

Venison stew

Paul Jaboulet Ainé Les Cèdres AC Châteauneuf-du-pape 97

Gilbeys

Full-bodied red

Rich concentration of mature cherry fruit and spices. Dry and warm with lots of spicy fruit and a long warm finish.

Venison stew with apples and blackcurrants

Red £20 - £25

J. Vidal-Fleury AC Châteauneuf-du-pape 94

Fitzgerald   C

Full-bodied red

Quite a big wine with aromas of tarry fruit and spice. Seductive rich fruit attack backed by a balanced structure. Will last well for a few years, but charming now.

Venison medallions with wine sauce

The South of France

The South of France, especially the Midi, is certainly the most exciting wine region in France for sheer innovation and soaring quality. This has been true now over many vintages, with each year bringing something new.

The Southern revolution started with well-made vin de pays varietals, New World lookalikes with a touch of Old World charm. More traditional regions such as Corbières and Fitou, originally VDQS status, then with appellations of their own, provided more substantial wines, supple and fruity yet with the added interest of a blend of grapes, local varieties and even oak-ageing.

White wines also began to impress, in part due to improved, often New World, technology, but more through the discovery of cooler vineyard locations and higher altitudes for slower ripening.

The regional appellations of the Languedoc, especially Corbières, Fitou and Minervois, have reached new heights of sophistication and complexity. Many will age delightfully over a few years and offer wonderful value for money. Some of the improved quality comes from older vines, better vinification and ageing methods, but also from the identification of individual sub-regions such as Lagrasse in Corbières.

Not all the excitement is in the Midi either. The South-West wine region, south of Bordeaux and north of the Spanish border, has made great strides in recent years. The whites are especially impressive from appellations such as Jurançon, Montravel and even Côtes de Gascogne, while the deep, brooding reds of Cahors and Madiran are still truly regional wines, totally traditional, individual and fascinating. One can only hope that popularity will not change this.

The whole South of France provides great quality, consistency and exciting variety in wines which combine modern polish with traditional character.

Languedoc-Roussillon

Fox Mountain Cuvée Lisette Sauvignon/ Chardonnay VdT nv
Wines Direct

Aromatic white

Ripe mango and honey on the nose. Fat, smooth-textured wine, very fruit-driven with balancing acidity and good length in the finish.
Warm mixed salad of cheese or poultry

Moulin de Gassac Terrasses de Méranée Sauvignon VdP d'Oc 98
O'Briens

Light fruity white

Peardrops and apples on the nose. Clean and fresh with citrus fruit, crisp acidity and a zippy fresh finish.
Canapés and finger food

Tesco Viognier VdP d'Oc 97
Tesco

Aromatic white

Very fruity on the nose— mashed bananas. Similar fruit on the palate with lemon and lime twists. Crisp and dry with good length of finish.
Cream of carrot and orange soup

Michel Picard Chardonnay VdP d'Oc 97
TDL ☆

Full-bodied white

Very intense and complex on the nose with oily, nutty aromas and ripe minerally fruit. Very good weight and mouthfeel with bread and citrus flavours and a long finish. Quite a classic.
Chicken with cream sauce

La Bergerie de L'Hortus VdP de Montferrand 98
Wines Direct C

Aromatic white

Intriguing aromatic nose with tropical fruit and floral tones. Full and rounded with honeyed fruit and spice and underlying nuttiness. Long, rather warm, finish.
Fish cooked with fennel

DLC Chevalière Chardonnay VdP d'Oc 97
Allied Drinks

Full-bodied white

Lovely inviting nose, ripe and full. Real fruit salad flavour with nicely balanced acidity and an attractive creamy finish.
Baked chicken or hake or brill with a light ginger sauce

Dom. de Valensac Chardonnay VdP d'Oc 98
Searson

Light fruity white

Ripe peach aromas. Good intensity of fruit on the palate with ripe peach and pear flavours. Nicely balanced with a fruity, clean finish.
Baked cod

Dom. des Lauriers Picpoul de Pinot AC Coteaux du Languedoc 98
Searson

Light dry white

Clean fresh aromas of stewed apple and citrus fruit. Good

weight of flavour, similar to the nose, with apple and citrus freshness and a clean finish.
Courgette soufflé

Dom. Piquemal Muscat Sec VdP Côtes Catalanes 98
Wines Direct
Aromatic white

Lovely aromatic, grapey nose with hints of white pepper. Grapey palate with overtones of spicy marmalade and bracing acidity. Nice weight and balance with a warm spicy finish.
Asparagus

Moulin de Gassac Eraus VdP de l'Hérault 98
O'Briens
Light fruity white

Fresh, restrained nose, slightly nutty. Ripe apple fruit with nicely balanced acidity and decent length of finish.
Salads

White £8 - £10

Roque Pertuise Chardonnay VdP d'Oc 96
Bubble Brothers   C
Full-bodied white

Lovely nose—ripe apples with a touch of artichoke. A big, fat wine with rounded, oily fruit and balancing acidity. Ripe flavours and a long finish. Could age well, too.
Smoked fish soup or casserole

DLC Chevalière Reserve Chardonnay VdP d'Oc 97
Allied Drinks
Full-bodied white

Ripe orchard fruits on the nose with a touch of creamy vanilla. Fresh and lively palate, not

quite as ripe as the nose but with a good finish.
Baked trout

Red £5 or less

Tesco Cabernet Sauvignon Reserve VdP d'Oc nv
Tesco   ££
Medium-bodied red

Ripe juicy blackberries with savoury tones. Delicious flavours of blackberry, mixed spice and orange peel. Well-balanced and long—great value.
Navarin of lamb

Tesco Merlot VdP d'Oc nv
Tesco   ££
Medium-bodied red

Brambly nose, earthy with a touch of pepper. Chewy berry fruit with balancing tannin, well-supported by alcohol. Good value.
Beef in beer

Ch. de Montrabech AC Corbières 96
Dunnes Stores
Medium-bodied red

Lots of jammy berry fruit on the nose; supple fruity palate with a nice touch of pepper. Good weight of flavoursome spicy fruit and nice balanced finish.
Spicy sausages

Ch. Grande Cassagne AC Costières de Nîmes 96
Dunnes Stores
Medium-bodied red

Liquorice fruit aromas. Simple, sound, easy-drinking wine with plenty of fruit and very well-priced. Good party stuff!
Hamburgers, meatloaf and the like

Dom. de Vignelaure Cabernet Sauvignon/Merlot VdP du Var 97

Dunnes Stores

Medium-bodied red

Fruity, slightly medicinal nose. Alcohol shows a bit on the palate with some under-ripe fruit but the wine is satisfactory at the price.

Liver and bacon or cold meats

Les Étoiles Organic VdP de l'Hérault nv

Tesco

Medium-bodied red

Slightly earthy ripe blackberry aromas. Same earthy hints on the palate with nice brambly, plummy fruit and a touch of tannin.

Meaty pasta

Red £5 - £6

Baron de la Tour AC Fitou 97

Tesco   C ££

Medium-bodied red

Rustic, complex nose with brambles, vanilla and spice. Rich, fleshy autumnal fruit with rounded tannins. Very long and a touch spicy to finish. Great!

Cassoulet

Louis Eschenauer Shiraz VdP d'Oc 98

MacCormaic   C ££

Medium-bodied red

Damson, plum and pepper aromas. Ripe spicy fruit with a nice grip of tannin. Well-structured with plenty of supporting fruit. A wine which will evolve further and is great value.

Steak and chips

Moulin de Gassac Terrasses de Méranée Merlot VdP de l'Hérault 98

O'Briens   C ££

Medium-bodied red

Ripe blackberries with a hint of vanilla on the nose. Similar flavours on the palate in a rich smooth texture with a lovely touch of white pepper spice. Lovely balance of longlasting flavours.

Calf's liver with shallots and herbs

Cuvée Antoine de Montpezad AC Coteaux du Languedoc 96

Dunnes Stores   ££

Light fruity red

Lots of character on the nose—dark fruits and herbs. The palate holds up well with plenty of ripe fruit and an impressively long finish.

Beef casserole

Ch. Belot AC St Chinian 97

Dunnes Stores

Medium-bodied red

Slightly vegetal fruit on the nose. Stalky fruit on the palate with soft, yielding tannin and dry finish.

Chicken braised with bacon and black olives

Ch. de Montesquieu AC Coteaux du Languedoc 97

Dunnes Stores

Medium-bodied red

Ripe chocolatey fruit aromas, cassis with a herbal touch. Dark, bitter cherry fruit with a firm bite of tannin and bal-

anced acidity. Dry finish with a spicy, bitter kick.
Aubergine pasta

Dom. Coste Rouge AC Coteaux du Languedoc 96
Dunnes Stores

Light fruity red

Some nice fruit and a touch of spice on the nose. Riper palate, easy-drinking and round with enough tannin to give it some grip; rich fruit balanced by savoury overtones. Dry finish.
Mediterranean-style chicken casserole

Louis Eschenauer Cabernet Sauvignon VdP d'Oc 98
MacCormaic

Medium-bodied red

Blackberries and blackcurrants on the nose. Ripe, up-front fruit with spicy plum flavours and stalky tannins. Good weight of flavour with a firm, dry finish.
Pizza

Louis Eschenauer Merlot VdP d'Oc 98
MacCormaic

Light fruity red

Fruit of the forest aromas. Flavoursome if slightly lean fruit but generally rounded and good value.
Pasta with a robust sauce

Moulin de Gassac Terrasses de Landec Syrah VdP de l'Hérault 98
O'Briens

Medium-bodied red

Earthy aromas with very ripe fruit. Similarly ripe palate bursting with blackcurrants finishing with a touch of cloves and pepper.
Cold raised game pie

Ptomaine des Blaguers Syrah VdP d'Oc 96
Oddbins

Light fruity red

Rustic nose, ripe fruit with a touch of pepper. Well-balanced with nice simple berry fruit and a touch of spice.
Party pleaser.

Red £6 - £8

DLC Chevalière Cabernet Sauvignon VdP d'Oc 96
Allied Drinks   ☆

Medium-bodied red

Intense blackcurrant and tar aromas. A flavoursome wine with plenty of ripe blackcurrant fruit and spice with balanced tannin and a good finish.
Garlicky lamb

Dom. Deshenrys AC Coteaux du Languedoc 95
Fitzgerald   ☆

Medium-bodied red

Mature rather gamey bouquet. Delicious dark peppery fruit filling the palate. Firm tannin and refreshing acidity. Beginning to develop but should hold well and improve further.
Noisettes of lamb and herbs

Foxwood Old Bush Vine Syrah VdP d'Oc 97
Wines Direct   ☆

Medium-bodied red

Intense dark fruit—typical Syrah nose. Well-structured with plenty of fruit and refreshing acidity. Bramble and berry flavours with spicy tones and a long, warm finish.
Intense tomato sauces for pasta or meat

Dom. Saint Germain AC Minervois 96

MacCormaic C ££

Medium-bodied red

Plum jam with a touch of herbs. Ripe, concentrated black fruits on the palate with lovely spice. Balanced tannins and a fresh lengthy finish. Needs a few years but great value to put away.

Mediterranean-style casserole

Ch. Viranel AC St Chinian 97

Wines Direct C

Medium-bodied red

Lovely loganberries and liquorice on the nose with a palate to match of spicy red berry and cherry fruit. Nicely balanced with a warm finish.

Lamb with garlic and herbs or spatchcocked fowl

Les Mâitres Vignerons de Cascastel Cuvée Speciale AC Fitou 95

Bubble Brothers C

Medium-bodied red

Intense baked, even slightly burnt, fruit aromas with a definite touch of rubber. Plenty of baked fruit flavours upfront and a long, warm finish. Good hot climate style.

Aubergine and tomato casserole

Les Meuliers AC Minervois 96

MacCormaic C

Medium-bodied red

Rustic bramble fruit with earthy tones. Spicy flavours with plum and bramble fruit. Well-balanced with nice firm tannin. Quite a complex style.

Lamb with flageolet beans

Bergerie de l'Hortus Pic St Loup AC Coteaux du Languedoc 97

Wines Direct

Medium-bodied red

Jammy juicy fruit jumps out of the glass. Not especially complex but smooth and well-balanced with honest fruit and lively acidity.

Robust casserole-type dishes; lasagne; sausages with lentils

Ch. de l'Amarine Cuveé de Bernis AC Costières de Nîmes 97

River Wines

Light fruity red

Ripe fruit of the forest nose. Juicy palate full of young berry fruit. Soft and gulpable.

Salami and mixed cold meats

Ch. La Baronne Montagne d'Alaric AC Corbières 97

Wines Direct

Medium-bodied red

Typical mix of jammy berry fruit and herbal aromas. Very much fruit first on the palate, but soundly made.

Salami or pepperoni pizza

Ch. Laville Bertrou AC Minervois 95

Fitzgerald

Medium-bodied red

Warm earth aromas with baked bramble fruit. Good weight of ripe bramble fruit with a touch of pepper and woody spice. Firm ripe tannin, and fresh acidity with nice supporting alcohol. Good all round.

Rabbit pie

Ch. Pech-Céleyran La Clape AC Coteaux du Languedoc 97

Findlater

Medium-bodied red

Slightly earthy vegetal aromas mixed with ripe concentrated fruit. Dark, brambly berry fruit with firm tannin. Long, pleasant finish.

Robust sausage casserole

Ch. St Marc d'Audéric AC Corbières 96

Dalton

Medium-bodied red

Spicy, earthy dusty nose. Dry and peppery with rather firm tannins and very earthy fruit. Chunky and savoury in a traditional style with plenty of character.

Potted hare

Clos du Pech de la Lune AC St Chinian 96

Cassidy

Medium-bodied red

Quite earthy and herbal with a touch of spice on the nose. Rich soft fruits on the palate with a touch of tannin. Very French food wine.

Veal chop with mushroom sauce

Dom. Clavel La Méjanelle AC Coteaux du Languedoc 96

Wines Direct

Medium-bodied red

Ripe fruit on the nose that really shows on the palate with good fruit intensity and a firm tannic frame.

Casserole of lamb and aubergines or chicken and peppers

Dom. Gardies-Tautavel AC Côtes du Roussillon-Villages 96

Wines Direct

Medium-bodied red

Bags of fruit with vanilla and spice. Chewy palate, richly textured with a touch of tannin and rather earthy, oaky fruit. Good food wine.

Hearty casserole of meat and beans—even cassoulet

Gabiam AC Coteaux du Languedoc 95

Dunnes Stores

Medium-bodied red

Very ripe berries with hints of pepper on the nose. Lots of fruit with firm dry tannin and decent finish.

Lamb and rice casserole

Luc Lapeyre L'Amourier AC Minervois 96

Wines Direct

Medium-bodied red

Aromas of white pepper and herbs along with fruit. Very ripe fruit with nice balancing acidity. Well-made wine.

Chunky rabbit or game terrine

Michel Picard Cabernet Sauvignon VdP d'Oc 97

TDL

Medium-bodied red

Very ripe fruit and a touch of new oak on the nose. Cool yet with plenty of upfront fruit and a touch of mint.

Lamb and rosemary kebabs

Michel Picard Merlot VdP d'Oc 97

TDL

Light fruity red

Ripe spicy fruit aromas. Light

and fruity with loads of berry flavours and dry finish.
Pasta with tomatoes, mushrooms and olives

Michel Picard Syrah VdP d'Oc 97
TDL

Medium-bodied red

Cool minty fruit upfront on nose and palate. Easy-drinking with nice balance.
Hamburgers with spicy relish

Moulin de Gassac Elise VdP de l'Hérault 97
O'Briens

Medium-bodied red

Very rich bouquet of ripe fruit with caramel and rubber nuances. Rich, super-ripe fruit on the palate with a touch of green pepper, highish alcohol and good length.
Rich stew of aubergines, pepper, onions and tomato

Red £8 - £10

Ch. de Gourgazeaud Reserve AC Minervois 97
Dunnes Stores   ☆

Full-bodied red

Elegant aromas of raspberry and loganberry fruit with liquorice and spice. Very round and smooth with plenty of flavoursome complex fruit and a long satisfying finish.
Couscous

Ch. La Voulte-Gasparets AC Corbières 95
Searson   ☆

Medium-bodied red

Lovely bouquet of leather, spice and blackcurrant pie. Intense black fruit flavours with spicy peppery tones and friendly

tannin. Beautifully balanced wine with tightly-knit flavour and long finish.
Calf's liver

Ch. La Bastide AC Corbières 97
Febvre   C ££

Medium-bodied red

Ripe yet slightly earthy and medicinal quality gives depth to the bouquet. Rounded palate with good weight of ripe fruit flavour and spice, damsons with a hint of pepper. Tannins beginning to yield but still young and will improve. Good value.
Hearty casserole of beef or lamb

Ch. des Estanilles Cuvée Prestige AC Faugères 96
Wines Direct

Medium-bodied red

Vegetal, stalky young aromas. Smoky plummy fruit with a touch of pepper. Dry, long finish.
Lamb and beans

Ch. Ricardelle Clos Sablières AC Coteaux du Languedoc 95
Karwig

Medium-bodied red

Intense ripe soft fruit aromas with spice and vanilla. Well-made wine, firmly structured with ripe fruit carrying through a long finish.
Rabbit with mustard

DLC Chevalière Grand Reserve VdP d'Oc 95
Allied Drinks

Medium-bodied red

Smoky, vegetal aromas with some ripe fruit showing too. Well-balanced with good ripe

fruit and supporting structure.
Pheasant casserole with tomatoes and sweet peppers

La Grange de Quatre Sous Lo Moulin VdP d'Oc 96

Wines Direct

Medium-bodied red

Intense aromas of ripe black-currant fruit. Quite firm tannin balanced by ripe fruit and peppery spice. Firm structure and nice weight with a long finish and future development.
Casserole of duck and olives

Red £10 - 312

Ch. de Flaugergues La Méjanelle AC Coteaux du Languedoc 96

Dunnes Stores

Medium-bodied red

Blackberry fruit and quite a bit of oak on the nose. Somewhat closed but with nice damson fruit and decent weight. Well-structured wine which should improve further.
Cassoulet and other robust casseroles

Dom. de l'Aigle Terres Rouges Pinot Noir VdP d'Oc 97

River Wines

Medium-bodied red

Redcurrant and cherry aromas. Peppery fruit in good concen-tration. Should develop lots more complexity in a year or so. At present slightly tarry but beautifully concentrated fruit with ripe tannin and long finish.
Cajun chicken

Red £12 - £15

Dom. l'Aiguelière AC Coteaux du Languedoc 94

MacCormaic ☆ ☆

Full-bodied red

Mature, meaty, farmyard aromas. Blackberry fruit, spice, menthol—great complexity and flavour. Big but very stylish. Sexy stuff, buy a case and enjoy its devlopment.
Game stew

Ch. des Estanilles AC Faugères 96

Wines Direct C

Medium to full-bodied red

Dark smoky fruit aromas with earthy hints. Firm, youthful tannin but enough ripe fruit to balance and show future potential.
Rabbit stew

Dom. de l'Hortus AC Coteaux du Languedoc 97

Wines Direct C

Medium to full-bodied red

Plum and damson aromas with inviting peppery spice. Good balance of ripe fruit, oak and tannin. Nice to drink now but will develop more complexity.
Steak

Prieuré de St Jean de Bébian AC Coteaux du Languedoc 94

Wines Direct C

Medium to full-bodied red

Plummy fruit aromas with white pepper. Plenty of damson and black cherry fruit with a backbone of tannin and spicy oak. Very well-balanced wine with impressive length of finish.
Couscous

Provence

Red £6 - £8

Les Matines AC Coteaux d'Aix en Provence 97
Grants
Light fruity red
Really ripe, almost sweet, fruit on the nose. Intense ripe blackcurrant fruit flavours with dry, light tannins and a good finish.
Rabbit cooked with basil

Red £8 - £10

Dom. des Béates AC Coteaux d'Aix en Provence 96
Grants
Medium-bodied red
Rich fruit aromas with caramel and spice in the background. Good weight of ripe fruit. Balanced, with nice length in the finish.
Good garlicky sausage

Red £10 -£12

Dom. de la Vallonge AC Les Baux-de-Provence 95
MacCormaic ☆
Full-bodied red
Lovely warm earth aromas with herbal influences. Great evolving flavours on the palate with very firm tannins but also spicy, tarry fruit and black pepper. Long satisfying finish.
Daube of lamb

Rosé £5 -£5

Dom. de Vignelaure VdP Coteaux du Verdon 98
Dunnes Stores
Rosé
Very pale 'pretty pink' rosé with ripe, slightly earthy berry aromas. Very dry palate with stalky berry fruit and a hint of spice. A touch green in the finish.
Aioli

South-West

White £5 - £6

Dom. du Rey VdP Côtes de Gascogne 98
Searson
Aromatic white
Lovely fresh young wine with clean floral and citrus aromas. Zippy fresh palate with nice broad citrus flavours and a crisp finish.
Fish mousse or pâté

Honoré de Berticot Sauvignon AC Côtes de Duras 98
Searson
Aromatic white
Quite elegant aromas of green fruit with mango and green-gage hints. Nice weight of green fruit flavour, well-balanced with a clean fresh finish.
Goat's cheese salad.

White £6 - £8

Ch. Pique-Sègue AC Montravel 98

United Beverages ☆

Light fruity white

Ripe green fruit with grassy, floral tones. Dry with plenty of crisp green fruit, lots of style and character. Very fresh and clean with lovely follow-through in the finish.

Fish and herb terrine

Ch. Jolys AC Jurançon Sec 96

Wines Direct C

Aromatic white

Lovely aromas of marmalade and spice, with honeysuckle hints. Rich, full palate with predominantly citrus fruit and spice flavours. Excellent balance of ripe fruit and acidity with elegant restraint. Long, spicy finish with a peppery twist.

Salad of grilled vegetables

Grain Sauvage AC Jurançon Sec 98

Searson C

Aromatic white

Elegant and quite complex nose with green fruit and a touch of honey. Good weight and roundness with slightly honeyed fruit similar to the nose and mineral notes in the background. Rounded and well-balanced, rich yet very fresh in the finish.

Warm salad of grilled vegetables

Red £6 - £8

Dom. Fleury Laplace AC Madiran 96

Molloy's

Full-bodied red

Slightly closed but quite concentrated nose of tarry black fruit. Firm tannin grips the palate with dark fruits in the background. A little austere, needs meat to tame the tannin but promises well.

Duck legs with herbs and garlic or confit

Red £8 - £10

Ch. Tour des Gendres AC Bergerac 97

MacCormaic

Medium-bodied red

Earthy, herby blackcurrant aromas. Slightly stalky black-currant flavours, balanced acidity and tannin. Good understated style.

Grilled lamb or mixed grill

Red £12 - £15

Ch. d'Aydie AC Madiran 94

Woodford Bourne ☆

Full-bodied red

Baked fruit aromas. Tarry fruit and firm tannins—a chunky structure. A big burly wine with lots of flavour and an intense impact.

Confit of goose

Germany

Away from its home, German wine remains a puzzle. The country has a very long tradition of fine wine production and for centuries a well-established export trade. True, following the Second World War the quality of exports went down as the economic benefits of cheap, off-sweet light wines went up. However, in the last decade, there has been a great upsurge in quality production and direct attempts to re-assure buyers of the new direction of German wine. The introduction of Trocken and Halbtrocken categories for dry wine, the simpler, more consumer-friendly labels (of some), and lower yields, riper fruit and better handling in vineyard and cellar have finally banished the Liebfraumilch syndrome. Or should have.

With the exception of real enthusiasts, consumers by and large fight shy of German wines as difficult to buy and understand. Now there are two kinds of German wine, three if you include the remnants of the cheap and cheerful brigade. Modern German winemaking has gone for low sugar, higher alcohol, drier, slightly fuller white wines. Often these are labelled by a brand name to simplify recognition and many are bottled in a consciously un-German style. A few manage a rather New World feel with tropical, fruit-driven flavour.

The traditional side of German winemaking is also part of the quality surge, ultimately its greatest strength. Well chosen Kabinett and Spätlese Riesling from the Rheingau, Mosel, Pfalz or even Rhineheissen is one of the few remaining great bargains in wine. These wines are elegant and understated, beautifully balanced between pure fruit and racy acidity with sweetness only a tiny part of their intricate balancing act. They are classic in style and their light fresh appeal is perfect with today's food. Many will last for a very long time and with prices soaring in most well-known regions, German wine makes an excellent cellar option.

You need to buy from a specialist who knows the regions and can provide a range, but with a trail of excellent vintages in the last decade, German wine to keep is a hot tip for the future.

White £5 or less

Tesco Kabinett Rheinessen QmP 97
Tesco

Aromatic white

Ripe peachy fruit on the nose. Fresh simple wine, off-dry style with nice fruit and good balance of acidity.
Oriental savouries

White £5 - £6

Bend in the River 98
Findlater

Aromatic white

Light fruit/floral nose. Dry crisp style with high acidity, apple and pear fruit and a clean, dry finish.
Good old prawn cocktail!

White £6 - £8

Deinhard Green Label Q 98
Woodford Bourne

Aromatic white, off-dry

Delicate nose of green apples with a touch of black pepper. Off-dry with refreshing, crunchy green apple fruit and a clean finish.
Spicy Oriental dishes

Hessische Bergstrasse Bensheimer Wolfsmagen Riesling Kabinett Halbtrocken QmP 97
Classic Wines

Aromatic white

Slightly floral nose with typical petrol tones. Orchard fruit nicely balanced by acidity and good weight of flavour. Very fresh and crisp.
Smoked duck salad

Hessische Bergstrasse Weisser Riesling Trocken Q 97
Classic Wines
Aromatic white

Distinct petrol nose with pear and apple fruit. Light in the mouth with green apple fruit, refreshing acidity and a clean, fresh finish.
Smoked fish and avocado salad

Hirt-Gebhardt Rheingau Rauenthaler Wulfen Riesling Kabinett QmP 96
Karwig
Aromatic white

Apples and custard on the nose. Very fresh start, softening into grapey fruit flavour and a crisp finish.
Stir-fried fish

Kendermann Dry Riesling Q 97
Gilbeys
Aromatic white, off-dry

Light aromatic nose, pears and candied lemon. Fresh, with plenty of uncomplicated citrus fruit. Easy-drinking and well-made.
Chinese pastries or noodles

White £8 - £10

Dürkheimer Steinberg Riesling Kabinett Halbtrocken QmP 98
Karwig   C
Aromatic white

Oily, grassy Riesling nose. Quite austere and minerally on the palate with lovely balance between fruit and acidity. Delicious wine with great length of flavour which should age beautifully.
Cold goose on St Stephen's Day!

Hessische Bergstrasse Heppenheimer Stemmler Riesling Kabinett Trocken QmP 98
Classic Wines
Aromatic white

Grapey, peardrop aromas. Quite minerally on the palate with apple and lemon hints. Short on the finish.
Aperitif

Hessische Bergstrasse Heppenheimer Stemmler Riesling Spätlese Trocken QmP 98
Classic Wines
Aromatic white

Youthful mineral and green fruit aromas. Nervy Riesling palate with high acidity and young fruit. Stylish potential which should age well.
Seafood pastry

Reichsgraf von Kesselstatt Piesporter Goldtröpfchen Riesling 96
Searson
Aromatic white

Aromas of lime and a touch of diesel. Crisp acidity and good weight of melon and green fruit flavours. Light and fresh with lasting taste.
Smoked trout salad

Weingut Joh. Haart Piesporter Treppchen Riesling Qba 97
Karwig
Aromatic white

Quite floral on the nose. Lively peach and citrus fruit flavours, with racy acidity and excellent balance. Very long, lovely finish.

Smoked trout

Weingut Unckrich Kallstadter Saumagen Riesling Spätlese QmP 96

Karwig

Aromatic white

Beeswax and honey on the nose. Lots of ripe fruit with a touch of honey, refreshing acidity and very good finish.

Poached sole with cream sauce

Werner Tyrell Ruwer Eitelsbächer Karthhäuserhofberg Kronenberg Riesling Kabinett 83

Searson

Aromatic white

Complex, very developed aromas of honey, petrol and

WINES

'Importing really superb German wines to the Irish market'
Tim Vaughan, *Examiner*

Telephone & Mail Orders welcome
Phone for the Wine List
Phone: 021-354888
Fax; 021 351010
Mobile: 087 2 85 9 983

ripe tropical fruit. Balanced and intriguing palate just beginning to fade. Drink up.

Smoked eel

White £10 - £12

Dr Burklin-Wolf Rupperstberger Riesling Trocken Qba 97

Karwig

Aromatic white

Ripe fruit on the nose beginning to develop. Austere stony fruit on the palate, intense and balanced if a bit young and unyielding. Give it a year or two for something really good.

Avocado mousse

Reichsgraf von Kessellstatt Josephshöfer Riesling Kabinett 97

Searson

Aromatic white

Slightly honeyed ripe fruit on the nose. Off-dry with refreshing acidity and excellent weight of ripe fruit with a honeyed aftertaste. Great length and cool dry finish.

Smoked salmon pâté

White £12 - £15

Weingut Schumacher Herxheimer Himmelreich Riesling Spätlese QmP 97

Mitchell

Aromatic white

Intensely aromatic ripe tropical fruit aromas. Off-dry with very fresh, crisp acidity, excellent weight of ripe fruit and a very long, impressive finish.

Goose pâté

Red £8 - £10

Dornfelfder Trocken Qba 97
Karwig

Light fruity red

Cherries and strawberries on the nose. Nice soft fruit flavours and balanced acidity. Flavour lasts well in the finish.
Cold ham

Hessische Bergstrasse Heppenheimer Eckwig Spatburgunder Spaätlese Trocken QmP 97
Classic Wines

Light fruity red

Good ripe berry fruit aromas. Quite rich cassis flavours with balanced acidity. Nice concentration of fruit which lasts well through the finish.
Stuffed field mushrooms

Red £10 - £12

Hessische Bergstrasse Wein und Stein Heppenheimer Stemmler Saint Laurent Trocken Qba98
Classic Wines

Light fruity red

Floral brambly aromas. Nicely balanced wine with ripe blackberries, almost fruit jelly flavours and a touch of vegetal complexity. A characterful wine with length.
Salmon with fennel and ham stuffing.

What the awards mean

☆☆☆ —exceptional wines of considerable complexity with classic balance from a very good vintage.

☆☆—elegant wines with character and complexity above expectations, showing balance, subtlety and 'typicité'.

☆—wines with character and style that are particularly good examples of their region and winemaking.

C—commendation: good, interesting wines that merit attention but not quite a star, including wines which are good examples of particular regional styles and wines which are a little young but show good potential.

££—value: wines offering exceptional value for money in their type/region; mainly lower-priced wines but including well-priced classics.

Greece

Although Greece is the oldest wine region in Europe, the modern Greek wine industry is still developing. Combined efforts of government, dedicated quality conscious-producers and outside expertise are just beginning to bear fruit on the export market. Holiday experience of Greek wine does not reflect the progress which has been made in the last half decade or so. There is still an abundance of oxidised or old-style sweet red wine and the quirky Retsina around tavernas, holiday bars and restaurants. Progressive winemakers are still a minority but are becoming increasingly vocal and dominant among exporters.

The big success of the moment is with red wines. Greece has some exciting red wine grapes—if you don't try to pronounce the names. Local varieties Xynomavro and Agiorgitiko and the imported Cabernet Sauvignon are currently making some lovely, great value reds which are worth seeking out and tasting. Like Portugal, Greece's relatively late entry to the export market has meant that its own grape varieties have been preserved and are a great strength for the future. More serious reds are already beginning to emerge which have subtlety and character and those from cooler regions will age well.

As with any traditional wine region, Greece has its specialities. The sweet wines, notably Muscat de Sammos and the Mavrodaphne are great value dessert wines with individual charm.

White £8 - £10

Gentielini Classico 97
Oddbins
Full-bodied white
Ripe fruit aromas. Oily and full with green apple fruit, citrus acidity and a spicy finish.
Seafood stews and casseroles

Red £6 - £8

Tsantali Syrah 96
Oddbins
Medium-bodied red
Earthy meaty nose with vanilla and toffee tones. Lots of super-ripe fruit with balanced tannins.
Lamb and runner bean stew

Red £8 - £10

Amethystos 97
Oddbins
Full-bodied red

Intense warm fruit aromas, very ripe. Full-bodied, fleshy and round with soft, ripe tannins and good weight of earthy fruit flavour.
Grilled lamb

Red £10 - £12

Megas Oenos Skouras 96
Oddbins ☆
Full-bodied red

Very ripe aromas, mulberries, tar and leather, developed and complex. Ripe tannins frame thick layers of rich fruit. Long peppery finish.
Robust meat/game casserole

Editor's choice: party wines

For large numbers and with the mixed tastes of a buffet or other such food, wines that are easy to drink, rounded and with plenty of fruit tend to please most people and complement the food. Easy-drinking means a wine with low tannin and moderate acidity and plenty of fruity flavours. It does not need to be bland or dull.

There's no need to pay more than £7 a bottle and there is a good range available well below this price.

Tesco Australian White Wine

Peter Lehmann Grenache 1998

Mount Hurtle Grenache Rosé 1998

Chapel Hill Balatonboglár Irsai Oliver 1997

Viu Manent Sauvignon Blanc 1997

Santa Emiliana Andes Peak Merlot 1998

Tesco Kabinett Rheinessen 1997

Elitaio DOC Montepulciano d'Abruzzo 1996

Ryland's Grove Chenin Blanc 1998

Agramont Tempranillo Navarra 1996

Italy

Apart from a few rising prices, the news from Italy is good. Traditional regions have taken a hard look at quality over the last decade and the results are beginning to show. At the same time forgotten and neglected regions are emerging, especially from the south. If in the past the variety of Italian wine was one of its problems, it is now a great strength, for throughout its vine-covered length, Italy has every possible style of quality wine you could ever want.

Italian white wines have been largely ignored in the wave of enthusiasm for Italian wine—and food—of recent times. They have their own style: crisp, refreshing and restrained. Their role is to sharpen the appetite and waken the palate which they do admirably and without distracting from food or following wines.

The boring side of Italian white wine came from the over-use of the Trebbiano grape. A majority of white could be simply labelled 'Trebbiano plus', and were dilute and neutral and tired quickly. Although it may take a lot to revive the image of Soave, white wines in general have improved. For one thing, they are younger and fresher on our shelves. The interesting Malvasia is beginning to replace the Trebbiano and a much better version of this infamous variety is making Lugano, the white wine from around Lake Garda, very trendy stuff. Pinot Grigio, from a top producer such as Lageder, is lightly aromatic and excellent, Muscats are increasingly dry and exciting, while new blends have emerged such as Masi's Serègo Alighieri Bianco di Garganega é Sauvignon.

Chianti has really come into its own in the nineties and the subzones Classico and Rúfina are in the lead. The wines are Sangiovese-dominated, intense and concentrated with ripe flavours and individual style. The Riservas combine lower yields with careful wood-ageing and have achieve a remarkable blend of traditional character and modern polish. With the exceptions of the 92 and 94 vintages most of these will age and develop in complexity over many years.

Lighter Italian reds have never had the same prestige as the blockbusters of Piedmont and Tuscany. However, new examples of carefully nurtured Dolcetto and Barbera show different, much more positive sides of the grapes. Good Dolcetto is richly fruity, soft and easy yet with appetising bite, while low-yield Barbera is vigorous and substantial with lovely savoury tone in its fruit. Other lighter styles to watch are Refosco, Teroldego and Breganze from the Veneto.

The biggest Italian news story has been the re-birth of the South. Puglia, and the whole of this region, is buzzing with exciting new wines, some in the soft, rich, spicy style that first made the region popular, others more structured and deep.

White £5 or less

Torresolada Settesoli IGT Bianco di Sicilia 97
Dunnes Stores ££
Light dry white
Good weight of citrus and melon fruit. Broad with balanced acidity and a crisp fresh finish. Good value.
Ravioli or gnocchi

Tesco DOC Frascati 98
Tesco
Light dry white
Very pleasant light aromas of apple and citrus with a touch of nuts. Bone-dry with nice balance of green fruit and crisp acidity. Very refreshing finish.
Seafood antipasta

White £5 - £6

Inama DOC Soave Classico Superiore 97
Italian Boutique Wines
Light dry white
Very fresh lemon and lemongrass aromas. Dry, light and delicate with peach kernel flavours and fresh lemon acidity.
Fried scampi—what else!

Pasqua Selection Vigneti del Sole DOC Soave 98
Woodford Bourne
Light dry white
Citrus fruit aromas. Apple fruit flavours with lively lemon acidity and a really crisp finish.
Deep-fried fish

White £6 - £8

Masi Serègo Alighieri Bianco di Garganega é Sauvignon DOC Veneto 97
Grants ☆
Aromatic white
Ripe citrus fruit and orange blossom aromas. Very well-balanced with an elegant palate of floral, citrus fruit and ripe pears. Lively acidity and a long finish.
Linguinni with sun-dried tomatoes

Alasia Muscate Sec VdT Piemonte 98
Findlater C
Aromatic white
Orange peel and apple blossom aromas. Apricot and peach fruit with balanced acidity and a clean warm finish. Different and stylish.
Asparagus salad

Bolla DOC Soave Classico 97
Dillon   C
Light dry white
Delicate aromas of hazelnut and biscuit. Dry and restrained palate with light citrus fruit flavours and a mineral core. A nutty edge adds interest and flavours last well.
Shelllfish salad

Alasia Chardonnay DOC Piemonte 98
Findlater
Light dry white
Honeyed melon with hints of pear and kiwi on the nose. Plenty of tropical fruit with balanced acidity. Well-made wine.
Simply cooked plaice or lemon sole

Alasia Cortese DOC Piemonte 97
Findlater
Light dry white
Hints of nettle and gooseberry on the nose. Nicely balanced wine with green and citrus fruit flavours. Lively and fresh.
Seafood risotto

Antinori Campogrande DOC Orvieto Classico 98
Grants
Light dry white
Fresh and rather floral nose. Zippy acidity well-balanced by fruit. Light, fresh and clean in the finish.
Simply cooked fish with butter and lemon

Le Grillaie DOC Vernaccia di San Gimignano 97
Gilbeys
Light dry white
Hints of yeast and toasted biscuit on the nose. Nice concentration of citrus and fruit pastille flavours and a clean finish.
Ravioli

Masi DOC Soave Classico Superiore 98
Grants
Light dry white
Light, citrus fruit aromas. Light and fresh with orange and almond flavours and zippy acidity. Refreshing and clean in the finish.
Deep-fried scampi

Pasqua Pinot Grigio/ Chardonnay IGT Venezie 98
Woodford Bourne
Light fruity white
Light tropical aromas with a touch of lemon sherbet. Light and dry with green fruit flavours and crisp acidity.
Canapés

Pietracolata DOC Orvieto Classico Secco 98
Ecock
Light dry white
Hints of peardrops and bubblegum. Nice weight of ripe fruit with crisp acidity and a dry finish.
Fish fritters or scampi

Vignetti Mancini DOC Verdicchio dei Castelli di Jesi Classico 98
Ecock

Light dry white

Clean fresh aromas with tropical fruit. Ripe melon and pear with fresh acidity. Well-balanced subtle wine.
Goujons of fish

Villa Antinori IGT Toscana 98
Grants

Light dry white

Aromas of nuts and herbs followed by an almost spicy palate with good weight and balance. Very fresh with bracing acidity.
Mixed shellfish in a salad, or deep fried

Zenato San Benedetto DOC Lugana 98
Searson

Light dry white

Citrus and apple hints on the nose. Delicate but attractive flavours of apple and pink grapefruit. Crisp acidity and impressively long finish.
Prawn wontons

White £8 - £10

Collavini Sassi Chardonnay IGT delle Venezie 96
Ecock

Light dry white

Tropical fruit, toast and honey on the nose. Excellent fruit flavour and length; very fresh with lively acidity.
Prawns in a light sauce

Collavini Villa del Canlungo Pinot Grigio DOC Friuli 98
Ecock

Light dry white

Citrus fruit aromas with hints of yeast and butterscotch. Lots of ripe stewed apple fruit, rounded and balanced with a clean dry finish.
Greek salad or cheesy pasta

Cormòns Isonzo Tocai Friuliano DOC Friuli 96
Select Wines from Italy

Light dry white

Fresh and clean on the nose. Mineral tones on the palate with citrus flavours beneath. Subtle and well-made.
Antipasta

La Vis Pinot Grigio DOC Trentino 98
Febvre

Light dry white

Youthful fragrant nose of honey and boiled sweets. Really ripe, ripe fruit but with balancing acidity—fresh and appetising.
Crostini

Masi Colbaraca DOC Soave Classico 97
Grants

Light dry white

Tropical fruit aromas with a touch of honey. Well-balanced fruit and acidity and a long, appetising finish.
Chinese dishes such as prawn toasts, spring rolls etc.

White £10 - £12

Liberna DOCG Vernaccia di San Gimignano Riserva 95
Select Wines from Italy ☆ ☆

Light dry white

Concentrated nose with butter, lemon and spice aromas. Dry and beautifully balanced with nutty fruit flavours and a long, lingering finish.
Sole cooked with butter and herbs

Kettmeir Pinot Grigio DOC Alto Adige 98
Select Wines from Italy ☆

Aromatic white

Quite complex aromas of marzipan, biscuits and straw! Well-balanced with concentrated broad fruit flavours and definite character which develops in the glass.
Buttered shrimps or prawns in pastry

Cormòns Ribolla Gialla DOC Colli 96
Select Wines from Italy

Aromatic white

Slightly oily character on the nose. Green fruit on the palate blends with richer, creamy fruit tones. Long and attractive.
Mussel stew

Eisacktaler Gewürztraminer della Valle Isarco DOC Alto Adige 98

Select Wines from Italy

Aromatic white

Floral nose, lychees and Turkish Delight. Impressively fresh, dry and charming with elegant balance of flavours and acidity. Well-made, polished example.
Salad of red peppers

Le Moie DOC Verdicchio dei Castelli di Jesi Classico Superiore 97

Select Wines from Italy

Light dry white

Fresh aromas, touch of green leaves. Quite nutty and herbal on the palate with fresh, lemony fruit. Broad and quite long.
Goujons of fish

White £12 - £15

Alois Lageder Pinot Grigio DOC Alto Adige/Südtirol 98

Febvre   C

Aromatic white

Floral orange blossom and roses on the nose. Lots of ripe peach and apricot fruit with honeyed tones. Clean crisp acidity. Different, stylish wine.
Fish in saffron sauce

Collavini Turian Ribolla Gialla DOC Colli Orientali del Friuli 98

Ecock

Aromatic white

Honeyed tropical fruit aromas with subtle vanilla and caramel. Plenty of ripe melon and peach fruit with a long, smooth well-

balanced finish.
Salmon or brill with a light herb sauce

White £15 - £20

Castel de Paolis Selve Vecchie IGT Lazio 97

Italian Boutique Wines

Full-bodied white, oak

Toasted, oaky aromas. Creamy-textured with plenty of new oak flavours balanced by ripe fruit. Good long finish and time should subdue the oak nicely.
Veal escalopes with lemon

Red £5 or less

Elitaio DOC Montepulciano d'Abruzzo 96

Gleeson   C

Medium-bodied red

Intense ripe bramble fruit aromas with chocolate and spice. Lots of ripe juicy black cherry flavours. Good body and lovely fruity finish.
Pasta with rich meaty sauce

Terre Verdi DOC Rosso Piceno 97

Dunnes Stores

Medium-bodied red

A burst of raspberry fruit on the nose, quite jammy and up-front. Firm structure with some weight of fruit; well-balanced with refreshing acidity and a good fruity finish. A good quaffer.
Pizza

Torresolada Settesoli IGT Rosso di Sicilia 96

Dunnes Stores

Medium-bodied red

Pleasant, clean red cherry

aromas with a touch of spice. Lively palate with plenty of straightforward cherry fruit, a bite of tannin and grapey acidity. Good value.
Pizza or salami

Red £5 - £6

Tioneo Conte di Monforte DOC Salice Salentino 96
Dunnes Stores   C ££
Full-bodied red

Lots of dark berries and chocolate on the nose with rich spicy tones. Mellow tannins and lovely rich autumn fruit with a lingering finish.
Venison stew

Il Vescovo Primitivo della Puglia IGT Puglia 98
Greenhills   C
Full-bodied red

Deep, dense aromas of fruit, liquorice and spice. Full-bodied with spicy plum and cherry fruit. A good backbone of tannin holds the richness and the creamy, full texture carries flavours right through to the finish.
Turkey with an olive sauce or poultry stuffed with fruit

Badia Frasca DOC Montepulciano d'Abruzzo 97
Greenhills
Medium-bodied red

Cherry and raspberry fruit aromas follow to the palate. Nice weight of fruit with real bitter cherry punch, balancing tannin and acidity and a typically bitter twist in the finish. A good example.
Richly sauced pasta

Pasqua Sangiovese di Puglia IGT Puglia 97
Woodford Bourne
Medium-bodied red

Minty chocolate aromas with black cherry fruit. Cherry flavours with refreshing acidity and a firm bite of tannin. Quite distinctive for the price.
Robust pasta

Pasqua Selection Vigneti del Sole DOC Valpolicella 97
Woodford Bourne
Light fruity red

Loads of cherry fruit aromas which carry through to the palate ending in a bitter twist. Good straightforward Valpol for simple quaffing!
Lentil patties

Red £6 - £8

Giacosa Fratelli DOCG Barolo 95
Tesco   C ££
Full-bodied red

Cherries and red berries on the nose with earthy woodland nuances. Balanced and approachable with nice weight of fruit and very well-priced. The modern face of Barolo.
Beef or game casserole

Alasia DOC Barbera d'Asti Superiore 95
Findlater   C
Medium-bodied red

Cherry and plum aromas with hints of caramel and herbs. Plenty of plum and damson fruit, typical bracing acidity and chewy texture. Good value, correct Barbera.
Kidneys or liver

Antinori Tenute Marchesi Antinori DOCG Chianti Classico Riserva 96

Grants   C

Full-bodied red

Very concentrated nose with chocolate, spice, blackcurrant and earth tones. Big, chewy palate with red fruit and spice framed by firm ripe tannins. Will improve further given time.

Rib of beef, grilled rare

Col di Sasso Sangiovese/ Cabernet IGT Toscana 96

Gilbeys   C

Medium-bodied red

Dark almost dried fruit aromas mixed with vanilla and spice. Firm tannin and plenty of texture with damson and bramble fruit flavours and a long, spicy finish.

Duck legs baked with herbs

Pasqua Negroamoro IGT Negroamaro Salento 97

Woodford Bourne   C

Full-bodied red

Meaty, leathery aromas with spicy dark fruit. Big and full with plenty of dark ripe fruit and spice, soft tannin and balanced acidity. Smooth, rich and chocolatey. A lot of taste for the price.

Earthy gratin of aubergines

Bolla DOC Valpolicella Classico 97

Dillon

Light fruity red

Cherry fruit aromas, plenty of similar cherry fruit flavour. Supple, easy-drinking.

Meat-based antipasta

Candido DOC Salice Salentino Riserva 96

Findlater

Full-bodied red

Spicy fruitcake aromas and similar fruit on the palate with high acidity and slightly rustic tannin. Appetising and typical with a warm alcoholic finish.

Rabbit stew or aubergine casserole

Coltibuono Cetamura DOC Chianti 97

Findlater

Medium-bodied red

Plummy black cherries on the nose—rather earthy. Cherry fruit with high acidity and firm tannin. Typical basic Chianti.

Roast pork with herbs

Duca di Castelmonte Cent'are IGT Sicilia 96

Oddbins

Full-bodied red

Blackberry and cherry aromas with hints of spice. Big, round and supple with rich flavours of baked fruit, firm tannin and a dry finish.

Mushroom stew

Il Vescovo Sangiovese IGT Rubicone 98

Greenhills

Medium-bodied red

Ripe fruit aromas with vegetal spicy undertones. Similar earthy fruit on the palate with soft tannin and rather chewy texture. Nice spicy finish.

Liver or kidneys with a flavoursome sauce

Le Masserie di Puglia IGT Primitivo Salento 98
Woodford Bourne

Full-bodied red

Lovely ripe bramble aromas mingling with rubber and smoke. Plenty of ripe dark fruit with balancing tannin and acidity. Quite mouthfilling with a long dusty finish.
Casserole of Mediterranean vegetables with olive oil and garlic

Melini Isassi DOCG Chianti Classico 96
Gilbeys

Medium-bodied red

Berry fruit and a touch of violet on the nose. Plenty of chewy, dark cherry fruit with lively acidity and a bite of tannin.
Salami and olives

MezzaCorona Merlot DOC Trentino 97
Mitchell

Light fruity red

Youthful ripe blackberry fruit on the nose. More restrained palate with crisp acidity and some tannin.
Coarse pâté or terrine

Sordo Giovanni DOC Dolcetto d'Alba 97
Gleeson

Light fruity red

Ripe elegant aromas of strawberry fruit. Lovely summer berry flavours. A light, fresh, fruity wine, very well-made.
Carpaccio

Tesco DOCG Chianti Classico Riserva 96

Tesco

Full-bodied red

Cherries and plums on the nose. Plenty of dark damson fruit with crisp acidity and firm tannin.

Roast pigeon for a bargain dinner party

Tesco DOCG Chianti Rúfina 96

Tesco

Medium-bodied red

Earthy, juicy fruit aromas. Dry with bitter cherry fruit, crisp acidity and dry tannin. Slightly astringent but good value.

Cold rare roast beef sandwich

Tesco DOCG Chianti Classico 96

Tesco

Medium-bodied red

Developed aromas of berries and liquorice. Good weight of fruit with balanced structure and a very dry finish which needs food.

Grilled chops

Red £8 - £10

Candido Capelle di Prete VdT Salento 95

Findlater ☆

Full-bodied red

Really intriguing mixture of plum and tobacco aromas with fragrant spice and great ripeness, very complex. Fleshy wine with well-cloaked tannins and huge weight of fruit with balancing acidity finishing with a bitter twist. Big and beautiful!

Game casserole

Barone Ricasoli San Ripolo DOCG Chianti Classico 96

Fitzgerald C

Medium-bodied red

Woody aromas with ripe morello cherries. Lots of cherry on the palate with firm tannin and refreshing acidity well-melded together throughout a long finish.

Pasta and truffles

Castellani Poggio al Casone DOCG Chianti Superiore 96

Cassidy C

Medium-bodied red

Ripe berry fruit and tobacco bouquet. Nice integration of berry fruit, fresh acidity and wood. Lingering flavours in the finish.

Roast pork

Colonna Bigio DOC Monferrato 96

Wine Warehouse C

Medium-bodied red

Mature, rich gamey scents. Mellow tannin and balanced acidity over cherry fruit with a long, earthy, tobacco-spiced finish.

Roast quail

Papà Celso DOC Dolcetto di Dogliani 97

Searson C

Medium-bodied red

Deep and inky with scents of mulberries and cinnamon. Ripe brambly palate with bitter chocolate, violet cream flavours. Very good structure with firm tannin behind all the fruit. Lovely, tempting Dolcetto.

Osso bucco

San Giovanni DOCG Chianti Classico Riserva 95

Dunnes Stores C

Full-bodied red

Dark cherry fruit with hints of liquorice and cedar. Firm structure; lots of fleshy black cherry fruit, mellow tannins and length of flavour.
Quail with mushrooms and sage

Taburno DOC Aglianico del Taburno Riserva 92

Ecock C

Full-bodied red

Earthy farmyard aromas— truffles and mushrooms. Very silky with ripe bramble and cherry fruit, balanced acidity and tannin. Elegant, under-stated wine with a long finish.
Pigeon with black olives

Villa San Andrea DOCG Chianti Classico 95

Gleeson C

Full-bodied red

Elegant yet rich aromas of black cherries. Well-structured with firm tannin and great weight of ripe fruit. Big robust wine with mouthfilling flavour.
Pheasant casserole

Alasia Nebbiolo DOC Langhe 96

Findlater

Medium-bodied red

Ripe fruit with quite nutty aromas. Dry with blackberry fruit, refreshing acidity and firm tannin. Well-structured around ripe fruit with a typical bitter twist in the finish.
Kidneys with cream and wine sauce

Barbaglio Rosso IGT Salento 95

Findlater

Full-bodied red

Very aromatic nose of spice, chocolate and mint with ripe fruit beneath. Chocolate influence continues to the palate which is firm with balancing acidity. A nice wine to drink now—a younger vintage might be even better!
Grilled steak or chops

Cantina Faccagnini DOC Montepulciano d'Abruzzo 97

Searson

Full-bodied red

Intriguing aromas of cherry fruit, smoke and nuts. Lots of similar fruit on the palate with lovely richness, balancing acidity and firm tannin. Impressively long lingering finish.
Pasta with rabbit or hare sauce

Cantina Tollo Colle Secco DOC Montepulciano d'Abruzzo 96

Febvre

Full-bodied red

Pronounced black cherries and other dark fruit aromas with a herbal twist. Plenty of quite fleshy fruit with juicy acidity and balanced tannins. Good and succulent to the end.
Robust pasta or casserole

Collavini Pucino Refosco dal Pedunculo DOC Friuli 98

Ecock

Light fruity red

Very fruity nose, maraschino cherry aromas. Smooth cherry

and blackcurrant fruit with satisfying length and stalky appetising tannins. Fresh and lively.
Escalopes of pork or veal with a rich sauce

Colonna DOC Barbera del Monferrato 96
Wine Warehouse
Light fruity red

Gentle aromas of violets and red berries. Juicy raspberry and redcurrant palate with easy tannins and balanced acidity.
Pizza

Fattoria il Palagio DOCG Chianti 97
MacCormaic
Full-bodied red

Black cherries, almond, chocolate and spice on the nose. Firm, typical Chianti character with lovely weight of ripe fruit and a dry finish.
Cold rare beef

Fazi-Battaglia Marche Sangiovese IGT Marche 97
Select Wines from Italy
Medium-bodied red

Black cherry fruit with spicy touches on the nose. Rich velvety palate with a weight of ripe fruit, balancing tannin and a bitter twist in the finish.
Robust pizza: try mozzarella and pepperoni

Kettmeir Tridentum DOC Teroldego Rotaliano 98
Select Wines from Italy
Medium-bodied red

Rich, ripe berry aromas with vegetal overtones. Mouthfilling fruit of the forest flavours balanced by acidity and tannin giving a clean appetising finish with a bitter twist.
Traditional pappardelle with hare

Leone de Castris DOC Salice Salentino Riserva 96
Select Wines from Italy
Full-bodied red

Slightly dusty aromas of black cherry, chocolate and nuts! Rich palate with concentrated cherry fruit and a nice bite of tannin. A winter warmer.
Venison stew

Taurino DOC Salice Salentino Riserva 96
Ecock
Full-bodied red

Jammy ripe fruit aromas with hints of tobacco. Ripe bramble fruit, not as intense as some from this area but with balanced tannins and acidity.
Good stew, rich in olive oil

Red £10 - £12

Castello di Volpaia DOCG Chianti Classico 97
Oddbins ☆

Full-bodied red

Ripe brambles on the nose, elegant and refined. Velvet palate with lovely soft fruit flavours integrated with chocolate and spice. Smooth and creamy with great length and should develop further.
Beef steak with a rich sauce

La Selvanella DOCG Chianti Classico Riserva 94
Gilbeys ☆

Full-bodied red

Rich cherry fruit, Christmas cake and cedar aromas. Full-bodied with lovely rich, developed fruit. Mellow and long with great balance.
Guinea-fowl with truffle sauce

Lamole di Lamole DOCG Chianti Classico 97
Select Wines from Italy ☆

Medium-bodied red

Cherry and vanilla aromas. Lovely balance of intense ripe fruit, acidity and ripening tannins. Lovely wine with long fruitcake flavoured finish.
Roast pheasant or quail for a dinner party

Villa Cerro DOC Amarone della Valpolicella 95
Tesco ☆

Full-bodied red

Chocolate, black cherries and smoke aromas. Layers of rich figgy fruit, date and coffee bean flavours. Well-balanced structure with a delicious chocolate finish.
After a meal

Le Pergole DOCG Vino Nobile di Montepulciano 95
Dunnes Stores C

Full-bodied red

Intense developed nose with black cherries, plums and cassis. Lots of warm, dark fruit flavours with mellow tannin and balanced acidity. Long finish too.
Roast pigeon

Ruffino Ducale DOCG Chianti Classico Riserva 95
Dillon

Full-bodied red

Mature, spicy vegetal aromas. Wonderful cherry and plum fruit wrapped around a vanillin core. Complex and attractive.
Roast or braised pheasant

Santa Sofia DOC Valpolicella Classico 97
Select Wines from Italy

Light fruity red

Cherry and violet aromas. Ripe cherry fruit flavours in a well-structured, rounded wine, silky in the mouth and fresh in the finish.
Grilled tuna steaks with black olives

Red £12 - £15

Rocca delle Macìe Ser Gioveto IGT Toscana 95
Fields ☆ ☆

Full-bodied red

Creamy, ripe cherry aromas with chocolate spice and a touch of leather. Excellent weight of baked fruit, in perfect harmony with structural frame. Delicious and forward but with lots of time to go.
Quail with polenta

Rocca delle Macìe Tenuta Sant'Alfonso DOCG Chianti Classico 96

Fields ☆

Full-bodied red

Earthy, ripe fruit with lovely Christmas cake aromas. Good weight of ripe berries cut through with acidity and firm tannin. Clean dry finish. Should age very well.

Venison medallions

Fassati Pasiteo DOCG Vino Nobile di Montepulciano 95

Select Wines from Italy C

Full-bodied red

Chocolate and spice on the nose. Robust full-bodied wine with plenty of dark damson fruit and balanced tannin. Long and flavoursome—a good wine.

Venison in a dark wine sauce

Frescobaldi Nipozzano DOCG Chianti Rúfina Riserva 96

Allied Drinks C

Full-bodied red

Fruitcake aromas with vanilla in the background. Good intensity of ripe, floral fruit; well-balanced with a typically bitter, long finish.

Pigeon or fillet of beef

Lamole di Lamole DOCG Chianti Classico Riserva 94

Select Wines from Italy C

Full-bodied red

Emerging aromas of forest fruits and spice. Beautifully balanced with intense ripe fruit flavour, good structure and long, slightly bitter, finish.

Rib of beef or roast game

Ocone DOC Piedirosso Taburno 96

Dalton C

Full-bodied red

Intense red fruit and cherry aromas with a medicinal touch. Complex style with good integration of wood and tannin and a long refreshing finish.

Lamb with mushrooms and sage

Castello Banfi Mandrielle Merlot IGT Toscana 95

Gilbeys

Full-bodied red

Plummy fruit and pepper on the nose. Quite intense on the palate with smoky plum flavours and firm tannin. A Merlot with typically Tuscan structure, different and rewarding with food.

Steak with basil sauce

Lamole di Lamole DOCG Chianti Classico 97

Select Wines from Italy

Full-bodied red

Heady concentrated aromas of ripe berry fruit. Redcurrant and raspberry flavours fan out over the palate with warming alcohol in the finish. Pleasing style.

Guinea-fowl with leeks and mushrooms

Santa Sofia Montegradella DOC Valpolicella Classico Superiore 96

Select Wines from Italy

Light fruity red

Bitter cherry aromas with a herbal twist. Lively fruity palate with plenty of ripe cherry and dark plum flavours. Finishes with a bitter twist—needs food.

Calf's liver and sage

Vistarenni Codirosso IGT Toscana 95

Select Wines from Italy

Medium-bodied red

Appealing, slightly toffeed berry fruit aromas. Mellow plum fruit flavours with toffee and chocolate and a peppery backdrop. Well-structured with good intensity of flavour.

Quail and polenta

Red £15 - £20

Bolla DOC Amarone della Valpolicella Classico 94

Dillon ☆

Full-bodied red

Voluptuous aromas of sweet fruit, vanilla and coconut. Mellow yet very concentrated flavours of bittersweet fruit. Firm tannin and long warm finish. Will develop further and very well.

Parmesan shavings at the end of a meal

Colonna Mondone DOC Monferrato 95

Wine Warehouse ☆

Full-bodied red

Seductive elegant bouquet of cedar and red fruits, mirrored on the palate. Velvet-smooth with silky tannins suffused with spice and a long classic finish.

Teal with wine sauce

Leone de Castris Donna Lisa DOC Salice Salentino Riserva 93

Select Wines from Italy C

Full-bodied red

Distinctly mature aromas of dried fruit, spice, leather and raw meat! Rich, liquoricey palate with ripe fruit and spice and still firm tannin. Full-bodied, complex and earthy. A rewarding wine.

Richly cooked game or a beef casserole

S. Orsola Tenuta Trerose DOCG Vino Nobile di Montepulciano 94

Fitzgerald C

Full-bodied red

Mature aromas of earthy baked fruit compote. Jammy strawberry fruit with still firm tannin. Finishes with a warm earthy, peppery flavour.

Roast boar or a game casserole

Tommasi DOC Amarone della Valpolicella Classico 95

Cassidy C

Full-bodied red

Ripe plum aromas. Quite peppery attack which softens to rich plummy fruit spiked with friendly tannins. Still young but potentially complex and intriguing.

Parmesan or after dinner

Fattoria del Cerro Vigneto Antica Chiusina DOCG Vino Nobile di Montepulciano 93

Febvre

Full-bodied red

Slightly closed on the nose, dark fruit and hints of violet. Earthy character with firm tannins and chewy fruit. Austere and classic, rewarding with food.

Pheasant casserole

Red £20 - £25

Marchesi di Barolo DOCG Barolo Riserva 93

Select Wines from Italy ☆

Full-bodied red

Chocolate and truffle aromas with an edge of burnt rubber. Mouthfilling concentration of dark fruit flavour to balance firm tannin and acidity. Complex and well-structured with a long finish.

Beef braised in wine, preferably Barolo

Serafini e Vidotto Pinot Nero IGT Colli Trevigiani 96

Italian Boutique Wines ☆

Medium-bodied red

Sweet bramble fruit aromas with hints of violets and earth Spicy black cherry fruit flavour with lively acidity and a long rich 'sweet' finish. Very complex and intriguing.

Braised wild duck or pigeon

Columbini Barbi DOCG Brunello di Montalcino 94

Select Wines from Italy C

Full-bodied red

Earthy fruit aromas—a real touch of the farmyard. Young palate with chewy tannins and emerging damson and cherry fruit flavours. Needs time to develop further.

If it must be drunk now, try it with venison

Marchesi di Barolo DOCG Barbaresco Riserva 91

Select Wines from Italy C

Full-bodied red

Tarry, medicinal aromas with a touch of violet. Mouth-puckering tannin covers some emerging, liquorice-flavoured fruit with hints of spice. Should develop well.

Rare, roast beef

Santa Sofia DOC Amarone della Valpolicella Classico Superiore 93

Select Wines from Italy C

Full-bodied red

Rich nose with raisins and sweet spices. Deep concentrated palate with dark chocolate tones and lots of raisiny fruit. Very elegant with a long complex finish.

After dinner

Serafini e Vidotto Rosso Dell'Abazia VdT del Veneto 96

Italian Boutique Wines C

Full-bodied red

Cherry and chocolate aromas with oak backdrop. Well-rounded with ripe fruit and mellow oak. Balanced tannins and acidity and a long finish.

Rack of lamb with garlic and herbs

Vigneto di Campolugno Lamole di Lamole DOCG Chianti Classico Riserva 94

Select Wines from Italy C

Full-bodied red

Restrained elegant nose with cherries and black chocolate. Cherries and chocolate persist on the palate in good concentration but as yet unevolved. Lots of potential.

Rare côte de boeuf

Foradori Granato VdT Atesino 96

Italian Boutique Wines

Medium-bodied red

Aromas of damsons, smoke and violets. Youthful concentra-

tion of berry and cherry
flavours. High acidity and firm
tannin. Definitely for food.
*Beef casserole or aubergine and
mozzarella pizza*

Mastroberardino Radici DOCG Taurasi 95
Select Wines from Italy
Full-bodied red

Very intense dark chocolate,
spicy, earthy aromas with
stalky fruit in the background.
Austere palate with very firm
tannin and a good weight of
concentrated fruit. Good finish
with plenty of grip, a good
keeper at a high price.
*Good steak or rich casserole to
tame the tannins*

Antinori Tignanello IGT Toscana 96
Grants   C
Full-bodied red

Youthful yet highly classic nose
with dark fruits, Oriental spice
and cedarwood all showing
through. Structured young
palate yet deliciously rich
flavours with depth and
concentration set off by new
oak spice. Excellent finish and
future.
*Typically Tuscan pigeon with black
olives*

Ornellaia Marchesi Lodovico A 94
Woodford Bourne   C
Full-bodied red

Complex bouquet of ripe
cherries, chocolate and spice. A
big wine with a weight of ripe
fruit and rich chocolate texture
yet elegant and refined with a
firm backbone of tannin. A
classic with a long time to go,
perfect for a special meal.
Pheasant, wild duck or quail

Sordo Giovanni DOCG Barolo Riserva 90
Gleeson
Full-bodied red

Intense rich dark fruit on the
nose with spice, chocolate and
vanilla. Very big with huge
treacly extract, bitter chocolate
and spice flavours.
Mouthfilling with plentiful
alcohol. Impressive, developed
Barolo.
*Game casserole in wine—
preferably Barolo!*

Umbrian Rosé IGT Umbria
Tesco
Rosé

Tinned strawberry aromas.
Good weight of fruit in the
mouth with spicy pepper and
clean crisp finish.
Salami and sausages outdoors

Lebanon

This ancient and fascinating wine-growing country is known to most of the outside world through the wine of Château Musar. The original inspiration came from lessons learned at the Barton estates in Bordeaux. The grape varieties and barrel-ageing remain definitely Bordelais but Château Musar has its own style. It is rich, deep, powerful, layered in taste and ages wonderfully. Older vintages are now much sought after. Remarkably the Château continued to produce wine through the conflict of the eighties, the 1984 vintage being the only casualty of war.

Red £10 - £12

Hochar Père & Fils Bekaa Valley 95
Grants
Full-bodied red

Spicy-sweet aromas of dried fruit. Rich super-ripe fruit flavours with touches of coffee and caramel. Chewy ripe fruit lasts right to the end. For those who like it rich.
Small fillet steaks with sweet-spicy sauce or garnish

Red £12 - £15

Gaston Hochar Ch. Musar 93
Grants   ☆ ☆
Full-bodied red

Very intense and complex nose with spice, chocolate, caramel and dark fruit. A touch volatile but with no fault. Huge and complex palate with intense sweet, spicy fruit. A power-house wine, with layers of super-ripe flavours and long lingering finish.
Game casserole or roast lamb

Mexico

Mexico is the oldest wine-producing country in the Americas and the newest on our market. The relatively large vineyard area is planted with a wide range of European varieties and Californian favourites such as Zinfandel and Petite Syrah, as well as the infamous Mission grape planted by the early Spanish settlers.

The combination of a long tradition, outside investment from wine and spirit companies and a strong Californian influence on viticulture, has created a promising base for an export wine industry. Mexico is certainly a country to watch as competition builds up in South America.

White £6 - £8

L. A. Cetto Chardonnay Reserva Limitada 97
Grants
Full-bodied white

Aromas of lime and melon. Refreshing fruit flavours—lime, citrus with a crisp dry finish.
Ceviche of salmon or bass

Red £6 - £8

L. A. Cetto Zinfandel 98
Grants
Full-bodied red, fruit-driven

Jammy, stewed rhubarb aromas. Stewed fruit flavours follow on the palate with spicy, peppery tones and a rather hot finish.
Hamburgers and fruity, spicy relishes

New Zealand

The sensation of Marlborough Sauvignon Blanc, which originally put New Zealand on the wine map, has had the unfor-
tunate effect of dominating the country's entire winescape.
Consumers tend to view New Zealand as just Sauvignon and
ignore the variety of interesting wines it now produces.

New Zealand Sauvignon is certainly intriguing, love it or
loathe it, see it as a new classic or total distortion, it simply
cannot be ignored. There is also a good deal of variety in
Sauvignon styles from the opulent tropical fruit bowl style,
streaked with mouth-watering lime, to the leaner nettle and
green pepper versions. None are understated or reserved,
many match brilliantly with Pacific Rim cooking, as popular
in New Zealand as the rest of the world.

Of the other white grapes, Chardonnay from Gisborne or
Hawkes Bay is firm and tightly-knit, very different to the
coolest Australian examples. Riesling is potentially brilliant,
with floral, citrus fruit and a steely mineral backbone. Late-
harvested examples especially from around Nelson on the
South Island, are quite stunning. Other varieties such as
Chenin Blanc, Gewürztraminer and Pinot Gris are also impressive, cool and aromatic, crisp and elegant. In fact the
watchword for New Zealand whites today is variety.

The main story of this year however, is red wine. New Zealand reds have developed much since the early days of unripe fruit and stalky tannins. The improvement has been helped
by really good, ripe vintages in 1997 and 1998. Good New
Zealand Cabernet/Merlot blends are now full of red berry
fruit with lean herbal tones and lovely spice, round and ripe
yet with cool reserve. They may never rival the jammy fruit
and sweet mint and vanilla of Australia, but perhaps the world
has enough super ripe Cabs to welcome a little restraint. Pinot
Noir is even more exciting. Light in body yet intense in flavour, spicy, earthy, rich and intriguing; it is not Burgundy, but
has all the Pinot magic.

White £6 - £8

The Sounds Marlborough Sauvignon Blanc 97

Dunnes Stores   C

Aromatic white, fruit-driven

Lots of blackcurrant leaf and nettle aromas. Good balance of green apple fruit and zippy fresh acidity. Very attractive, inviting wine.

Seafood with herb mayonnaise

Azure Bay Chardonnay/ Semillon 98

Tesco

Full-bodied white

Ripe, tropical fruit aromas and plenty of ripe fruit flavour to follow. Intense and mouthfilling with nice crisp green fruit in the finish.

Lobster with butter/cream sauce

White £6 - £8

Babich Marlborough Pinot Gris 98

Gleeson

Aromatic white, fruit-driven

Pronounced aromas of lemon and apricot, and a touch of almond. Rich, with mouthfilling weight and balancing crisp acidity. Slightly honeyed fruit flavours linger right through.

Vegetable tart or strudel

Babich Marlborough Sauvignon Blanc 98

Gleeson

Aromatic white, fruit-driven

Ripe stewed gooseberry aromas. Bracing green fruit flavour with crisp clean finish.

Seafood mayonnaise

Montana Marlborough Chardonnay 98

Grants

Full-bodied white

Quite restrained and elegant on the nose with a touch of steeliness. Follows through on the palate with stylish, subtle fruit, very well-balanced and elegant with a long finish.

Chicken with a cream or mildly spiced sauce

Montana Marlborough Sauvignon Blanc 98

Grants

Aromatic white, fruit-driven

Ripe gooseberry aromas. Plenty of punchy ripe fruit flavour with lively acidity. Well-balanced and long with lasting green fruit flavours.

Smoked fish chowder

Te Whetu Gisborne Dry White 97

Allied Drinks

Light fruity white

Lime zest and honeysuckle on the nose. Refreshing, fruity style with lively acidity and a crisp finish.

Seafood starter; Chinese prawn toasts

The Sounds Marlborough Chardonnay 97

Dunnes Stores

Full-bodied white

Attractive nose of honey and ripe tropical fruit. Crisp refreshing acidity and mouthfilling flavours of pineapple and apricot. Clean finish.

Smoked fish pie

White £8 - £10

Millton Gisborne Te Arai Vineyard Chenin Blanc 98

Tesco ☆

Aromatic white, fruit-driven

Lovely rich aromas of wild honey and lavender. Clean, lively acidity and a nice weight of honey and pineapple flavours which linger right through the finish.

Seafood curry

Framingham Marlborough Dry Riesling 98

Gleeson C

Aromatic white, fruit-driven

Oily, ripe fruit aromas with hints of marzipan. Good weight of rounded tropical flavours cut through with refreshing citrus acidity.

Japanese tempura

Montana Reserve Marlborough Barrique-fermented Chardonnay 97

Grants C

Full-bodied white, oak

Aromas of ripe melon and butterscotch. Well-balanced palate with good weight of elegant fruit. Silky textured with a long, stylish finish.

Well-flavoured chicken with cream sauce

Morton Estate Hawkes Bay Chardonnay 96

Dillon

Full-bodied white

Honeysuckle and lemon aromas, with a nutty element. Layers of tropical fruit flavour with a hint of white pepper. A nicely balanced, elegant wine.

Chicken and bacon pie or a gratin

of smoked fish

Morton Estate Hawkes Bay Sauvignon Blanc 98

Dillon

Aromatic white, fruit-driven

Stewed apples and nettles from the nose. Nice weight of Bramley apple fruit with citrus acidity and a clean finish.

Snapper and tomatoes

Nobilo Fall Harvest Sauvignon Blanc 98

Barry & Fitzwilliam

Aromatic white, fruit-driven

Aromatic aromas of nettles and gooseberries. Flavours of gooseberry and green apple fruit set off by lively acidity and a crisp clean finish.

Warm salad of roasted asparagus

Selaks Gisborne Fumé 97

Karwig

Aromatic white, fruit-driven

Very intense gooseberry aromas. Good concentration of fruit with an oily background and a long smoky finish. Full but restrained, a lovely style of wine.

Barbecued red snapper with grilled vegetables

Selaks Premium Selection Sauvignon Blanc 98

Karwig

Aromatic white, fruit-driven

Tomato plant aromas. Ripe palate with rich gooseberry and elderflower tones. Good weight of flavour and refreshing citrus acidity cutting through the finish.

Thai seafood

Shingle Peak Marlborough Riesling 97
Mitchell

Aromatic white, fruit-driven

Limes and grapefruit on the nose with a touch of kerosene creeping in. Crisp and zippy with a streak of lemon acidity cutting right through the green fruit flavours. Balanced and beautifully long.
Fish cakes with lemongrass and coriander

Shingle Peak Marlborough Pinot Gris 97
Mitchell

Aromatic white, fruit-driven

Apple and melon aromas follow to apple, greengage and lemon flavours. Very crisp with a long refreshing finish.
Little vegetable flans

St Clair Marlborough Sauvignon Blanc 98
Greenhills

Aromatic white, fruit-driven

Fresh green fruit aromas, which follow on the palate. Nice balance and clean, crisp finish.
Zesty seafood salad

Villa Maria Private Bin Riesling 98
Allied Drinks

Aromatic white, fruit-driven

Juicy fruits on the nose with floral touches; ripe fruit flavours with lively citrus acidity. Good depth and length of flavour.
Tempura and spicy fishcakes

Villa Maria Private Bin Sauvignon Blanc 98
Allied Drinks

Aromatic white, fruit-driven

Pronounced gooseberry aromas. Really fresh green apple and nettle flavours with balanced acidity and a delicious fruity finish.
Baked stuffed red peppers

White £10 - £12

Nautilus Marlborough Sauvignon Blanc 98
Cassidy   C

Aromatic white, fruit-driven

Blackcurrant leaves and green fruit aromas, very cool. Youthful with loads of gooseberry fruit and crisp refreshing acidity.
Thai noodles with seafood

Hunter's Sauvignon Blanc 98
Gilbeys

Aromatic white, fruit-driven

Very aromatic nose. Lively green fruit flavours. Full, with good weight of mouthwatering green fruit and lively, citrus acidity. Long crisp finish.
Smoked fish chowder

Lawson's Dry Hills Marlborough Gewürztraminer 98
Febvre

Aromatic white, fruit-driven

Floral spicy aromas, rose petals and orange peel. Dry and full with very spicy flavours and zippy fresh acidity. Lots of citrus peel and honey, and a really spicy finish. Quite a mouthful!
Oriental dishes especially Chinese

Lawson's Dry Hills Marlborough Sauvignon Blanc 98

Febvre

Aromatic white, fruit-driven

Fresh grassy floral aromas with a touch of lemon. Well-balanced wine with elegant green fruit and rounded, full body. Stylishly understated!

Mussels in cream and ginger sauce or chicken with mustard

Red £6 - £8

Montana Marlborough Cabernet Sauvignon/Merlot 98

Grants   C

Full-bodied red

Earthy aromas mingle with berry fruit and hints of vanilla. Good weight of ripe blackberry fruit and chewy texture. Young and should develop very well.

The youthful style is good with a grilled lamb steak

Red £8 - £10

Te Whetu Hawkes Bay Red 97

Allied Drinks   C

Medium-bodied red

Stalky red berry fruit aromas with shades of green pepper. Dry with plenty of stalky berry fruit with spicy overtones. Well-balanced tannin and acidity and nice complexity.

Good Irish stew

St Clair Marlborough Merlot 98

Greenhills

Light fruity red

Slightly spicy herbal nose. Clean fresh style with soft berry fruit flavours and mild tannin. Easy-drinking style.

Pasta with spicy sausage

Red £10 - £12

Montana Reserve Marlborough Barrique-fermented Merlot 96

Grants   ☆

Full-bodied red, fruit-driven

Red fruit aromas with a touch of black pepper. Plenty of weight on the palate with red fruit flavours and spice balanced by tannin. Complex and elegant with a very long finish.

Noisettes of lamb

Babich Irongate Cabernet/Merlot 96

Gleeson   C

Full-bodied red, fruit-driven

Blackcurrant jam with a touch of oak. Mouthfilling fruit and very ripe berry flavours with refreshing acidity to balance and a good structure. Nice finish with a touch of pepper.

Spicy lamb noisettes

Babich Marlborough Pinot Noir 97

Gleeson

Medium-bodied red

Slightly earthy, farmyard tones. Crisp acidity and good weight of rounded fruit. Some cherry and spice overtones. Good finish.

Deliciously different with roasted salmon

Portugal

No country's wine industry has benefited so much from money and modernisation as that of Portugal. For a long time, Portuguese reds were the wine world's best kept secret. Always impressive in a rather rustic way, they were labelled an acquired taste. Now fourteen years on from EU membership and the break up of the co-ops, Portugal's wines are ready to take the world by storm.

The basis for Portugal's achievement is the quality and variety of its indigenous grape varieties. Preserved through isolation, grapes such as the Baga, the Touriga Nacional, the Periquita, are world class and unique. Portugal's own geography is another factor. This is not just another hot country wine region. Certainly summer in the Douro is a real scorcher, but Portugal is essentially Atlantic and has a range of altitudes which provide varied microclimates.

The natural resources, combined with money and freedom, needed only a little inspiration to realise Portugal's potential. This was provided by winemakers such as Dirk van der Nieport and Jão de Almeida in the Douro, Alvaro Castro in Dão, David Baverstock in the Alentejo and, in a more commercial way, by the Bright Brothers. Possibly most creative of all is Luis Pato in Bairrada who produces the intriguingly complex Vinho Barro and brooding, oaky Vinho Pan as really top examples of serious age-worthy wine.

The story is not all red either. Portuguese white wines have also taken a quality leap. Look out for re-invented Vinho Verde as the trendy white of the next millennium.

Red £5 or less

JP Barrel Selection Red VR Terras do Sado 93
Tesco ☆
Medium-bodied red

Earthy, baked fruit aromas. Rich, round and full on the palate with a lovely, long spicy finish.
Pork with clams

Aristocrata VR Estramaduranv
Karwig
Medium-bodied red

Meaty earthy nose. Lively acidity with dusty dark fruit flavours developing into chewy, earthy fruit. Nice spicy tones and long dry finish.
Kidneys with wine sauce

Segada VR Ribatejo 97
Oddbins

Medium-bodied red

Dark berry fruit on the nose. Stalky tannins tend to dominate the palate with dusty fruit flavours and high acidity. Quite dry and austere in the finish. Very good with rich, fatty food.
Lamb and bean stew

Red £5 - £6

Aliança Palmela VQPRD 94
Oddbins

Medium-bodied red

Ripe bramble aromas. Dry and firm with good weight of quite plummy fruit developing into cherry rich flavours. Nice bite of balancing tannin and good finish.
Kidneys and sausages

Caves Bonifácio VdM nv
Dalton

Full-bodied red

Ripe brambly fruit on the nose, slightly hot. Baked brambles backed up by firm tannin and balancing acidity. Well-made wine.
Pork and tomato stew.

Charamba DOC Douro 96
Karwig

Full-bodied red

Tart cherry fruit on the nose. Good weight of fruit, with lively acidity and ripe tannin. Nicely balanced palate with slightly dusty bramble flavours and good finish.
Sausage and bean casserole

Tesco DOC Dão 96
Tesco

Medium-bodied red

Smoky baked fruit on the nose. Jammy palate with firm tannin and spicy tones. Dry, appetising wine, slightly short on the finish.
Stuffed lamb's heart with garlic

Red £6 - £8

Quinta de Parrotes VQPRD Alenquer 96
Dunnes Stores   C

Medium-bodied red

Attractive plums and chocolate on the nose. Good weight of baked plummy fruit; well-structured with weight, body and a clean refreshing finish.
Game casserole

Casa Cadaval Muge Tinto VR Ribatejo 96
Molloy's

Full-bodied red

Nice strawberry fruit on the nose with well-structured palate and good weight of baked fruit flavour. Quite big and mouthfilling with a long fruity finish.
Lamb and aubergine casserole

Fonseca Periquita VR Terras do Sado 96
Gilbeys

Full-bodied red

Dusty nose--scorched earth and baked fruit. Firm tannic structure well-supported by fruit. A well-balanced, integrated wine with a warm jammy finish.
Pork ribs with beans

Quinta de Vila Freire DOC Douro 96
River Wines
Full-bodied red

Baked plummy fruit on the nose. Firm tannin but with plenty of fruit similar to the nose with rich baked spicy flavours and a long warm finish.
Lentil lasagne

Quinta do Ribeirinho DO Bairrada 96
Karwig
Full-bodied red

Opulent nose of dark berry fruit, spices, mint and other herbs. Very firm tannin and high acidity at present masking the fruit. Typically Portuguese--lots of character.
Pork and aubergines

Red £8 - £10

ACTV Torres Vedras Reserva VQPRD 89
Karwig ☆ ☆
Full-bodied red

Black cherries, allspice and figs on the nose. Chunky fruit and ripe tannin; delicious mouthfilling complexity with mellow fruit and spice flavours developing on the palate. Very long and lingering.
Roast leg of pork

Calcos do Tanha DOC Douro 95
River Wines C
Full-bodied red

Intense ripe fruit--blackcurrant, berries and cherries. Big and flavoursome with well-structured tannins and hints of vanilla and chocolate spice. Delicious now with plenty of time to go.
Pheasant with chestnuts

Fonseca Quinta de Camarate VR Terras do Sado 94
Gilbeys
Full-bodied red

Developed aromas of warm autumn fruit. Firm structure with just yielding tannins, fresh acidity and good fruit. Well-balanced, properly-structured wine.
Pot-roasted pigeon

Red £10 - £12

Casa Cadaval Muge Cabernet Sauvignon VR Robato 96
Molloy's ☆
Full-bodied red

Lovely fresh blackcurrant and vanilla aromas. Firm and structured with excellent ripe fruit beginning to show. A very good wine now which will repay keeping for a few years.
Game casserole

Casa Cadaval Muge Pinot Noir VR Ribatejo 95
Molloy's C ££
Full-bodied red

Complex and ripe with tinned strawberry and cigarbox aromas. Lovely balance of tannin, acidity and ripe fruit mingling with spice and hints of chocolate. Long and delicious and great value.
Wild duck with Port

Casa Ferreirrinha Vinha Grande Ferreira DOC Douro 95

Karwig   C

Full-bodied red

Spicy raisins and black chocolate on the nose. Mouthfilling flavours with peppery spice, firm and well-structured with potential to develop further.
Grilled lamb with garlic and rosemary

Casa Cadaval Muge Trincadeira Preta VR Ribatejo 96

Molloy's

Full-bodied red

Ripe blackcurrant aromas. Plenty of ripe summer pudding fruit with balancing acidity and tannin filling the mouth with delicious lasting flavours.
Lambs' kidneys in Madeira sauce

Red £15 - £20

Quinta dos Rogues Touriga Nacional DOC Dão 96

River Wines   ☆ ☆

Full-bodied red

Developed bouquet with fig, cherry and blackcurrant fruit. Big and mouthfilling with firm tannins and loads of blackcurrant fruit with delicious vanilla, toffee and chocolate nuances. Long and fruity with plenty of time to go.
Pigeon with wine and olives

Red £20 - £25

Luis Pato Vinha Pan DOC Bairrada 95

Karwig   C

Full-bodied red

Deep intense aromas of cedary fruit. Firm dry tannins with bramble fruit flavours. Big and bold with plenty of flavour behind the structure. Drinks well now with robust food and should age gracefully.
Rare roast venison

Wines of
Portugal

A New World of
Unexpected Pleasures

Portugal

'The Cork Wine Merchants'

- Over 500 quality wines
- Quality staff on hand for advice
- 8 shops to choose from
- Full party/function service
- Wine consultancy service available
- Corporate and private tastings arranged
- Direct wine deliveries nationwide arranged
- Wholesale price-list for on-trade available on request
- Wine list available on request
- Wine Club—Douglas and Bishopstown Wine Club

Main Office
Unit 27, St Patrick's Mill Douglas, Cork
Phone: (021) 895 227/746
Fax: (021) 893 391
Wine consultant—Gary O'Donovan 087 263 2211

Branches
Douglas (021) 363 650 Bishopstown (021) 343 416
Blackpool (021) 398 177 Summerhill (021) 505 444
Oliver Plunkett St (021) 277 626
Shandon St (021) 399 121 Midleton (021) 613 001
Riversdale Shopping Centre (021) 613 792

'We have all the wine in the world'

South Africa

South Africa had a very difficult task to re-enter the world wine market after an absence of twenty odd years during which time the whole New World revolution had taken place. The structure of its industry, the lingering restrictions on the import of vines, constant pressure on the rand, made development slow and difficult. A handful of quality-motivated producers persevered in the struggle to respond to market needs and finally succeeded; their main problem was tiny quantities.

In reality, quality South African wines will be in short or inconsistent supply for some time. Now the honeymoon of goodwill which greeted the new South Africa is beginning to subside and more pragmatic market forces are likely to become the driving force. Yet the picture is a lot more positive than all this might suggest. The quality of South African wine is extremely high. Since the early nineties, the number of wineries in the Cape has increased from 170 to 300. Many are run by a new generation who have bypassed the growing pains of New World viticulture and are going straight for cool climate areas, less clinical vinification methods and more attention to 'making wine in the vineyard'.

Cabernet Sauvignon, after some rather weedy early examples, has emerged sleek and balanced with lovely herbal tones and restrained fruit. Pinot Noir is a revelation, at least in the hands of Peter Findlayson whose Walker's Bay vineyards produce the best in the country if not in the entire southern hemisphere.

Lower-priced wines are a bit more difficult and more sensitive to shortages in supply. Pinotage has not quite captured consumer imagination and off-dry Chenin was even less successful. A number of companies such as the Australian-influenced Long Mountain, Nederburg, and the lesser labels of the Bergkelder group, have succeeded remarkably.

White £5 or less

Simonsig Adelblanc 98
United Beverages ££
Light fruity white

Clean, soft and round with hints of peach and lemon. Quite intense melon fruit. A well-balanced wine and great value.
Salads or without food

Long Mountain Chenin Blanc 97
Fitzgerald
Light fruity white

Slightly damp wool aromas, typical Chenin. Ripe, slightly tropical fruit with very crisp lemon acidity and a good finish.
Spring rolls

Tesco Cape Chenin Blanc nv
Tesco
Light fruity white

Nice fresh honey and citrus-style fruit with balanced acidity and a refreshing dry finish.
Canapés

White £5 - £6

Ryland's Grove Chenin Blanc 98
Tesco ☆
Aromatic white, fruit-driven

Complex developed aromas with floral and toffee apple notes. Good weight of ripe rich fruit, honeyed apple, and brisk balancing acidity. Fresh, long finish. An interesting wine.
Courgette soufflé

Cape Mountain Chardonnay 98
Gleeson
Light fruity white

Stewed apple aromas with a touch of lemon. Apple fruit flavours follow through with crisp acidity and a dry finish.
Chicken pastries or vol-au-vents

Goiya Kgeisje Chardonnay/ Sauvignon Blanc 99
Tesco
Aromatic white, fruit-driven

Ripe dessert apple aromas with a hint of nuts. Flavour of sweetened stewed apple with plentiful supporting alcohol and a crisp finish.
Chicken salad

Long Mountain Chardonnay 98
Fitzgerald
Full-bodied white

Melon and pineapple aromas which carry through in flavour. Crisp green fruit acidity cuts through. Long, warm finish.
Creamy pasta

White £6 -£8

Bellingham Chardonnay 98
Dunnes Stores
Full-bodied white

Honey and tropical fruit with a hint of lime on the nose. Ripe, big and mouthfilling with pineapple-like fruit and a lovely clean finish.
Pork kebabs

De Wetshof Bon Vallon Chardonnay Sur Lie 98
Oddbins
Light fruity white
Fresh, crisp and full of fruit with a clean pleasant finish. Nice easy-drinking style but a touch expensive.
Avocado salad

Drostdy Hof Steen Chenin Blanc 98
Febvre
Light fruity white
Clean, rather candied nose. Very fresh palate with lively fruit flavours and a crisp finish.
Party curry

Fair Valley Bush Wine Chenin Blanc 99
Oddbins
Light fruity white
Soft, floral nose. Nice weight of apple fruit with crisp acidity Light, easy-drinking style..
Chicken with apricots

Hoopenburg Sauvignon Blanc 99
O'Brien's
Aromatic white, fruit-driven
Aromatic nose, gooseberry and riper tropical tones. Very fruit-driven; green fruit, gooseberry flavours with clean, balanced finish.
Smoked cheese salad

Impala Chenin Blanc 98
Allied Drinks
Light fruity white
Rather neutral on the nose, slightly oily. Dry and crisp with citrus and apple flavours. Clean finish.
Salad or spicy Indian pastries

Ken Forrester Chenin Blanc 98
Oddbins
Light fruity white
Concentrated honey and lemon aromas, slightly smoky. Honeyed fruit; rounded long and satisfying.
Escalope of pork with lemon and coriander

Simonsig Sauvignon Blanc 98
United Beverages
Aromatic white, fruit-driven
Grassy green apple fruit aromas. Crunchy green fruit with mouthwatering acidity and a clean crisp finish.
Herby mussels or other seafood

Weltevrede Estate Gewürztraminer 98
Wine Warehouse
Aromatic white, fruit-driven
Pungent nose with rose petal, honey and lychee aromas. Ripe tropical fruit with peach and pineapple fruit. Nicely balanced with well-integrated flavours; not overpowering.
Grilled red pepper canapés

Weltevrede Rhine Riesling 98
Wine Warehouse
Aromatic white, fruit-driven
Aromatic peach-like fruit on the nose. Apple and citrus flavours with crisp acidity. Nicely balanced wine.
Prawns in filo pastry with drinks before dinner

White £8 - £10

L'Avenir Chardonnay 97
Dunnes Stores C

Full-bodied white

Elegant aromatic nose. Palate laden with ripe tropical fruit, pineapples and mangoes in a lovely creamy texture. Nice oaky background and great length.
Brill or turbot in a cream sauce

Dieu Donné Chardonnay 97
Gleeson

Full-bodied white, oak

Aromas of ripe apples and honey. Big and broad with ripe apple and peach flavours and a hint of oak. Well-made, attractive wine.
Chicken with spicy noodles

White £10 - 312

Stellenryck Chardonnay 97
Febvre C

Full-bodied white

Ripe melon, butterscotch and toast on the nose. Buttery, smooth palate with mouthfilling flavours of fruit, vanilla and toast and a warm mellow finish that goes on and on.
Chicken in a seafood sauce and other OTT sorts of dishes

Klein Constantia Chardonnay 96
Gilbeys

Full-bodied white, oak

Buttery fruit and oak on the nose. Ripe and buttery and quite oaky on the palate. Well-structured and may well improve with another year in bottle.
Baked chicken with a herb crust

White £12 - £15

Cathedral Cellar Chardonnay 97
TDL ☆

Full-bodied white, oak

Attractive smoky bouquet with vanilla notes. Delicious concentrated melon and peach fruit with creamy vanilla. Long harmonious finish to a very classic wine.
Salmon with a cream sauce

Plaisir de Merle Chardonnay 96
Dillon

Full-bodied white, oak

Butterscotch aromas with ripe, slightly floral fruit. Citrus fruit flavours in a creamy texture, with a caramel-toffee finish.
Roast chicken; rich fish and shellfish dishes

Red £5 or less

Adelberg Cabernet Saivignon Merlot 98
United Beverages

Medium-bodied red

Brambles and blackcurrants on the nose. Soft, ripe fruit with crisp acidity and a bite of tannin. Nice spicy background and decent length.
Stir-fries or bobotie

Red £5 - £6

Cape Indaba Pinotage 98
Barry & Fitzwilliam C

Medium-bodied red

Berry and cherry fruit mix with floral aromas and a touch of spice. Complexity follows

through with flavoursome fruit and chewy texture. Satisfying long finish.
Barbecues and most grilled meats

Long Mountain Cabernet Sauvignon 98
Fitzgerald

Medium-bodied red

Upfront fruit of the forest aromas. Nice ripe fruit and crisp acidity with a touch of tannin. Pleasant, easy-drinking style and well-priced.
Mexican tacos with meat

Long Mountain Merlot/ Shiraz 98
Fitzgerald

Light fruity red

Slightly vegetal bramble fruit. Round plummy palate with hints of spice. Light and easy-drinking.
Pasta with tomato, pepper, ham and chili sauce

Tesco International Wine Maker Cabernet Sauvignon/Merlot nv
Tesco

Medium-bodied red

Smoky blackcurrant fruit on the nose. Good concentration of stewed fruit flavour with balanced tannin. Dry and slightly dusty in a typically South African way.
Lamb, bacon and pepper kebabs

Red £6 - £8

Fairview Zinfandel Carignan 98
Oddbins   C

Full-bodied red, fruit-driven

Spicy blackberry and plum aromas. Oozes soft fruit flavours, fruitcake richness

with spice lingering into the finish. Soft and easy to drink, a forward style.
Spicy meat, especially Oriental duck

Ariston Ruby Cabernet/ Merlot 98
Findlater

Medium-bodied red

Ripe fruit with quite nutty aromas. Dry with ripe blackberry fruit, refreshing acidity and firm tannin. Well-structured with a typical bitter twist in the finish.
Kidneys with cream and wine sauce

Cape Mountain Pinotage 97
Gleeson

Medium-bodied red

Jammy, rubbery nose. Well-structured with nice berry fruit, spice and balanced tannins. Quite hot and peppery in the finish.
Kebabs

Clos Malverne Cabernet/ Shiraz 98
Dunnes Stores

Full-bodied red, fruit-driven

Quite vegetal and farmyardy on the nose with a dash of burnt rubber. Ripe fruit and soft tannins on the palate with a long ripe, fruit-driven finish.
Tagine of lamb with prunes

Clos Malverne Pinotage 98
Dunnes Stores

Medium-bodied red

Plummy fruit aromas with hints of mint. Tarry black fruits on the palate and soft tannin. Rather dusty feel, but well-made and drinking now.
Chunky grilled sausages

Nederburg Paarl Cabernet Sauvignon 96
Dillon

Medium-bodied red

Ripe bramble fruit with a hint of smoke. Good weight of blackcurrant fruit flavours, creamy vanilla and a long dry finish.

Grilled, marinated ostrich steaks

Niel Joubert Pinotage 97
TDL

Medium-bodied red

Quite medicinal and smoky on the nose; richer palate with chocolatey fruit and spice.

Skewered kidneys with bacon

Schoone Gevel Merlot 98
Tesco

Medium-bodied red

Nice plummy intensity on the nose. Very fruit-driven with plums and cherries coming through. Soft structure with slight astringent twist in the finish.

Spicy kebabs or kefte

Simonsig Pinotage 97
United Beverages

Medium-bodied red

Meaty, earthy fruit aromas. Chewy style with big fruit extract and firm tannin. Rather baked character, burnt toffee hints in the fruit. Interesting and long.

Pot-roasted beef and beer

Tesco Beyers Truter Pinotage nv
Tesco

Medium-bodied red

Very ripe baked nose with hints of rubber tyres. Stewed tea, Pinotage style with plummy spicy fruit underneath and a good bite of tannin.

Hamburgers

Tesco Cabernet Sauvignon Reserve nv
Tesco

Full-bodied red, fruit-driven

Very ripe nose. Real cookies and cream stuff, very soft and fruity, just holding together. Crowd-pleasing, easy style.

Stir-fried beef or lamb

Red £8 - £10

Hoopenburg Cabernet Sauvignon 97
O'Briens   C

Full-bodied red, fruit-driven

Complex, meaty and rich on the nose with ripe fruit aromas mixed with tar and leather. Well-integrated fruit and elegant structure with long complex character.

Steak or roast beef

Hoopenburg Merlot 98
O'Briens   C

Medium-bodied red

Ripe berry fruit on the nose. Palate of concentrated berry fruit, spice and yielding tannins. Approachable but classic style.

Duck in a fruity sauce or Chinese style

Bellingham Pinotage 98
Cassidy

Medium-bodied red

Herbal fruit on the nose with chewy liquorice palate, firm tannin and high acidity adding an astringent note. Good, longlasting flavours.

Leg of autumn lamb with garlic and herbs

Fleur du Cap Merlot 96
Febvre

Medium-bodied red

Ripe plummy aromas with spice and earthy tones. Rich plummy fruit with earthy, savoury side. Firm tannin provides a good structure to balance the rich fruit.
Gammon steaks or a robust casserole

Villiera Cabernet Sauvignon 96
Grants

Full-bodied red, fruit-driven

Lovely ripe autumnal fruit aromas with underlying vanilla and allspice tones. Well-rounded and balanced with nicely integrated fruit and spice flavours.
Duck breast with a fruity sauce

Villiera Cru Monro Cabernet Sauvignon/Merlot 97
Grants

Medium-bodied red

Blackcurrant and summer pudding aromas with woody hints. Chewy and well-structured; tannins still very firm and dominating the fruit, but should develop well.
Shoulder of lamb with herbs or lamb kebabs

Red £10 - £12

Stellenzicht Merlot/ Cabernet Franc 94
Fitzgerald   C

Full-bodied red

Ripe, fruit pastille and blackberry juice aromas. Good concentration of ripe plummy fruit spiked with tart redcurrant

flavours. Firm tannin. Elegant, restrained style—a wine for food.
Partridge with chestnuts

Groot Constantia Pinotage 94
Fitzgerald

Medium-bodied red

Rather medicinal, farmyard aromas. Slightly dusty fruit but well-balanced with ripe tannin and plenty of individual character.
Beef in Guinness

Stellenzicht Shiraz 96
Fitzgerald

Full-bodied red, fruit-driven

Dark fruit aromas with tar and rubber nuances. Rather chewy palate though tannins are softening and are balanced with plenty of fruit. Long, spicy finish.
Lamb and potato casserole

Red £12 - £15

Cathedral Cellar Cabernet Sauvignon 94
TDL   C

Full-bodied red, fruit-driven

Slightly stalky, twiggy blackcurrant aromas. Good weight of restrained blackberry and blackcurrant fruit with subtle oak spice. Long and elegant, very classic style which will improve over time.
Crown of lamb with dried fruit stuffing

Plaisir de Merle Cabernet Sauvignon 96
Dillon   C

Full-bodied red, fruit-driven

Bramble fruit aromas with earthy tones of damp under-

growth. Mouthfilling fruit flavours—cherry, blackcurrants—well-supported by alcohol. Rounded balanced structure, and a long finish with spice and chocolate coming through the fruit.
Medallions of beef with port and shallots

Hamilton Russell Vineyards Pinot Noir 97
Gilbeys
Medium-bodied red

Quite rich fruit aromas with hints of chocolate and earthy tones. Ripe cherry fruit and balanced tannin and acidity. Slightly warm in the finish.
Spiced dishes of lighter game, such as glazed quail

Red £15 - £20

Hartenberg Estate Merlot 95
Fields
Full-bodied red, fruit-driven

Spicy herbaceous touch on the nose. Smooth and big mouthfeel with fruit following from the palate with similar spicy nuances. Big and chunky with plenty of length.
Guinea-fowl with a mushroom sauce

Editor's choice: New World bargains

Most New World countries established themselves originally as value for money. But in the last year or so prices as well as quality and range have increased and Australian wine seems likely to rise further. Our top ten bargains offer great value in different styles and types of wine, demonstrating character and interest ahead of their price range.

Rosemount Estate Shiraz/Cabernet 1998

Antu Mapu Sauvignon Blanc Reserva 1998

Las Casas del Toqui Chardonnoy Grand Réserve 1997

Villard Pinot Noir

Montana Marlborough Cabernet Sauvignon/Merlot 1998

L'Avenir Chardonnay 1997

Inglenook Estate Cellars Cabernet Sauvignon

Gallo Sonoma Sonoma County Pinot Noir 1995

Peter Lehmann The Barossa Semillon 1997

Lindauer Brut nv

Spain

The last few years have been a success story for Spanish wine: improved quality, the opening up of new regions and revitalising of areas such as Navarra and the Penedès. In the past decade Rioja has doubled its home sales and increased its export market by three. However, Spain now faces the challenge of its own success, to preserve its markets in the face of inevitable price rises.

Rioja went through a difficult patch in the seventies and early eighties, quality dipped and the market with it. But the response of big investment and the pursuit of excellence—specifically, lower yields, more fruit extraction and more careful use of better oak—have brought Rioja back on the world stage with a number of super wines, helped along the way by a few terrific vintages. For several years now, Rioja has been unable to meet the demand for its wines. Most producers do not own their own vineyards and with demand at a premium grape prices have risen steadily. In 1998 grapes were simply auctioned off to the highest bidder and with such pressure on volume, fruit quality was not even considered. A bad frost this year threatens a very short harvest and even more pressure on prices. All this is bad news for the winemaker, and threatens to accompany higher prices with uneven quality for the consumer.

A region such as Rioja with a long tradition and unique product is likely to survive these difficulties. Quality producers are already beginning to acquire their own vineyards and to absorb extra costs rather than pass them on to the customer. However, price rises are not confined to Rioja. Navarra, which has a new and trendy market, has also had a number of very short harvests and prices have gone up and are likely to increase further. Producers hope the rises in Rioja will help them to maintain their market though the new and trendy rarely comes with loyalty.

Other fashionable newcomers such as Priorato and Ribera del Duero began with high prices and have generally gone higher, though are still better hunting grounds for well-priced quality than the well-known areas. The south, La Mancha, Valdepeñas and the smaller DOs such as Yecla and Jumilla, do offer great value, moderately priced wines. Replanting of these areas has meant more decent, well-made reds from Cencibel, Garnacha and a number of other quality grape varieties in place of the dull whites from the infamous Airen

White £5 or less

Las Campañas Chardonnay DO Navarra 98

Dunnes Stores   ££

Light fruity white

Appealing ripe fruit on the nose. Dry but with very ripe apple and fruit cocktail flavours. Nicely balanced wine and good value.
Quiche or buffet food

Castillo San Simon DO Jumilla 97

Greenhills

Full-bodied white

Slightly oxidized bouquet with nutty, burnt citrus aromas. Full weighty palate with burnt fruit and salty flavours and balancing acidity. Typical old-style Spanish with lots of character.
Rich, garlicky fish stew

White £5 - £6

Con Class Especial DO Rueda 98

Searson

Aromatic white

Fresh gooseberry aromas and crisp green apple and gooseberry flavours. Well-balanced with a dry refreshing finish.
Fishcakes or Szechuan prawns

White £6 - £8

Herederos del Marqués de Riscal DO Rueda 98

Findlater   ☆

Aromatic white

Intense yet elegant aromas of green fruit. Full, ripe palate with slightly waxy feel; nettle and gooseberry flavours. Well-balanced acidity and good length of flavour.
Seafood with garlic and herbs

Raimat Chardonnay DO Costers del Segre 98

Grants   C

Full-bodied white

Very honeyed aromas, aromatic and floral. Oily, smooth texture with a weight of honeyed lemon fruit--lemon meringue pie flavours! Layers of flavour with balanced, refreshing acidity and a long impressive finish.
Baked chicken with apricots or mangoes

Chivite Gran Feudo Chardonnay DO Navarra 98

TDL

Light fruity white

Ripe fruit with hints of toast and honey. Nicely balanced with good weight and balancing acidity. Long fruity finish.
Spanish omelette

Herederos del Marqués de Riscal Sauvignon DO Rueda 98

Findlater

Aromatic white

Clean grassy nose. Smooth and nicely balanced acidity and fruit, green fruit flavours and some length in the finish.
Seafood and rice

Mantel Blanco Sauvignon Blanc DO Rueda 98
Approach Trade
Aromatic white

Aromatic nose with ripe gooseberries and hints of nettle. Quite herby green apple fruit, fresh and crisp.
Prawns in garlic

Mantel Blanco Verdejo-Sauvignon Blanc DO Rueda 98
Approach Trade
Aromatic white

Very aromatic grassy character leaping out of the glass. Ripe apple and peach fruit, very fresh and clean with a crisp finish.
Goat's cheese and pepper salad

Marqués de Cáceres DOC Rioja 98
Grants
Light dry white

Fresh and yeasty aromas with a touch of quince. Nice weight of mouthwatering fruit offset by alcohol and refreshing acidity. Smooth and elegant mouthfeel with a long finish.
Baked plaice or sole with butter and herbs

Torres Gran Viña Sol Chardonnay DO Penedès 98
Woodford Bourne
Full-bodied white

Clean fresh aromas of lemon and lime with floral tones. Lively palate with orange marmalade and honeysuckle flavours. Well-balanced, round and long.
Mussel stew

Torres Viña Sol DO Penedès 98
Woodford Bourne
Light dry white

Fresh, very clean aromas of green fruit with floral hints. Well-balanced with ripe pear fruit and balanced acidity. Easy summer drinking.
A variety of salads

White £8- £10

De Muller Chardonnay DO Tarragona 98
Karwig
Full-bodied white

Ripe tropical fruit with a touch of oak on the nose. Very rounded with concentrated fruit, toast and vanilla with a lovely fresh fruity finish to balance.
Spicy chicken with almonds and cream

Guitian Godello DO Valdeorras 97
Approach Trade
Full-bodied white

Ripe apples and melon on the nose. Dry and full with flavours of apple and herbs, slightly smoky. Round and long.
Fish soup or stew

Torres Waltraud Riesling DO Penedès 98
Molloy's
Aromatic white

Aromatic and grapey. Dry with refreshing acidity and lovely weight of ripe fruit well supported by alcohol.
Prawns with peppers

White £12 - £15

Enate Chardonnay DO Somantano 97
Febvre ☆
Full-bodied white

Marzipan, red apple and vanilla aromas, complex and inviting. Full with rich flavours of apples, butter and toast. Smoky oak cuts in through the long finish.
Grilled swordfish or snapper with a robust sauce

Jean Leon Chardonnay DO Penedès 95
Woodford Bourne
Full-bodied white

Complex aromas of marmalade and buttery fruit with floral notes. Full-bodied and round with a good weight of fruit, tightly-knit structure and long finish.
Sauced fish or smoked fish cakes

Lagar de Cervera Albariño DO Rías Baixas 97
Molloy's
Light dry white

Lemon fruit aromas with hints of toast and nuts. Great weight of very different fruit flavour, pineapple and banana tones. Good length and finish.
Grilled or baked sardines

Red £5 or less

Las Campañas Tempranillo DO Navarra 98
Dunnes Stores
Medium-bodied red

Brambly, plummy nose; youthful palate full of berry fruit flavours; refreshing acidity and a nice touch of tannin.
Baked ham or bacon

Red £5 - £6

Las Campas DO Navarra 94
Dunnes Stores C ££
Medium-bodied red

Earthy spicy fruit on the nose. Lots of spicy cherries on the palate with ripe tannins in the background. Good finish and great value.
Vegetable couscous

Agramont Tempranillo/ Cabernet Sauvignon DO Navarra Crianza 96
Dunnes Stores C
Medium-bodied red

Clean well-defined fruit on the palate with good, balanced structure. Straightforward and good with plenty of taste and character.
Couscous with lamb

Agramont Tempranillo DO Navarra 96
Dunnes Stores ££
Medium-bodied red

Lovely mature aromas of ripe strawberry, vanilla and coffee. Well-rounded with delicious plummy fruit laced with oaky vanilla. Great value.
Jambalaya or Basque-style chicken

Agramont Garnacha de Viñas Viejas DO Navarra 96
Dunnes Stores
Medium-bodied red

Ripe plummy fruit on the nose. Chewy cherry and plum flavours with tannic frame. Dry finish.
Spicy sausages and pizza

Agramont Merlot/ Tempranillo DO Navarra 96

Dunnes Stores

Medium-bodied red

Spicy savoury nose. Satisfying wine with lots of flavour and a nice tannic grip. Warm and lingering finish.

Spaghetti and meatballs

Marqués de Aragon Old Vine Garnacha DO Calayatud 98

Searson

Medium-bodied red

Ripe, slightly earthy fruit with baked cherry and raspberry aromas. Ripe and intense cherry fruit on the palate with plenty of youthful vigour, balanced acidity and warm finish.

Merguez sausages or spicy meatballs

Marqués de Chivé DO Utiel-Requena 94

Tesco

Medium-bodied red

Jammy fruit on the nose; rather baked brambly fruit, stalky backdrop. Nicely balanced and with decent length but a little hard.

Gammon steaks

Red £6 - £8

Marqués de Vitoria DOC Rioja Crianza 96

Remy
C ££

Full-bodied red

Mature dark fruit aromas, plums and cedar. Soft mellow tannin and fresh acidity with good weight of fruit. Excellent value.

Lamb casserole with Parma ham and tomato

Marqués de Griñon Durius VdM Ribera de Castillo y Léon 96

Fitzgerald   C

Full-bodied red

Ripe dark fruit aromas with hints of chocolate and tobacco. Rich black cherry flavours with a spicy, peppery backdrop. Balanced acidity and firm tannins show in the finish.

Steak and kidney pie

Campillo DOC Rioja Crianza 93

Barry & Fitzwilliam   ££

Medium-bodied red

Some complexity on the nose, strawberry fruit with vegetal undertones. Smooth silky palate with nice fruit intensity, spicy tones and a long finish.

Beef medallions or roast pheasant for a dinner party

Añares DOC Rioja 96

Allied Drinks

Medium-bodied red

Spicy, jammy aromas. Balanced and well-structured wine with a long, fruity finish.

Rabbit stew or another country casserole

Campo Viejo DOC Rioja Crianza 96

Cassidy

Full-bodied red

Floral red fruits on the nose, not especially oaky. Good weight of soft ripe fruit on the palate, balanced and well-made with a certain charm.

Chicken and bacon

Corchelo DO Jumilla 98
Searson
Full-bodied red
Plenty of earthy, jammy plum and cherry aromas. Full and rich with flavours similar to the nose. Mellow tannins frame the flavours which last well through the finish.
Herby baked pork with garlic

Huge Juicy Red DO Calatayud nv
Tesco
Medium-bodied red
Ripe jammy fruit aromas. Nice weight of fruit with highish acidity and quite firm tannin. Good value.
Pork casserole

Marqués de Griñon DOC Rioja 96
Fitzgerald
Full-bodied red
Ripe spicy nose with lots of dark fruit aromas. Rich and ripe with lovely spicy flavours and a pleasant bite of tannin.
Pork and prunes

Montecillo Viña Cumbrero DOC Rioja 96
Dillon
Medium-bodied red
Meaty aromas mix with ripe red fruits. Pleasantly creamy palate with ripe strawberry fruit and spicy vanilla tones. Enough tannin to hold it together and some length in the finish. Popular style of Rioja.
Navarin of lamb or pan-fried turkey fillet with mushrooms

Nekeas Tempranillo/ Cabernet DO Navarra 96
Grants
Medium-bodied red
Blackcurrant with exuberant caramel, vanilla and toffee aromas. Savoury blackcurrant fruit flavours with lots of spice well-supported by tannin and alcohol. Long warm finish.
Turkey fillets or chicken baked with bacon

Palacio de la Vega DO Navarra Crianza 96
Fitzgerald
Full-bodied red
Meaty, developed nose with hints of spice and vanilla. A robust, chunky wine with plenty of flavour and warming weight.
Basque-style lamb with peppers and beans

Paternina Banda Azul DOC Rioja Crianza 96
Barry & Fitzwilliam
Medium-bodied red
Lots of slightly tarry fruit aromas. Plenty of fruit, coconut and spice flavours, a bit short on concentration. Balanced, easy-drinking.
Roast ham or a black pudding dish

Petit Caus DO Penedès 96
Approach Trade
Medium-bodied red
Summer pudding aromas and plenty of fruit on the palate. Spice, tannin and crisp acidity make the palate a touch harsh.
Robust lamb or pork casserole

Raimat Abadia DO Costers del Segre 96

Grants

Full-bodied red

Complex medicinal fruit on the nose which is still slightly closed. Quite high tannin but good weight of ripe blackberry fruit and nice length of finish.
Char-grilled lamb steaks with garlic and herbs

Torres Coronas Tempranillo DO Penedès 97

Woodford Bourne

Medium-bodied red

Smoky brambles on the nose. Smooth, ripe and fruity with a pleasant finish. Decent wine.
Kidney or sausage casserole; bistro food

Torres Las Torres Merlot DO Penedès 95

Molloy's

Full-bodied red

Sweet, ripe, jammy plum aromas with hints of spice. Full-bodied with plenty of ripe plum-like fruit and spice. Quite chewy tannins and a good dry finish.
Carbonnade or other beef in beer

Torres Sangre de Toro DO Penedès 97

Woodford Bourne

Medium-bodied red

Ripe fruity aromas with a touch of vanilla and spice. Nice depth of cherry compote fruit, medium weight and length with quite fiery spice in the finish.
Robust stew of beef or lamb

Viña Mara DOC Rioja Reserva 94   *Tesco*

Full-bodied red

Brambly fruit on the nose. Rounded, plummy palate with nice fruity finish. Popular Rioja style.
Lamb shanks cooked in beer

Red £8 - £10

Viña Hermina DOC Rioja 96

Bacchus   ☆

Full-bodied red

Quite elegant aromas with bramble fruit and cedar tones, Mellow tannin harmonises with the rich soft fruit. Flavours continue to a long lingering finish.
Braised pheasant with apples

De Muller Scala Dei Legitim DO Priorat 95

Karwig   C

Full-bodied red

Figs and dates on the nose. Smooth silky palate with lots of fruit well-integrated with spicy oak. Very nice richness followed by smoky oak on the finish.
Roast turkey, traditional style

Palacio de la Vega Cabernet Sauvignon DO Navarra Reserva 94

Fitzgerald   C

Full-bodied red

Quite meaty on the nose. Plenty of deep blackcurrant fruit and toasty oak flavour. Very intense fruit with firm structure and refreshing acidity. Long and impressive in the finish.
Rib of beef

Palacio de Muruzabal Cosecha Particular DO Navarra Crianza 95

Approach Trade   C

Full-bodied red

Aromas of strawberry laced with vanilla and spice. Palate follows through with dense black and red fruit flavours, peppery spice and firm tannin. Concentrated, flavoursome Navarra.

Roast leg of lamb with beans and peppers

Campo Viejo DOC Rioja Reserva 95   *Cassidy*

Full-bodied red

Traditional ripe fruit and caramel aromas. Ripe developed fruit flavours with hints of spice, well-supported by alcohol. Quite a big Rioja with a long finish.

Steak pie

De Muller Cabernet Sauvignon DO Tarragona 96   *Karwig*

Full-bodied red

Ripe, spicy plum fruit on the nose. Velvet mouthfeel with loads of blackberry and plum fruit, chocolate and spice in the finish. Rich and tasty.

Char-grilled beef

Faustino V DOC Rioja Reserva 95

Gilbeys

Medium-bodied red

Meaty and dark fruit aromas. Rather meaty palate also with spice and some fruit showing. A bit hot in the finish, but nice length.

Casserole

Guelbenzu DO Navarra 96

Searson

Full-bodied red

Complex black fruit aromas, a little closed and young as yet. Lashings of tightly packed blackcurrant fruit, chewy and robust with well-defined tannin and balancing acidity. Very good but needs a little more time.

Pheasant and mushroom pie

Ijalba Múrice DOC Rioja Crianza 96

Greenhills

Medium-bodied red

Very attractive aromas of blackberry, currant and cherry fruit with hints of chocolate. Fine weight of fruit on the palate with well-balanced acidity and firm tannin. Rounded and mellow with nice long spicy flavours in the finish.

Baked or roast ham with a fruity sauce

Marqués de Cáceres DOC Rioja 95

Grants

Medium-bodied red

Aromas of meadow flowers and boiled sweets! Creamy and very approachable with loads of ripe fruit. Very pleasing.

Steak pie or casserole

Marqués de Murrieta Coleccion 2100 DOC Rioja 96

Gilbeys

Full-bodied red

Pleasant aromas of jammy fruit with hints of chocolate. Firm structure balanced by a good weight of autumn berry fruit.

Well-rounded finish. A nice wine.

Basque-style braised rabbit with red peppers

Raimat Cabernet Sauvignon DO Costers del Segre 95

Grants

Full-bodied red

Earthy medicinal nose with a touch of eucalyptus and chocolate. Good concentration of ripe fruit with firm tannin and a long finish.

Robustly flavoured duck with a good sauce

Ramón Bilbao DOC Rioja Crianza 96

Approach Trade

Full-bodied red

Spicy Christmas cake fruit with mint and basil. Plenty of fruit, but a lot of wood. Good spicy, chocolate flavours with lingering vanilla. For those who like oak.

Guinea-fowl and bacon in red wine

Vega Sauco DO Toro Crianza 96

Approach Trade

Full-bodied red

Intense aromas of black fruit with touches of dark chocolate and meaty tones. Well-structured with plenty of spicy, chewy fruit, firm tannins and a long hearty finish.

Hearty beef or game pie

Red £10 - £12

Emilio Moro DO Ribera del Duero Crianza 95

Approach Trade   C

Full-bodied red

Layers of cherry and raspberry

fruit, spice and vanilla. Similar weight of flavour on the palate with spice, chocolate and rich ripe fruit with softening tannins. Finishes well and will go on improving.

Venison with a rich sauce

La Rioja Alta Viña Alberdi DOC Rioja 94

Molloy's   C

Full-bodied red

Perfumed, aromatic oak and strawberry nose. Silky and elegant with good balance of fruit, oak and acidity and a firm well-structured frame.

Roast ham

Marqués de Murrietta Ygay DOC Rioja Reserva 95

Gilbeys   C

Full-bodied red

Mature jammy blackberry and cassis aromas. Mature flavours continue on the palate with nice vegetal hints creeping in. Well-balanced with a smooth, round finish.

Baked ham with wine and grape sauce

Vega Sauco DO Toro Reserva 95

Approach Trade   C

Full-bodied red

Very meaty, robust nose with dark fruit and chocolate aromas. Nice balance between dark spicy fruit and tannin. Big and full-bodied with plenty of alcohol, structure and flavours.

Game with a rich sauce

Añares DOC Rioja Reserva 94

Allied Drinks

Full-bodied red

Spicy oak and strawberry

aromas. Palate of spicy red fruits merging with creamy oak and vanilla. Nice balance of fruit and acidity with a touch of tannin. Spicy warm finish.
Lamb boulangère for Sunday lunch

Enate Tempranillo/ Cabernet DO Somantano Crianza 96
Febvre
Full-bodied red

Earthy, gamey nose with ripe soft fruit in the background. Very well-balanced with concentrated fruit wrapped around a cedary core. Long and spicy to finish.
Rich casserole of rabbit, peppers and chorizo

Florentino De Lecanda DOC Rioja Reserva 91
Approach Trade
Full-bodied red

Brambles, cherries and soft spices on the nose. Good weight of baked fruit flavour, backed by tannins. Well-made savoury wine with nice length.
Game and mushroom casserole

Ijalba DOC Rioja Reserva 94
Greenhills
Full-bodied red

Lovely autumnal aromas of blackberries and plums with creamy vanilla and nutmeg underneath. Well-structured with a weight of fruit under-pinned by acidity and firm tannins. Long and mellow in the finish. Stylish wine.
Lamb navarin or other casserole or leg of lamb

Marqués de Griñon Colleccion Personal DOC Rioja Reserva 93
Fitzgerald
Full-bodied red

Slightly medicinal nose with tobacco spice. Intense and complex with lots of oak backed by plenty of silky fruit. Balanced, elegant Rioja.
The very best black pudding available!

Marqués de Griñon Dominio de Valdepusa Cabernet Sauvignon VdM Toledo 96
Fitzgerald
Full-bodied red

Lots of spicy, cedary blackcur-rant on the nose, quite classic aromas. Young palate with chewy, earthy blackcurrant fruit with hints of spice. Firm youthful tannins and a dry finish.
Duck with tapenade

Marqués de Riscal DOC Rioja Reserva 95
Findlater
Full-bodied red

Mature aromas of strawberry and cherry fruit, spice and cedar. Rather oak-dominated palate with balancing tannins and spicy fruit.
Roast duck

Montecillo Viña Monty DOC Rioja Gran Reserva 87
Dillon
Full-bodied red

Lovely mature bouquet of sweet, cedary fruit. Very soft, elegant palate with rich, ripe fruit, coconut and vanilla spice.

Good example of a mature Rioja.
Braised or roast pheasant

Siglo DOC Rioja Reserva 93

Cassidy

Full-bodied red

Mature, developed bouquet. Attractive blackberry fruit on the palate, mellow but still holding together well with good balance and length.
Guinea-fowl and mushrooms

Torres Gran Coronas DO Penedès Reserva 95

Woodford Bourne

Full-bodied red

Earthy palate with definite hints of rubber. Spicy baked fruit flavours and firm tannin but well-balanced with nice length.
Lamb chops or medallions with a sauce

Red £12 - £15

Montecillo DOC Rioja Gran Reserva 70

Dillon ☆ ☆

Full-bodied red

Mature complex aromas, fruit, woodland, spice. Wonderful palate—balanced, complex mingling of fruit, spice, earthy tones. Still holding after thirty years! Quite a treat.
Simply cooked lamb or beef--let the wine star

La Rioja Alta Viña Alberdi DOC Rioja Reserva 95

Woodford Bourne ☆

Full-bodied red

Oak-led nose with dominant spice and earth aromas over rich strawberry and bramble

fruit. Lovely complexity just emerging. Seductively sweet fruit opens the palate with spice and chocolate hints developing into earthy flavours. Long lingering finish.
Roast pheasant and truffles on New Years Eve!

Arzuaga DO Ribera del Duero Crianza 96

Searson C

Full-bodied red

Spicy black fruits on the nose with smoky touches. Very smooth and rich with plenty of baked fruit flavour and spicy nuances. Silky and appealing yet with loads of character.
Beef en croûte

Faustino I DOC Rioja Gran Reserva 92

Gilbeys C

Full-bodied red

Intense aromas of spice, tar and black fruit. Spicy, meaty flavours, fruitcake and oak. Well-structured with firm tannins—will develop further.
Big, rich stew of game or beef

Les Terrasses DO Priorat 96

Approach Trade C

Full-bodied red

Very fragrant nose abounding in vanilla and chocolate. Full-bodied with plenty of structure, extract and firm tannin which needs time for the fruit to really show. Young but with great potential.
Game casserole

**Marqués de Griñon
Dominio de Valdepusa
Petit Verdot VdM Toledo 95**
Fitzgerald C
Full-bodied red

Spicy, cedary fruit aromas. Ripe berry and blackcurrant fruit with spicy flavours and firm ripe tannin. Rich and succulent fruit which should develop very nicely.
Duck and bean stew

Remelluri DOC Rioja 95
Approach Trade C
Full-bodied red

Ripe, with farmyard aromas mingled with the fruit. Very rich, luscious blackberry palate cloaking firm tannins to give a smooth rounded wine. Drink-ing beautifully now and will improve.
Pheasant with Madeira sauce

**Conde de Valdemar DOC
Rioja Reserva 94**
Febvre
Full-bodied red

Very ripe spicy, oaky fruit aromas. Impressive palate full of forest fruits and vanillin oak with balanced acidity and soft tannin.
Pheasant with mushrooms or lamb with a sauce

**Guelbenzu Evo DO
Navarra 94**
Searson
Full-bodied red

Intense vanilla, spice and red

fruit nose. Good weight of ripe, concentrated dark fruit with a firm frame and a long flavoursome finish.
Roast wild duck

Jean Leon Cabernet Sauvignon DO Penedès 91
Woodford Bourne

Full-bodied red

Very mature medicinal character. A big wine with flavours of stewed fruit and spice. Still holding and balanced with plenty in the finish.
Roast pheasant

Marqués de Cáceres DOC Rioja Reserva 92
Grants

Full-bodied red

Earthy aromas with baked or dried fruit and touches of vanilla. Very ripe plum and damson fruit and firm tannins. Good finish.
Roast meat for a special Sunday lunch

Ramón Bilbao DOC Rioja Reserva 94
Approach Trade

Full-bodied red

Jammy strawberry and blackcurrant nose with hints of vanilla. Darker, more liquoricey, on the palate with some dry, bitter chocolate flavours. Robust wine with decent length.
Roast lamb with herbs and beans

Red £15 - £20

Alión DO Ribera del Duero 95
Mitchell ☆

Full-bodied red, fruit-driven

Very ripe, deep aromas of new oak and fruit, still young. Strong fruit attack but with very firm tannin and plenty of oak. Needs time to shine. Keep, don't drink now.
Pheasant with Port

Gran Caus DO Penedès 94
Approach Trade

Full-bodied red

Very claret-like nose with ripe blackcurrant, cedar and spice. Ripe fruit flavours, similar to nose, framed by firm tannin and cedary wood. Very structural wine.
Roast wild duck or pheasant

Imperial DOC Rioja Reserva 94
Findlater

Full-bodied red

Complex, elegant aromas of spice and cedary fruit. Mature flavours with plenty of mellow berry fruit in a silky texture with a background of oaky vanilla and a warm spicy finish.
Richly cooked turkey

Palacio de Muruzabal DO Navarra Reserva 92
Approach Trade

Full-bodied red

Grassy floral notes on the nose with mature dark fruit aromas. Mature flavours of stalky fruit with coffee and spice. A classic but expensive.
Richly cooked lamb

Red £20 - £25

Emilio Moro DO Ribera del Duero Reserva 94

Approach Trade ☆

Full-bodied red

Wonderful aromas of strawberries, cherries and oak, intense but elegant. Spicy cherry fruit on the palate with oaky backdrop and chocolate-tinged spice and richness. Firm tannins and a complex, lengthy finish suggest a long and delicious future.

Fillet of beef or venison

Chivite Coleccion 125 DO Navarra Gran Reserva 92

TDL C

Full-bodied red

Meaty aromas with a whiff of chocolate. Still young and not fully knit but shows potential balance and promises to develop well.

Loin or saddle of lamb

La Rioja Alta Viña Ardanza DOC Rioja Reserva 90

Woodford Bourne

Full-bodied red

Aromas of cherries, chocolate and mint, complex and inviting. Big, mouthfilling wine. Structured style of Rioja but with good balance of fruit and excellent use of wood. Fine example of a traditional wine for those prepared to pay.

Good corned beef--an eccentric combination!

Red £25 - £30

Finca Dofi DO Priorat 96

Approach Trade ☆ ☆

Full-bodied red

Still slightly closed on the nose but lovely shades of rich fruit and spice. Plenty of ripe berry fruit on the palate with subtle oak, spice and chocolate flavours. Very concentrated yet elegant with real style which should mature beautifully.

Wild duck

Red £35 - £40

Vega Sicilia Valbuena DO Ribera del Duero 93

Mitchell C

Full-bodied red, to keep

Very pungent leathery nose with dense black fruit and spice. Super concentration of fruit and tightly-knit structure with nice oak and a very long finish.

Venison with redcurrant sauce

Rosé £10 - £12

Gran Caus Merlot DO Penedès 97

Approach Trade C

Rosé

Rather slow on the nose but really opens up on the palate. Ripe and plummy with amazing weight of flavour and mouthfilling presence for a rosé. Plum and red berry flavours dominate with savoury spice and a good finish.

Paella

United States of America

The hot tip for white wine is 1997 cool Californian Chardonnay. Many winemakers have taken to the hills, coast and cooler regions like Carneros and Santa Barbara for their Chardonnay vineyards and the wines have changed character. The best Californian Chardonnay of today is lean, fresh and complex in flavour. These are wines which complement food and which will age gracefully in a way that the voluptuous Chardonnays of earlier years could not.

California and US winemaking as a whole seem to thrive in adversity. Not only did the past decade see the replanting of almost all Napa due to phylloxera, and the emergence of strong competition from South America, but also continued pressure from the unrelenting anti-alcohol lobby. However, there now seem to be better wines all round and greater energy and innovation among the producers than ever before.

California's most famous grape, Cabernet Sauvignon, was the wine that started it all when Bordeaux cru classé was beaten hands down in blind tastings by Mondavi's Cabernets. That sort of competition is (thankfully) in the past and so is the insecurity which needed to copy Bordeaux. California now has its own style, its own classics and is starting to establish its own regional categories.

Terroir is the driving force behind much recent development which is strange when you consider how the earlier generation dismissed the notion as a French conspiracy. Nevertheless, the discovery and research into different vineyard sites has greatly increased the potential of the whole quality wine industry. Californian Cabernet now has elegant fruit and suave tannin, silky but structured, ripe but never fruit-driven. Beyond this there are subtle regional styles from Sonomo and Napa, from Stag's Leap District and the Alexander Valley.

Probably the best of all news from the sunshine state is the spread of grape varieties. At last Zinfandel is being treated with due seriousness. There is plenty of the fruity, juicy barbecue wine, and even more of the notorious pink, but more producers are moving to serious, deep, brooding wines with real character and ageing potential. Rhône varieties and Italian grapes such as Sangiovese are also gaining ground with impressive results.

As the new century approaches and Californian winemaking comes of age, the future looks very exciting.

The new emphasis on cool climate wines areas within California has tended to overshadow the original cool regions of the United States, those of the Pacific Northwest Region and Washington State. Cool in Californian terms is a relative statement, and the more northern coastal regions have produced a very different style of wine.

Oregon and Washington make up a fairly small vineyard area. They are chiefly known for Pinot Noir which is exceptional in quality. These states are often tiresomely said to produce the only Burgundian Pinot to rival Burgundy. In fact, the wines for all their classic direction have excellent style of their own. As well as Pinot Noir, Chardonnay and Cabernet both states produce classic, cool-climate wines with lower alcohol, higher acidity and, in the case of the reds, firmer structure, than the majority of California.

Yields are low and vintages vary in these regions and prices are high. However, from producers such as Rex Hill, whose wines are a veritable showcase for the wines of the Williamite Valley, or the Burgundian Drouhin's Oregon winery or any other quality producer, the wines rarely disappoint and are certainly stars of the future.

California

White £6 - £8

Columbia Crest Chardonnay 96
Tesco
Full-bodied white, oak
Super-ripe tropical fruit salad aromas, following to the palate with similar gusto and white pepper spice. Nice, if not subtle, and good value.
Pork barbecued in a pineapple shell!

Ernest & Julio Gallo Turning Leaf Chardonnay 97
Fitzgerald
Full-bodied white, oak
Oily, buttery peach aromas. Big fruit flavours, melon and peach with well-balanced acidity and a rather nutty edge to the finish.
Lobster salad with mangoes

Inglenook Estate Cellars Chardonnay nv
Dillon
Full-bodied white
Tropical fruit aromas followed by similar flavours with refreshing acidity and balanced alcohol. Slightly honeyed fruit and a long finish add interest.
Chicken cooked with mango or lime; fish with pineapple or coriander salsa

Wente Vineyards Chardonnay 96

Dunnes Stores

Full-bodied white

Ripe tropical fruit aromas with a touch of vanilla. Fruit-driven with stewed apples and cream flavour and a crisp finish though a touch short.

Marinated chicken from the barbecue

White £8 - £10

Canyon Ridge Chardonnay 96

Greenhills

Full-bodied white, oak

Complex toasty nose with melon and peach fruit. Well-structured and rounded with smoky tones beneath the fruit and a smoky/spicy finish.

Char-grilled poussin with a zesty sauce; similar mid-Atlantic food

Robert Mondavi Woodbridge Chardonnay 96

Febvre

Full-bodied white, oak

Subtle vanilla and restrained tropical fruit aromas. Elegance follows on the palate with smooth texture and refined fruit. Smoky toast flavours underneath add interest.

Monkfish with a rich saffron sauce or chicken with mangoes

Shale Ridge Monterey Chardonnay 97

Woodford Bourne
Full-bodied white, oak

Oaky vanilla on the nose. Buttery fruit with citrus overtones and well-balanced acidity. Crisp, clean finish.

Creamy pasta dishes

White £10 -£12

Beringer Appellation Collection Napa Valley Fumé Blanc 96

Allied Drinks

Aromatic white, fruit-driven

Oaky aromas of spice and butter. Full and creamy with tropical fruit flavours overlaid by smoky oak. Quite mouthfilling with oily, concentrated palate and long spicy finish.

Something over the top like Lobster Thermidor

White £12 - £15

Geyser Peak Gewürztraminer 97

Dalton ☆

Aromatic white, fruit-driven

Very aromatic rosewater and lychees with spice. Highly individual with lots of ripe fruit and spice flavour and long rewarding finish.

Red pepper compote

Clos du Bois Sonoma County Chardonnay 97

Grants C

Full-bodied white, oak

Youthful aromas of green and citrus fruits. Well-balanced palate with plenty of refreshing acidity and apple and citrus fruit flavours. Good weight and length of finish.

Creamy lobster supper

Kendall-Jackson Vintner's Reserve Chardonnay 97

Cassidy

Full-bodied white, oak

Lots of melon fruit and ripe buttery aromas. Quite rich on the palate with sweetly spicy

oak. Full and round with a nutty background. Very ripe but well-made.
Smoked fish pie

White £15 - £20

Robert Mondavi Napa Valley Fumé Blanc 97
Febvre
Aromatic white, fruit-driven

Green fruit and smoky aromas with a hint of rosemary. Rather grassy. Oily, green fruit flavour with high acidity. Good length of flavour.
Barbecued fish kebabs

White £20 -£25

Gallo Estate Northern Sonoma Chardonnay 93
Fitzgerald   C
Full-bodied white, oak

Tropical fruit and honeycomb nose. Lovely ripe sunny fruit and well-integrated oak. Long and full with refreshing acidity cut right through the wine.
Lobster Thermidor

Red £5 - £6

Diamond Grove Shiraz 98
Dunnes Stores   ££
Medium-bodied red

Ripe berry fruit with a smoky edge. Very fruit-driven with soft, well-integrated tannins. Lovely spicy edge to the ripe fruit. Warm peppery finish.
Pizza with sausage and mushrooms

Garnet Point Zinfandel/ Barbera 96
Fitzgerald   ££
Medium-bodied red
Light jammy fruit aromas

which follow on the palate with spice and slight smokiness. Easy-drinking but diverting and very good value.
Pasta with sundried tomato and olive sauce

Red £6 - £8

Inglenook Estate Cellars Cabernet Sauvignon nv
Dillon   ££
Full-bodied red

Blackcurrant aromas with a touch of cigar-box spice give quite a classic impression. Ripe fruit with well-masked tannins. Balanced and stylish for the price.
Roast lamb, steaks and grilled meats

Ernest & Julio Gallo Turning Leaf Merlot 96
Fitzgerald
Medium-bodied red

Vegetal autumnal fruit, which follows through on the palate. Quite plummy with a touch of coffee flavour and soft tannin. Rather short.
Medallions of lamb with red pepper, ginger and rosemary sauce

Fetzer Home Range Zinfandel 96
Dillon
Full-bodied red, fruit-driven

Spicy fruit of the forest aromas, very ripe character. Plenty of soft fruit on the palate, spicy, juicy flavours. Very up-front and appealing with easy tannins.
Barbecued ribs with barbecue sauce or kebabs with sweet peppers

Vendange Cabernet Sauvignon 97
Barry & Fitzwilliam
Medium-bodied red

Blackcurrant pastilles dominate a pronounced, ripe and fruity nose. Similar palate: very fruity, super-ripe cassis flavours and friendly tannins. Balanced, with a good finish.
Meatloaf, hamburgers or pasta and meatballs; also good party wine

Vendange Zinfandel nv
Barry & Fitzwilliam
Full-bodied red, fruit-driven

Cherry and bramble aromas with a definite hint of leather. Soft blackberry fruit on the palate with white pepper spice and the warmth of alcohol in the finish.
Barbecues, especially hamburgers and ribs

Wente Vineyards Cabernet Sauvignon 97
Dunnes Stores
Medium-bodied red

Fruit of the forest, slightly baked aromas. Good ripe fruit with balanced tannin and good dry finish.
Hamburgers or meatballs with plenty of flavour

Red £8 - £10

Gallo Sonoma Sonoma County Pinot Noir 95
Fitzgerald ☆
Medium-bodied red

Gamey, meaty aromas showing maturity. Gorgeous ripe fruit and lots of spice. Lovely Pinot style.
Duck with fruit

Stratford Cabernet Sauvignon 95
Barry & Fitzwilliam ☆
Full-bodied red, fruit-driven

Aromatic fruit on the nose—blackcurrant and rhubarb. Lovely ripe, summer fruit flavours balanced by tannin and acidity. Well-integrated wine with a long finish.
Beef cooked with wine and herbs

Gallo Sonoma Sonoma County Zinfandel 94
Fitzgerald C
Full-bodied red, fruit-driven

Earthy dark berry fruit and vanilla on the nose. Lots of redcurrant and loganberry flavour with dry tannin and crisp acidity. Peppery, slightly bitter finish.
Anchovy and olive pizza

Wente Vineyards Charles Wetmore Reserve Cabernet Sauvignon 96
Dunnes Stores C
Full-bodied red, fruit-driven

Full fragrant aromas of earthy fruit and wood. Lots of enjoyable ripe and characterful fruit on the palate with nice balance of acidity and tannin. Some length, too.
Duck with a fruit sauce

Canyon Ridge Cabernet Sauvignon 95
Greenhills
Full-bodied red, fruit-driven

Plenty of ripe blackcurrant fruit aromas. Firm tannin with a good weight of ripe fruit and balanced acidity. A smoky influence and spicy finish add interest.
Grilled chops or kebabs

Fetzer Valley Oaks Cabernet Sauvignon 95
Dillon

Full-bodied red, fruit-driven

Ripe blackcurrant and vanilla with a touch of smoke (the nose. Full-bodied with well-rounded tannins and ripe fruit flavours. Drinking well.
Steaks

Frog's Leap Cabernet Sauvignon 95
Findlater

Medium-bodied red

Ripe fruit with quite nutty aromas. Dry with blackberry fruit, refreshing acidity and firm tannin. Well-structured around ripe fruit with a typical bitter twist in the finish.
Kidneys with cream and wine sauce

Ironstone Vineyards Shiraz 95
Gilbeys

Full-bodied red, fruit-driven

Earthy, maturing fruit aromas. Full-bodied with mature soft fruit flavours, rounded tannin and balanced acidity. High alcohol burns slightly but good length in the finish.
Lamb and aubergines from the barbecue

Ironstone Vineyards Sierra Foothills Cabernet Sauvignon 96
Gilbeys

Medium-bodied red

Stalky red fruit aromas. Plenty of full-flavoured red fruit with spicy overtones. Smooth-textured with a long finish.
Barbecued steak

Robert Mondavi Woodbridge Zinfandel 97
Febvre

Full-bodied red, fruit-driven

Bramble and cherry aromas with underlying mint. Intensely ripe cherry and berry fruit with smoky wood and tight structure. Distinctive yet subtle style of Zinfandel.
Char-grilled ribs and steaks

Shale Ridge Monterey Merlot 97
Woodford Bourne

Medium-bodied red

Rather steely and medicinal on the nose with a touch of rubber. Medium weight with firm, pronounced tannins, good weight and length. An unusual Merlot.
Grilled steaks or chops to tame the tannins

Shale Ridge Monterey Sangiovese 97
Woodford Bourne

Medium-bodied red

Cherries and blackcurrant on the nose with vegetal nuances, quite elegant. Jammy, ripe and mouthfilling with a spicy kick in the finish. Balanced tannins. Attractive, well-made wine.
Robust meat-based pasta or a casserole

Stratford Zinfandel 97
Barry & Fitzwilliam

Full-bodied red, fruit-driven

Aromas of bitter cherries and rhubarb. Juicy and soft with good weight of brambly, berry fruit flavour and hot, spicy finish.
Mustard-glazed steaks or beef stir fry

Red £10 -£12

Bonterra Cabernet Sauvignon 95
Dillon ☆

Full-bodied red, fruit-driven

Ripe blackcurrant aromas with mint and vanilla. Good weight of pure blackcurrant fruit, with hints of black pepper and vanilla beneath. Well-structured with a long finish. Will shine even more with food.
Roast duck with dried fruit stuffing

Sebastiani Sonoma County Cabernet Sauvignon 96
Barry & Fitzwilliam ☆

Full-bodied red, fruit-driven

Intense blackcurrant with a hint of black pepper. Ripe berry and currant fruits with nicely woven oak flavours and a firm structure. Very satisfying now but will improve further.
T-bone steak or a similar piece of meat

Cardinal Zin 97
Oddbins C

Aromatic white, fruit-driven

Big earthy nose with a hint of rubber. Rich berry flavours, skins and all, with layers of different tastes--mineral, vegetal. Lots going on and very different.
Stir-fried beef with blackbean sauce

Geyser Peak Merlot 97
Dalton C

Medium-bodied red

Plummy fruitcake nose and flavours of ripe soft fruit with spicy layers. Well-integrated wood and mild tannins pull together a balanced, elegant wine.
Pork with plums or dried fruit sauce

Bonterra Zinfandel 96
Dillon

Full-bodied red, fruit-driven

Spicy cooked fruit aromas, slightly earthy tones. Plenty of juicy dark fruit flavours and spicy, smoky tones. Moderate tannin and an impressively long finish.
Robust highly-flavoured pizza such as aubergine and goat's cheese

Pedroncelli Mother Clone Dry Creek Valley Zinfandel 95
Dunnes Stores

Full-bodied red, fruit-driven

Peppery fruit aromas. Ripe soft fruit with firm tannic structure. Quite meaty and substantial. Drinks well now.
Barbecue steak.

Red £12 - £15

Gallo Sonoma Frei Ranch Vineyard Zinfandel 95
Fitzgerald ☆ ☆

Full-bodied red, fruit-driven

Enticing nose of blackberries and leather with tar in the background. Fruit carries through to the palate with chewy liquorice flavours and balanced rounded tannins. Long and lingering and totally delicious.
Venison casserole with fruit

Kendall-Jackson Vintner's Reserve Pinot Noir 97

Cassidy ☆

Medium-bodied red

Classic raspberries and beetroot on the nose. Intensely fruity but with an attractive mineral backbone which gives a classic edge.

Roast salmon

Clos du Bois Sonoma County Merlot 95

Grants C

Full-bodied red, fruit-driven

Mellow aromas of autumn fruit and spice. Round and well-structured with peppery spice underlying rich fruit flavours. Smooth-textured with complex maturing style and excellent length of finish.

Fillet of beef

Robert Mondavi Coastal Pinot Noir 96

Febvre C

Medium-bodied red

Complex concentrated aromas of strawberry fruit with hints of coffee. Soft fruits on the palate with elegant spice and warm peppery finish. Silky smooth and highly seductive. Almost too easy to enjoy!

Game, especially with a fruit/spice sauce

Ravenswood Vintners' Blend Zinfandel 97

Woodford Bourne

Full-bodied red, fruit-driven

Aromas of figs and raisins mix with tar and leather for added complexity. A big wine, ripe and jammy with firm tannin to balance the luscious flavours. Very long and utterly seductive.

Venison casserole

Red £15 - £20

Francis Coppola Diamond Series Black Label 97

Woodford Bourne ☆

Full-bodied red, fruit-driven

Earthy, smoky, spicy fruit nose. Good fruit flavours with spice, chocolate and vanilla emerging on the palate. Soft and fresh,a very fruit-driven style but with amazing length of flavour.

Beef and wine casserole

Gallo Sonoma Frei Ranch Vineyard Cabernet Sauvignon 93

Fitzgerald C

Full-bodied red, fruit-driven

Great concentration of black-currant and cedar aromas. Explosive cassis and bramble flavours backed by very friendly tannins. Long tarry, fruity finish.

Barbecued ribs of beef

Red £20 - £25

Ravenswood Sonoma County Merlot 94

Woodford Bourne

Full-bodied red, fruit-driven

Fragrant tobacco and cigar box aromas. Ripe fruit flavours with firm yet balanced tannins and Christmas pudding spice. Very big structure, weight and length.

Pheasant casserole or roast beef

Red £25 - £30

Kent Rasmussen Carneros Pinot Noir 96

Fields

Medium-bodied red

Typical Pinot nose with rich fruit, farmyard and vegetal

aromas. Well-structured with nice balance of fruit and spice and structure. Only the price jars a little.
Wild duck with red onion compote

Red £40 and over

Gallo Estate Northern Sonoma Cabernet Sauvignon 94
Fitzgerald C
Full-bodied red, fruit-driven
Mint and blackcurrant aromas. Smooth palate with rich dark fruit, chocolate and vanilla flavours. Balanced tannin and a long mint-infused finish. A lovely wine beginning to show.
Middle-Eastern lamb casserole with apricots and aubergines and black olives

Oregon

Red £12 - £15

Rex Hill Kings Ridge Pinot Noir 95
Searson
Medium-bodied red
Rather jammy strawberry aromas with a smoky vegetal edge. Lots of ripe fruit with a mineral streak, slight stalkiness and crisp acidity. Young but complex and promises well.
Game terrine

Washington

White £10 - £12

Ch. St Michelle Chardonnay 95
United Beverages
Full-bodied white, oak
Slightly closed, restrained on the nose. Appealing cool fruit with crisp balancing acidity. Elegant, good accompaniment to food.
Prawns and other shelllfish served hot

Red £12 - £15

Ch. Ste. Michelle Cold Creek Vineyard Cabernet Sauvignon 95
United Beverages ☆
Full-bodied red, fruit-driven
Restrained aromas with a delicious whiff of cedar. Great concentration of tarry black fruit, tempered by mineral flavours and spice. Long and impressive finish. Should get even better.
Noisettes of lamb with herbs

Ch. St Michelle Cabernet Sauvignon 93
United Beverages
Full-bodied red
Dumb and sleepy on the nose. Slightly green palate evolving into riper fruit flavours. Firm tannin and balanced acidity. To drink now.
Casserole of beef or lamb

Editor's choice: Champagnes for
New Year's Eve

*This is our selection of options for New Year's Eve 1999,
a day when there will be more Champagne drunk than
ever before.*

*The list includes favourite non-vintage wines that are
excellent representatives of their house style. They have
been chosen for roundness, complexity and ability to
drink well with or without food.*

*For vintage Champagne the most important criterion
is readiness to drink—and many of the 1990s are potentially very fine but relatively young and under-devel-
oped. Our selection includes exceptional wines from the
generally lighter—therefore more forward—years of the
early 90s, one good value 1988 and those 90s that are
now mature.*

Perrier-Jouët Grand Brut 1992

Alfred Gratien Brut 1988

Cuvée William Deutz Brut 1990

Piper Heidsieck Brut 1990

Champagne Louis Roederer Brut Premier nv

Moët & Chandon Brut Imperial Rosé 1992

Joseph Perrier Cuvée Royale Brut nv

Deutz Brut Classic nv

Bollinger Special Cuvée nv

Laurent Perrier Rosé Brut nv

GOLD WINNERS

International Wine and Spirit
Competition 1998

International Wine and Spirit
Competition 1999 (non-vintage)

MOËT & CHANDON
Fondé en 1743

Nederburg

Barton & Guestier
La passion du vin depuis 1725

LUPÉ-CHOLET

I.L. RUFFINO

CONTI SERRISTORI

BLUE NUN®

SANDEMAN

BOLLA

FOUNDED IN 1850
CARMEN

FetzeR.

FONTANA CANDIDA

MONTECILLO

Fine wines from Edward Dillon.

Champagne and other sparkling wines

There is a general consensus that Champagne is the only possible wine choice for New Year's Eve 1999 (the Millennium, in case you had forgotten). The decision seems to be between non-vintage and vintage, and then which house and/or which year.

Non-vintage and vintage Champagne have two quite different intentions. Non-vintage is an expression of the house style; it is Champagne Moët et Chandon, Pol Roger, Krug etc. Such Champagne is the supreme example of a blended wine. In fact the skill of the Champagne master blender is one of the greatest in the world. In a grande marque house, the blander may work with more than one hundred different wines from different vineyards, grapes and years to achieve the taste which represents that house.

There are three grape varieties used in Champagne : Pinot Noir which gives complexity, character and weight, Pinot Meunier which is supposedly less fine, though the great Krug uses quite a lot, and Chardonnay for fruit and elegance. These come from different regions within Champagne principally the Côtes de Blancs, the Montagne de Reims and the Vallée de la Marne. Each grape variety, from each individual parcel of vineyard, is vinified separately until the final blending. Reserve wines, wines from previous vintages, are also introduced at this stage to complete the house style and erase the hallmarks of vintage variation common in a northern region.

Vintage Champagne is intended to express the character of the year and is produced from a single harvest, although small portions of reserve wines are sometimes used. A vintage Champagne also reflects the house, but the main intention is to make a wine to compare and contrast with other vintages. Such Champagne ages and develops in bottle just like any other fine wine. It is more full-bodied than non-vintage and acquires layers of taste and complexity in maturity.

Choosing a Champagne house is a question of personal taste. Non-vintage Champagnes differ fundamentally in term of body and weight from the lightest, most ethereal, styles to the full-bodied, rich and broad. Each house has its own subtlety from the blending and ageing of the wine. Reading the notes and descriptions for each house will help, but if you are buying for a party, taste a bottle first.

The right vintage for New Year is also a matter of personal taste and of the degree of maturity preferred. The 1985 and 1988 are probably the most classically mature vintages on the market. 1990 is somewhat problematical. It is an excellent year, but many of the best Champagnes are still quite young in taste and though enjoyable now will be much better in a few years' time. 1990 is expensive and it seems a pity to drink it so young. The lighter years of 1991, 1992 and 1993 have some really lovely wines which are forward and ready and though they lack the depth and potential of the better year, are excellent now and much better value.

Our Top Ten list of Champagnes for the midnight hour is on page 220.

On a practical note—Champagne, or any sparkling wine, needs careful handling. It is essential that it is properly chilled for both taste and safe opening. At room temperature the fizz is much more aggressive and therefore more likely to 'pop' the cork unexpectedly (and dangerously). Place the bottles overnight in a domestic fridge or put into a combination of two-thirds water, one-third ice for about thirty minutes.

When removing the cork remember there is considerable pressure inside. Remove the foil and wire, clamping the cork in place with your left thumb (if you are right-handed); if you are out of practice, protect everyone in the room by placing a cloth over the cork before starting to remove it. Then with your other hand twist the bottle until you can feel the pressure behind the cork. Gently release your thumb so that the cork is removed with a subtle hiss, not a pop. Never try to pull a cork and always point the bottle away from people or fragile objects. A night in A&E is not the way to start the new Millennium!

Some of the truly great Champagnes rank with the world's finest wines. However, fizz of any kind is usually bought for reasons other than its taste and quality as a wine. Bubbles are for celebration rather than appreciation and while there are occasions for good Champagne there are many more occasions for good sparkling wine, of which there is plenty to be found. Buying Champagne is buying an illusion of luxury and extravagance. Judging by this year's tasting, one might do well to set aside such prejudice and snobbery and vote with the palate for a really good sparkler at half the price of nv champers.

There are a huge number of sparkling wines available from Europe and the New World. Quality varies considerably from country to country and within producing regions. In selecting a sparkling wine, too much emphasis can be placed on production method. That a wine is made by the traditional or Champagne method is not a guarantee of quality. The final wine is influenced as much by the quality of the base wine— the still wine from which it is made—as by the production. Fairly boring grape varieties from young vines will end up as fairly boring sparkling wine. Having said that, the traditional or transfer method (a variation on the Champagne method of vinification), combined with a tasty base wine, is a pretty good bet for quality.

Australian and Californian sparkling wines tend to be extremely well-made with lovely ripe fruit and well-sustained mousse. Recently the dosage seems to have bcome quite high which makes for easy drinking but can rob the wine of some of its clean-cut, refreshing elegance.

New Zealand, on the other hand, makes very lean, thoroughly elegant sparklers. At the top of the scale, Pelorus from Cloudy Bay is complex and delicious while a more modest example such as Lindaur from Montana manages perfect balance and style. South Africa, too, has some impressive sparklers.

Perhaps the biggest improvements in sparkling wine can be seen in the cavas from Spain, the crèmants of France and the German Sekt. These are no longer simply cheaper alternatives to Champagne but are serious wines in their own right. They are options of choice not cost.

Champagne

Champagne £15 - £20

J. Charpentier Brut Tradition AC Champagne nv
Wines Direct ☆
Very fine well-sustained mousse. Lactic yeasty nose and lovely citrus flavours to follow. Mouthfilling and creamy with a long finish.

Charles Heidsieck Brut Réserve AC Champagne nv
Remy
Fruity, citrus nose. Lemon and citrus flavours follow on the palate. A crisp and nicely balanced wine.

Comte L. de Ferande Brut AC Champagne nv
Dunnes Stores
Toasty, nutty aromas, quite developed. Dry and firm with nice stewed apple flavours,

clean mousse and well-rounded finish.

Marie Stuart Brut 1er Cru AC Champagne nv

Wines Direct

Lively mousse and subtle biscuity aromas. Citrus fruit with a touch of toasted almond on the palate. Crisp with good weight and nice apple flavours in the finish.

Champagne £20 - £25

Canard-Duchêne Brut AC Champagne nv

TDL ☆

Hints of nuts and yeast on the nose. Layers of fruit and yeast flavours, complex and creamy with a long lingering finish.

Henriot Souverain Brut AC Champagne nv

Wine Warehouse ☆

Cream and biscuits on the nose with berry aromas in the background. Full and rich with excellent weight of fruit and crisp elegant finish.

Bernard Gentil Réserve Brut AC Champagne nv

Bubble Brothers C

Lovely complex aromas of toast and almonds. Creamy, full-bodied palate with flavours of biscuit and pineapple nicely balanced by acidity.

Delbeck Brut Heritage AC Champagne nv

Mitchell C

Quite subtle nose with hints of bread dough. Elegant yeasty fruit on the palate with crisp acidity and excellent balance.

Laurent-Perrier Brut AC Champagne nv

Gilbeys C

Reassuringly mature bouquet of spring flowers and buttery biscuits. Delicate, ripe and creamy palate with a long finish.

Billecart-Salmon Demi-Sec AC Champagne nv

Oddbins

Fresh pear aromas with biscuit tones. Off-dry with very nice ripe fruit and balancing acidity. Pleasant well-sustained mousse and firm long finish.

Canard-Duchêne Brut AC Champagne nv

Oddbins

Yeast on the nose with citrus and vanilla. Full expanding mousse and enough fruit to balance crisp acidity.

Demilly de Baere Brut AC Champagne nv

Bubble Brothers

Full bouquet of apple and yeast aromas. Crunchy Granny Smith apple flavours but a little short on finish.

Jean-Claude Vallois Assemblage Noble Blanc de Blancs Brut AC Champagne nv

Bubble Brothers

Subdued lemon and lime fruit with hints of nuts and toast.

Nicely balanced fresh acidity and a biscuity finish.

Mumm Cordon Rouge Brut AC Champagne nv

Barry & Fitzwilliam

Aromas of buttery fruit with a touch of honey. Nice weight on the palate with honey and lemon fruit, lively balanced acidity and long finish.

Piper-Heidsieck Cuvée Brut Year 2000 AC Champagne nv

Remy

Fruit and bread on the nose. Nice weight of citrus fruit flavours with fresh acidity and yeasty flavours through the finish.

Champagne £25 - £30

Louis Roederer Brut Premier AC Champagne nv

Searson ☆ ☆ ☆

Baked brioche and vegetal aromas, dominant Pinot Noir. Complex yeast and fruit flavours follow through on the palate with lovely refreshing citrus acidity and an endless finish.

Joseph Perrier Cuvée Royale Brut AC Champagne nv

United Beverages ☆

Hazelnut and biscuit aromas. Dry and full with a lovely weight of fruit flavour. Clean soft mousse and rich elegant finish.

Piper-Heidsieck Brut AC Champagne 90

Remy ☆

Fresh bread, toast and yeast on the nose. Excellent fruity palate

with subtle hints of toast and a delicate, yeasty finish. Beautifully knit and ready to drink now.

Deutz Brut Classic AC Champagne nv

Febvre/Oddbins C

Mature bouquet with biscuit and almond aromas. Lovely mouthfilling mousse and plenty of ripe fruit. Excellent nv with plenty of character.

Mumm Cordon Rouge AC Champagne 90

Oddbins C

Complex nutty, biscuity aromas. Cooked apples, spice and fresh bread flavours. Very fruity and crisp with yeast flavours on the finish. Nice now.

Veuve Clicquot Ponsardin Brut AC Champagne nv

Findlater C

Delightful nose of ripe pear and yeast undertones. Rich and full with mouthfilling mousse and ripe fruit. Well-balanced Champagne.

Brown Thomas Millennium De Venoge Blanc de Noirs Brut AC Champagne nv

Brown Thomas

Fruity aromas with vegetal and bread dough hints. Plenty of citrus and green apple flavours,

well-sustained mousse and crisp acidity. Very crisp yeasty finish.

Canard-Duchêne Brut AC Champagne 90   *TDL*

Ripe citrus aromas with a biscuit background. Harmonious palate with a lively mousse, fresh acidity and an elegant finish.

De Venoge Cordon Bleu Brut Sélect AC Champagne nv

Bacchus

Elegant mineral and citrus aromas. Lively mousse and rich nutty fruit. Nice but a bit overpriced.

Heidsieck Monopole 'Blue Top' Brut AC Champagne nv

Allied Drinks

Lovely fragrant nose of jasmine and elderflowers. Rather floral fruit flavours with gentle acidity, quite full and round to taste.

Moët et Chandon Brut Imperial AC Champagne nv

Dillon

Steady flow of bubbles in the glass. Delicate aromas of bread with hints of marzipan. Lemon, pear and toast flavours and balanced rather than crisp acidity.

Perrier-Jouët Grand Brut AC Champagne nv

Fitzgerald

Toasted aromas of nuts and peaches. Good weight of creamy fruit with slightly lactic, honeyed flavours, refreshing

acidity and a long finish.

Pommery Brut Royal AC Champagne nv

Grants

Pronounced biscuity nose with a touch of earthiness. Plenty of weight with mineral, chalk and fruit flavours and decent length.

Champagne £30 - £35

Bollinger Special Cuvée AC Champagne nv

Oddbins   ☆ ☆

Quite complex bready aromas with honey and toast. Big, nutty and complex, managing both power and elegance. Great weight of ripe fruit with balancing acidity in a lovely creamy mousse. Long elegant finish.

Joseph Perrier Cuvée Royale Brut AC Champagne 90

United Beverages   ☆ ☆

Developed aromas of biscuits and yeast. Fresh, lively elegant character. Very flavoursome wine with yeasty hints and a long, long finish.

Alfred Gratien Brut AC Champagne nv

TDL

Citrus fruit and yeast aromas. Full with rich, ripe fruit flavours and buttered toast. Elegant and long with clean,

bracing acidity right the way through.

Laurent-Perrier Brut AC Champagne 90
Gilbeys
Stewed fruit aromas and palate of toast and creamy apples. Full-bodied with smooth, oily texture. Delicious!

Perrier-Jouët Grand Brut AC Champagne 92
Fitzgerald
Lovely aromas of freshly baked bread. Balanced elegant palate with a strong Pinot accent. Crisp and toasty and goes on and on.

Moët et Chandon Brut Impérial AC Champagne 93
Dillon
Brioche and lemon curd aromas. Very rich and full with lemon and jasmine flavoured fruit and a crisp, citrus finish.

Taittinger Brut AC Champagne 92
Febvre
Ripe apple fruit and hints of biscuit and bread aromas. Lively with a creamy mousse and fresh citrus and yeast flavours.

Champagne £35 - £40

De Venoge Brut Blanc de Blancs AC Champagne 90
Bacchus ☆ ☆
Elegant aromas of citrus, baked apple and toast. Creamy textured with a lively mousse and fresh acidity. Complex flavours of biscuit and yeast emerging. Will improve for two to three years.

Pol Roger Brut AC Champagne 90
Oddbins ☆ ☆
Very lively well-sustained mousse and aromas of fresh bread and citrus fruit. Plenty of elegance and finesse with layered complexity not yet totally evolved.

Billecart-Salmon Cuvée Nicolas-François Billecart AC Champagne 91
Oddbins
Toasty aromas and a lovely creamy palate with persistent lively mousse, balancing acidity and a toasty finish.

Champagne £50 - £60

Alfred Gratien Brut AC Champagne 88
TDL ☆
Toast and citrus fruit on the nose. Full and finely balanced on the palate. Lively mousse with plenty of fruit and a biscuity finish. Mature and drinking well now but will hold.

Bollinger Grande Année AC Champagne 90
Woodford Bourne ☆
Wonderful aromas of brioche and yeast. Creamy and elegant with an abundance of rounded fruit. Finely poised with a very long finish. Lovely but even better in a year or so.

Cuvée William Deutz Brut AC Champagne 90
Febvre ☆
Slightly dumb at first on the nose. Very fresh lively style with flavours of green fruit, yeast and toast and a touch of

honey. Complex lactic character is appealing.

Champagne £60 - £70

Perrier-Jouët Belle Epoque Brut AC Champagne 90
Fitzgerald   C
Lactic, yeasty nose with similar bready, doughy flavour on the palate. Gentle mature mousse and long finish. For drinking now.

Champage £70 and over

Dom Pérignon AC Champagne 92
Dillon   C
Bright, lively streams of bubbles and a wonderful bouquet of nettles and new-mown grass. Toasty, tangerine fruit, balanced by crisp, elegant acidity. Harmonious, luxurious Champagne at a price!

Rosé Champagne £15 - £20

Comte L. de Ferande Brut Rosé AC Champagne nv
Dunnes Stores
Apple skins and pear drops on the nose. Fresh with nice weight of rather green fruit. Balanced but a bit short on finish.

Rosé Champagne £20 - £25

Delbeck Brut Heritage Rosé AC Champagne nv

Mitchell
Very fine mousse with strawberry fruit aromas. Good weight of restrained fruit flavours and fresh acidity. Fine length in the finish.

Rosé Champagne £25 - £30

Moët et Chandon Brut Imperial Rosé AC Champagne 92
Dillon   ☆
Alluring, heady aromas of red fruit and woodlands. Full, quite complex palate with layers of minerally fruit and lively acidity. Long, intriguing finish.

Rosé Champagne £30 - £35

Laurent-Perrier Brut Rosé AC Champagne nv
Gilbeys   ☆
Mature and developed on the nose with aromas of liquorice and caramel. Well-made with layers of ripe red apple flavours well-balanced by acidity. Long, flavoursome finish.

Billecart-Salmon Rosé AC Champagne nv
Oddbins
Lovely rich elegant nose of crushed strawberries with almond and biscuit tones. Dry, fresh and full, with classic structure, lively mousse and a long finish.

Joseph Perrier Cuvée Royale Brut Rosé AC Champagne nv
United Beverages
Interesting toffee apple, strawberry aromas. Plenty of ripe fruit and soft balancing acidity with underlying richness and good length in the finish.

Other sparkling wines

Tesco Sweet Asti DOCG Asti nv
Tesco   C
Grapey, floral nose. Light and delicate with plenty of sweet grapey fruit and refreshing acidity. Great value for a lovely wine in a neglected style.

Jacob's Creek Chardonnay/ Pinot Noir Selected Reserve nv
Fitzgerald
Buttery yeast aromas, a bit heavy on the nose but delivers on taste. Smooth, oily and well-balanced palate with refreshing acidity, fine structure and mousse and a long finish.

Orlando Carrington Brut nv
Fitzgerald
Mellow toasty brioche aromas. Clean and fresh palate with citrus fruit. Good weight of flavours and well-balanced with a long finish.

Cave de Lugny Blanc de Blancs Brut AC Crémant de Bourgognenv
Oddbins   ☆ ££
Citrus fruit and toast on the nose. Good mousse and firm structure with nice balance of ripe fruit and acidity. Well-made and excellent value.

Gran Troya Brut DO Penedès nv
Greenhills
Muted nose; digestive biscuits and slightly tropical hints, clean crisp finish.

Freixenet Medium Dry Cava nv
Woodford Bourne
Touch of Turkish Delight on the nose!. Light and easy-going with a relatively short finish. Uncomplicated, decent fizz.

Seaview Brut nv
Findlater
Punchy yeasty nose, ripe and mature, quite bready style with flavours carrying through well to the finish.

Seppelt Salinger Brut 92
Dunnes Stores
Intense and nicely developed bouquet. Quite complex with creamy rich mousse and ripe flavours. Good crisp finish.

Codorníu Cuvée Raventós Cava Brut nv
Grants
Fresh, zesty aromas of apples and lemon with hints of yeast. Lively green fruit on the palate with fresh acidity. Light and youthful.

Ackermann-Laurance Brut Royal AC Saumurnv
Barry & Fitzwilliam   C
Lovely drifts of bubbles rising through the wine. Mature aromas of lanoline and beeswax. Lively in the mouth with green apple fruit and a toasty edge.

Blaners Brut AC Blanquette de Limouxnv

Wines Direct ££

Nice mix of fruit and yeast on the nose. Dry and crisp with lovely fresh fruit coming through the mousse and lasting right to the end.

Gratien & Meyer Brut AC Saumurnv

Gilbeys

Wet wool on the nose with slightly floral hints. Delicate palate with rounded, dessert apple flavours. Fresh and long in the finish.

Lindauer Brut nv

Grants ££

Aromas of ripe melons, tropical and exuberant on the nose. Good weight of fruit with balancing acidity. Crisp and clean with excellent length. Gorgeous sparkler!

Freixenet Cordon Negro Brut nv

Woodford Bourne ££

Aromas of lemon and lime. Crisp, tart palate with flavours of green apples and lemons. Clean and refreshing.

Dom. de l'Aigle Tradition Brut AC Limouxnv

River Wines ☆

Fine, well-sustained mousse; yeasty aromas. Excellent balanced palate with elegant structure and restrained, refined fruit. Lovely, classic sparkler.

Hardys Nottage Hill Sparkling Chardonnay 97

Allied Drinks

Aromas of ripe honeydew melon and lemon meringue pie. Creamy with ripe fruit flavours and balancing acidity.

Sparkling £12 - £15

Hessische Bergstrasse Sekt Schloss Starkenburg Heppenheimer Schlossberg Riesling Trocken 96

Classic Wines ☆

Very fine vigorous mousse. Very clean and fresh with elegant aromas.. Beautifully balanced and stylish with abundant fruit, delightfully crisp in the mouth with a very long finish.

Faustino Martinex Cava Brut Reserva nv

Gilbeys C

Lively glass with aromas of freshly baked bread and apple fruit underneath. Good weight of fruit with balancing crisp acidity and smooth elegant texture.

Deutz Marlborough Cuvée Brut nv

Oddbins

Lemon and green fruit aromas. Harmonious blend of youthful fruit, acidity and freshness.

Seaview Pinot Noir/ Chardonnay Brut 94

Findlater

Warm toasty aromas. Good weight of ripe, honeyed fruit and biscuit flavours in the finish.

Mumm Cuvée Napa Brut nv

Barry & Fitzwilliam C

Lively fine mousse, light toast aromas. Delicate flavours of apple fruit with chalky overtones. Refreshing with excellent length of flavour.

Shadow Creek Blanc de Noirs nv
Oddbins
Apple peel and strawberry with undertones of yeast. Clean and fruit-driven with good mousse and texture and lots of really ripe fruit flavours.

Gratien & Meyer Cuvée de Minuit Brut AC Saumur 96
Gilbeys ☆
Earthy aromas of crusty baked bread. Wonderfully crisp and zippy with lively acidity and a nice weight of apple fruit. Excellent refined mousse and elegant structure with a long classic finish.

Gran Caus Cava Brut Natural Reserva 96
Approach Trade
Light fruit aromas with a mineral overtone. Clean and fresh with ripe fruit and a refreshing citrus twist. Long clean finish.

Sparkling £15 - £20

Hessische Bergstrasse Sekt Heppenheimer Stemmler Riesling Brut 96
Classic Wines ☆ ☆
Very complex nose, kerosene beneath green apple aromas. Elegant, exquisitely poised palate with smooth, full texture, plenty of evolved character and lingering flavours.

Green Point Brut 95
Febvre ☆
Complex aromas of yeast, mineral and honey. Smooth mellow palate with lovely concentration of flavour and an endless finish.

Pelorus 94
Findlater ☆
Complex elegant nose with mineral overtones and underlying ripe fruit. Creamy and subtle with ripe biscuity fruit offset by crisp acidity and a very long finish.

Deutz Blanc de Blanc 94
Oddbins C
Elegant mousse with yeast and green fruit aromas. Zippily fresh and clean with green fruit in abundance and a long flavoursome finish.

Sparkling Rosé £8 - £10

Orlando Carrington Brut Rosé nv
Fitzgerald
Light nose, slightly floral with a touch of honey. Fuller on the palate with a weight of ripe pink grapefruit flavours and a toasty edge. Nice and rounded with a good finish.

Sparkling Rosé £10 - £12

Freixenet Cava Brut nv
Woodford Bourne
Redcurrant and strawberry aromas with yeast underneath. Refreshing with plenty of strawberry fruit. Rounded with nice weight, sustained mousse and long, mellow finish.

Gran Caus Cava Brut DO Penedès 97
Approach Trade
Complex toffee, berries and honey on the nose with herbal hints. Very refined rounded palate, beautifully balanced with wonderfully even, sustained mousse. Layers of flavours and good weight.

Sparkling Rosé £12 - £15

Hessische Bergstrasse Sekt Spätburgunder Rosé Sec 97

Classic Wines

Quite complex mingling of toffee and ripe berries. Palate is quite evolved and rounded with good weight and decent length.

Mumm Cuvée Napa Rosé nv

Barry & Fitzwilliam   C

Fine bubbles in an onion skin hue, brioche and faint redcurrant aromas with more obvious redcurrant and raspberry fruit on the palate. Crisp acidity and a long finish.

Sweet wines

At one time a quality sweet wine, to serve with or after the sweet course, was almost inevitably a Sauternes or fine Beerenauslese from the Rhine. Today the range of wines from far-flung sources is impressive indeed. In the history of viticulture, sweet wines have always held a special place and regional styles proliferate throughout traditional areas. The general enthusiasm for wine has led to the revival of historic gems such as Tokay and Vin Santo, while New World producers have developed highly individual styles of their own.

In a sweet wine, quality means balance. The wine may be intensely sweet, rich and luscious, yet it must have that essential nervy acidity to give it excitement and prevent a cloying taste. This balance is the great difference between properly-handled, naturally sweet wines and the others.

Apart from the glorious wines of Sauternes and Barsac, France provides many lesser-known sweet wines which up to now remained principally of local interest. Jurançon is a very old sweet wine made near the town of Pau towards the Spanish border. It is luscious and delicious with delightfully complex spicy fruit from the Petit Manseng grape.

The Coteaux du Layon in the Loire is another source of excellent value sweet wines from the Coteaux appellation or the smaller zones of Bonnezeaux and Quarts de Chaumes. These wines do not have the intensity of Sauternes and are often better with sweet food. From a good vintage they can age for decades.

The revival of Hungary's Tokay has re-introduced another noble name to the modern world of wine. These wines are made by a very special vinification process and are unique. They have great intensity and complexity and age beautifully. From Portugal, Muscatel de Setúbal is becoming increasingly popular for its sweet, rich flavour, reminiscent of caramelised oranges and warming, full-bodied style. At present—though one suspects not for long—it is very good value.

The New World makes lovely late-harvested/botrytised Riesling and Semillon. Sometimes slightly simple or one-dimensional in fruit, these wines are excellent with sweet foods and the best can develop attractive complexity. The dark

Muscats of Australia are yet another style and great value, highly popular wines to accompany chocolate tart or Christmas pudding.

£6 - £8

Langlois-Château AC Coteaux du Layon 97
Woodford Bourne ££
Honey and beeswax on the nose with underlying ripe pears. Fresh, rather elegant style with rich honeyed fruit and crisp acidity in the finish. Full-bodied with a nice touch of spice to add complexity. Good value.
Super apple crumble

Ch. Jolys AC Jurançon 96
Wines Direct
Honey and apricot aromas with a touch of spice. Full and rounded, with creamy apricots, crisp refreshing acidity and a long, lingering finish.
Fruit pastries, blue cheese and rich pâtés

£8 - £10

Penfold's Magill Tawny nv
Findlater ☆
Toffee, caramel and raisins on the nose with nuts and spice. Sweet and spiritous character-- toffee, nuts and caramel abound; smooth and unctuous with raisiny fruit and spicy caramel in the finish.
Chocolate and nut pudding especially

Royal Tokaji Tokaji Aszu 5 Puttonyos (Blue Label) 93
Findlater C
Slightly sherry-like aromas with caramel tones. Toffee and caramel with refreshing citrus crispness in the background. Very long, nutty, caramel flavours.
Strudel or plum tart

Bethany Barossa Select Late Harvest Riesling 98
O'Briens
Very pronounced petrol/ kerosene nose. Opening spritz on the plate with quite crisp acidity and marmalade fruit. A little fragmented in taste but fresh and pleasing with a citrus finish.
Orange pudding

Brown Brothers Late-Harvested Muscat 97
Woodford Bourne
Aromas of spring flowers and grapes. Sweet and honeyed with plenty of ripe fruit, balancing acidity and an off-dry finish.
Melon; light fruit puddings

Brown Brothers Late-Harvested Riesling 95
Woodford Bourne
Lovely aromas of super-ripe honeyed fruit and caramel. Good concentration of taste with caramel and honey offset by citrus, marmalade flavours. Clean, crisp finish with good length.
Sweet foods; pastries; fruit; simple cakes, especially Tarte Tatin and strudel

Fonseca Alambre Moscatel de Setúbal DOC Setúbal 91
Gilbeys
Rich fruit and nut aromas with sultanas and dried fruit in the background. Big and full-bodied, with dried fruit similar to the nose and a long warm finish.
Orange pudding or mincepies

£10 - £12

Marchesi di Barolo Zagara DOCG Moscato d'Asti 98
Select Wines from Italy
Lemon peel and candy nose. Ripe, very sweet apples on the palate. Lovely, simple sweet fruit and refreshing acidity.
Simple fruit pudding eg strawberry cheesecake

£12 - £15

Ch. La Bouade AC Sauternes 95
Dunnes Stores ☆ ☆
Honey and beeswax with botrytis tones on the nose. Sweet and delicate with crisp acidity giving perfect balance. Luscious honeyed fruit with citrus hints. Clean and long in the finish. Stunning value.
Pear and almond tart

Rymill Botrytis Gewürztraminer 96
Gleeson ☆ ☆
Fragrant rose petal and lychee fruit nose. Honeyed sweetness with spicy fruit and refreshing lively character. Soft, yielding finish—and long.
Warm ginger pudding with vanilla cream

Sipp-Mack Cuvée Lucie-Marie Gewürztraminer Vendange Tardive AC Alsace 96
Mitchell ☆
Clean spicy aromatic nose. Very rich with super-ripe exciting fruit and excellent balance.
Foie gras

Brown Brothers Reserve Muscat nv
Woodford Bourne
Christmas pudding aromas: nuts, raisins and spice with chocolate and butterscotch. Very sweet, rich and raisiny palate with plenty of kick from alcohol. Not subtle but very good and good value.
Chocolate and nut pudding or Christmas fare

£15 - £20

OremusTokaji Aszu 5 Puttonyus 93
Mitchell ☆ ☆
Intense butterscotch and marmalade on the nose. Lovely ripe apricot and orange fruit with perfectly balanced acidity.
Apricot tart

£25 - £30

Ch. Filhot AC Sauternes 90
Oddbins ☆ ☆
Lovely rich golden colour with complex aromas of honey, nuts and obvious botrytis. Layers of luscious fruit, spice and nut flavours evolve into a lovely developed style. Full and rich with an endless finish. Delicious now.
Almond cake

Herxheimer Himmelreich Riesling Beerenauslese 90
Mitchell
Delicious butterscotch and honey aromas. Smooth almost creamy palate with rich sweet fruit which will develop more complexity in time. Nicely balanced acidity prevents cloying.
Dessert crèpes

Ch. Climens AC Sauternes-Barsac 1er Cru 94
Febvre ☆
Mellow honeyed aromas with obvious botrytis tones. Very mellow honey and fruit flavours balanced by refreshing citrus acidity. Finish seems to last forever.
Roquefort cheese

Importers of listed wines

Some of the wines recommended in this book are widely available, others only from specific locations. This section lists the distribution arrangements of the importers of wines listed in this book

Allied Drinks Ltd, Windsor Hill House, Glounthaune, Co. Cork. Tel (021) 353 438 Fax (021) 354 362; JFK Road, JFK Industrial Estate, Dublin 12 Tel (01) 450 9777 Fax (01) 450 9699
Wines are widely available.

Approach Trade Ireland Ltd, South Quay, Carrick-on-Suir, Co. Tipperary. Tel (051) 640 164 Fax (051) 641 1580
Wines are available direct and also from
Don Angel, 7 D'Olier St, Dublin 2. Tel (01) 679 3859
Karwig Wines, Carrigaline, Co. Cork. Tel (021) 372 864
Quay St Wine Bar, Galway. Tel (091) 565 662
Patrick Egan, Liscanor, Co. Clare. Tel (065) 81430

Bacchus Wine & Spirit Merchants Ltd, Unit T, 28 Stillorgan Industrial Park, Blackrock, Co. Dublin. Tel (01) 294 1466 Fax (01) 295 7375
Wines are available from off-licences and wine merchants.

Barry & Fitzwilliam Ltd, Glanmire, Cork. Tel (021) 320 900 Fax (021) 320 910; 50 Dartmouth Square, Dublin 6. Tel (01) 667 1755/660 6984 Fax (01) 660 0479
Wines are widely available.

Brown Thomas
Champagne is available from Brown Thomas, Moons and selected off-licences.

Bubble Brothers, 43 Upper John St, Cork. Tel 1800 [28 22 53] Freefone [BU BB LE] email: info@bubblebrothers.com website: www.bubblebrothers.com
Champagne and wines are available direct and from off-licences and wine merchants.

Cassidy Wines Ltd, 1B Stillorgan Industrial Park, Stillorgan, Dublin 18. Tel (01) 295 4157/4632 Fax 295 4477
Wines are widely available.

Classic Wines, 3 Annmount, Glounthane, Co. Cork. Tel (021) 354888 Fax (021) 351010 Mobile 0872 859983
Wines are available by mail order.

Peter A. **Dalton Food & Wine,** 'Loch Grein', Ballybetagh, Kilternan, Co. Dublin. Tel (01) 295 4945 Fax (01) 295 4945 email padwines@indigo.ie Website www.daltonwines.com
Wines are available from off-licences and wine merchants.

Edward **Dillon & Company,** 25 Mountjoy Square East, Dublin 1. Tel (01) 836 4399/819 3300 Fax (01) 855 6064
Most wines are widely available but some only from specialist outlets.

Dunnes Stores, Head Office, 67 Upper Stephen Street, Dublin 8. Tel (01) 475 1111 Fax (01) 475 1441
Wines are only available from branches of Dunnes Stores.

Ecock Wines, Unit 6, Riverview Park, Dublin 12. Tel (01) 460 0511
Wines are widely available.

Febvre & Co. Ltd, 15–17 Maple Avenue, Stillorgan Industrial Park, Blackrock, Co. Dublin. Tel (01) 295 9030 Fax (01) 295 9036
Most wines are widely available but some only from specialist outlets.

Fields Wine Merchants Ltd., 1B Birch Avenue, Stillorgan Industrial Park, Stillorgan, Co. Dublin. Tel (01) 295 4423 Fax (01) 295 4452
Wines are widely available.

Findlater (Wine Merchants) Ltd., The Harcourt Street Vaults, 10 Upper Hatch Street Dublin 2. Tel (01) 475 1699 Fax (01) 475 2530
Wines are widely available.

Fitzgerald and Co. Ltd, 11–12 Bow Street, Dublin 7. Tel (01) 872 5911 Fax (01) 872 2809
Most wines are widely available and others only from specialist outlets.

Gilbeys of Ireland, Gilbey House, Belgard Road, Dublin 24. Tel (01) 459 7444 Fax *(01) 459 0188*
Wines are widely available.

M. & J. **Gleeson & Co.,** 15 Cherry Orchard Estate, Ballyfermot, Dublin 10 Tel (01) 626 9787 Fax (01) 626 0652
Wines are widely available.

Grants of Ireland Ltd, St Lawrence Road, Chapelizod, Dublin 20. Tel (01) 626 4455 Fax (01) 626 4680
Wines are widely available.

Greenhills Wines & Spirits, Aisling House, Shanowen Road, Santry, Dublin 9. Tel (01) 842 2188 Fax (01) 842 2455

Wines are widely available.

Italian Boutique Wines Tel (01) 671 7450 Mobile 868 390 533
Wines are available by mail order.

Karwig Wines, Kilnagleary, Carragaline, Cork. Tel (021) 372
864 Fax (021) 372 864 email info@karwig-wines.ie Website
www.karwig-wines.ie
Wines are available direct and from off-licences and wine merchants.

Koala Wines, 25 Seatown, Dundalk, Co Louth. Tel (08) 016937
52804   Fax   (08)   016937   52943   email
koalawines@ireland1.fsbusiness.co.uk
Wines are widely available.

B. **MacCormaic Vintners,** 116a Terenure Road North, Dublin
6. Tel (01) 490 7928 Fax (01) 490 7930
Wines are widely available.

Mitchell & Son, 21 Kildare Street, Dublin 2. Tel (01) 676 0766
Fax (01) 661 1509 54 Glasthule Road, Sandycove, Co. Dublin. Tel (01) 230 2301 Fax (01) 230 2305 email
wines@mithcellandson.com Website http://mitchellandson.
com
*Wines are available only from Mitchells Wine Shops or through
the Internet at http://mitchellandson.com*

Molloy's Liquor Stores, Head Office, Block 2, Village Green,
Tallaght, Dublin 24. Tel (01) 451 5544 Fax (01) 451 5658
*Wines are available only from branches of Molloy's Liquor Stores,
or through the Internet at www.liquorstore.ie.*

O'Briens Fine Wines, 30-32 Donnybrook road, dublin 4 Tel
(01) 269 3139 Fax (01) 269 3033 email obrinesfw.ie
Wines are available from branches of O'Briens.

**Oddbins 31-33 Weir Road, Wimbledon London SW19 8UG,
Tel 0181 944 4400 Fax 0181 944 4411**
Wines are available from branches of Oddbins.

Remy Ireland Ltd, 101 Monkstown Road, Co. Dublin. Tel (01)
280 4341 Fax 2801805
Wines are widely available.

River Wines, Sandpit House, Termonfeckin, Co. Louth. Tel
1850 794 637, Fax 041 982 2820 email: rvrwines@indigo.ie
Wines are available by mail order.

Syrah Wines, 11 Rowanbyrn, Blackrock, Co. Dublin. Tel
(01)289 3670 Fax (01)289 3306
Wines are widely available.

Tesco Ireland, Gresham House, Marine Road, Dun Laoghaire,
Co. Dublin. Tel (01) 280 8441 Fax (01) 280 0136
Wines are available only from branches of Tesco.

Searsons Wine Merchants, 6a The Crescent, Monkstown, Co. Dublin. Tel (01) 280 0405 Fax (01) 280 4771
Wines are available only from Searsons Wine Merchants.

Select Wines from Italy Ltd, 12 Balally Close, Dundrum, Dublin 16.Tel (01) 294 2858 Fax (01) 294 2858
Contact Select Wines from Italy for details of retail outlets

TDL, 47–48 Pearse Street, Dublin 2. Tel (01) 677 4381 Fax (01) 677 4775
Wines are widely available.

United Beverages, Finches Industrial Park, Long Mile Road, Dublin 12. Tel (01) 450 2000 Fax (01) 450 9004
Wines are widely available.

Wines Direct, Lisamate, Irishtown, Mullingar, Co Westmeath. Tel 1800 579 579 Fax (044) 40015 email winesdirect@wines-direct.com Website http://www.wines-direct.com/
Wines are available by mail order

Wine Warehouse, Unit D1 Dunshaughlin Business Centre, Dunshaughlin, Co. Meath Tel (01) 824 0050 Fax (01) 824 0065 Mobile 087 2505929
Wines are available direct by mail order.

Woodford Bourne (inc. Mitchells Wholesale, 79 Broomhill Road, Tallaght, Dublin 24. Tel (01) 404 73700 Fax (01) 459 9342
Wines are widely available.

Index of wines

Index to food suggestions